LIMINAL ACTS

LIMINAL ACTS

A Critical Overview of Contemporary Performance
and Theory

SUSAN BROADHURST

CASSELL
London and New York

Cassell
Wellington House, 125 Strand, London WC2R 0BB
370 Lexington Avenue, New York, NY 10017-6550

First published 1999

British Library Cataloguing in Publication Data
A catalogue record for this book is available from the British Library.
ISBN 0 304 70585 3 Hardback
      0 304 70586 1 Paperback

Library of Congress Cataloging-in-Publication Data
Broadhurst, Susan.
      Liminal acts : a critical overview of contemporary performance and
theory / Susan Broadbent.
            p.   cm.
      Includes bibliographical references and index
      ISBN 0–304–70585–3 (hardcover). — ISBN 0–304–70586–1 (pbk.)
      1. Experimental theater.   2. Experimental films—History and
criticism.   3. Avant-garde (Music)   I. Title.
      PN2193.E86B76   1999
      792'.022—dc21   99-20180
                                                                          CIP

Typeset by BookEns Ltd, Royston, Herts.
Printed and bound in Great Britain by Biddles Ltd, Guildford and King's Lynn

For my mother and sister

Contents

Acknowledgements   ix

Introduction   1

1   The Liminal: A Preliminary View   12

2   The Problem of Aestheticization: Kant, Nietzsche and Heidegger   26
    Kant   26
    Nietzsche   31
    Heidegger   35

3   Contemporary Aesthetics   43
    Foucault   43
    Derrida   47
    Baudrillard   53
    Lyotard   59

4   Liminal Theatre   69
    Tanztheater: a dancing across margins   69
    'Theatre of images': *Einstein on the Beach*   82
    'Synthetic fragments': Müller's *Hamletmachine*   90
    'Social sculptures': Viennese Actionism   99

5   Liminal Film   109
    'Painterly' aesthetics: *Prospero's Books*   109
    Liminal politics: the 'queer' aesthetics of *Edward II*   115
    Transgressing borders: *Der Himmel über Berlin/Wings of Desire*   121
    Limits of fragmentation: *Europa/Zentropa*   130

6   Liminal Music   139
        Digital sampling: the techno music scene   139
        Digitized Performance: the 'acid' rave   149
        Destructive aesthetics: neo-gothic sound   152
            Nick Cave and The Bad Seeds   152
            Einstürzende Neubauten   158

7   Conclusion: Liminal Performance   168

References   180
Index   191

Acknowledgements

I wish to give thanks to Professor Horst Ruthrof. I would also like to thank Heather Mearns, Cindy Leon, Alan Petersen, Malissa Helms, Shelley James, Peter Eadie, David McKay and Harry Denton, who have provided me with professional expertise, friendship and entertainment. Appreciation to my MA Creative Arts students from the Western Australian Academy of Performing Arts within Edith Cowan University, particularly Lesley Wheeler and Melanie Knight-Smith; also to the Wray Avenue Bookshop, Freemantle. A special acknowledgement to my parents, my mother who will see the end results of this process and my father who will not, and for James and Raman.

Finally, special thanks to my dear friend, and fond memories of Ben and Alan, wherever they may be.

The author and publisher would like to thank the following for permission to use copyright material in this book.

Bonnie Marranca at PAJ Publications for the extracts from Heiner Müller's *Hamletmachine and Other Texts for the Stage* (1984). A special mention to Kathy Onofrio at PAJ for her help and interest. Einstürzende Neubauten and Nick Cave for their kind permission to quote from various lyrics. A special thanks to Klaus Maeck at Freibank Music Publishing and Sam Campbell at Mute Song Ltd.

Introduction

In recent years, certain marginal performances have become increasingly experimental and technological in their performative modes. I believe that this has led to a noticeable lacuna between such practices and current critical theory, with its heavy emphasis on linguistic explanation. In *Liminal Acts*, I offer a description of a range of performative types which I have provisionally assembled under the heading of 'liminal performance'. In the absence of any effective critical tools with which to interpret such works, traditional aesthetics and current critical theory are surveyed for an appropriate analysis.

Quintessential aesthetic features of the liminal appear to be hybridization, indeterminacy, a lack of 'aura'[1] and the collapse of the hierarchical distinction between high and popular culture. A central characteristic is the utilization of the latest developments in media technology, which has led to increased creative possibilities. Other quasi-generic traits are experimentation, heterogeneity, innovation, marginality, a pursuit of the almost chthonic and an emphasis on the intersemiotic: that is, a significatory practice which involves such non-linguistic modes as those provided by the corporeal *gesta*, certain performances becoming 'a writing of the body itself' (Derrida, 1978a, p. 191). Foucault could be referring to this gestural signification when he writes, 'the body is the inscribed surface of events (traced by language and dissolved by ideas), the locus of a dissociated self (adopting the illusion of substantial unity), and a volume in disintegration' (Foucault, 1977, p. 148). A certain sense of excitement is generated by the liminal: for instance, in many of the works, feelings close to disquiet and discomfort are experienced. A certain 'shift-shape',[2] stylistic promiscuity favouring pastiche, is signalled, together with repetition (a repetitiveness which foregrounds not sameness but difference), parody, playfulness and a delegitimation of authorial authority. Moreover, liminal performance strives to play to the edge of the possible, continually challenging not only performance practice but also traditional aesthetic concepts.

I would argue that liminal performance, by creating a scene of immediate aesthetic intervention, has an *indirect* effect on the political. Much of the performance, by problematizing reference activity, involves an 'impossible complicity' with what it seeks to deconstruct.[3] Furthermore, it provides certain 'perceptive strategies' by being parodic and questioning (Féral, 1987, p. 471), attempting to create non-'docile bodies' of non-performance (Foucault, 1986, pp. 135–69). Therefore, liminal performance, in keeping with all avant-garde art, though not in the separatist sense of that term, is an experimental extension of our social, cultural and political milieu.

Typical liminal acts, which I will discuss in detail in Chapters 4–6, are; in theatre, the hybridized performances of Robert Wilson's operatic 'theatre of images' and Pina Bausch's *Tanztheater*; the 'synthetic fragments' of Heiner Müller's *Hamletmachine* and the 'social sculptures' of the Viennese Actionists; in film, the 'painterly' aesthetics of Peter Greenaway's *Prospero's Books* (1991), transgressing borders with Wim Wenders's and Peter Handke's *Der Himmel über Berlin/Wings of Desire* (1987); the liminal politics of Derek Jarman's *Edward II* (1991) and the limits of fragmentation in Lars von Trier's *Europa/Zentropa* (1991); and, in music, the digitized performance of sampled music and the neo-gothic sound of Einstürzende Neubauten and Nick Cave and The Bad Seeds.

It is my belief that present performative theory is inadequate in providing a suitable description of such practices. For instance, historically, Western theatre has traditionally based its theory and practice on Aristotle's *Poetics*. The Aristotelian concept of drama is a drama of illusion, which creates events that represent the 'absent' as being 'totally present'. It is a drama of catharsis by terror and pity; a drama of spectator-identification with actors. It presupposes a dramatic structure that will have coherence, self-inclusiveness and the possibility of a recognizable sequence; in short, a beginning, middle and end. The dramatic action (*praxis*) and plot (*mythos*) assume both a 'teleological and an eschatological basis'.[4] For Aristotle, 'Tragedy in its essence is an imitation, not of men as such, but of action and life, of happiness and misery. ... In a play ... the agents do not perform for the sake of representing their individual dispositions; rather the display of moral character is included as incidents of the plot' (Aristotle, 1947, p. 24).

Bertolt Brecht, in refuting the Aristotelian 'theatre of illusion' and deception, attempted to create an 'epic' theatre; a theatre of calm contemplation and detachment; of critical thoughtfulness; a theatre emphasizing narrative structure; and a theatre that produced active participation by its audience.[5] Brecht believed that he could achieve a double political strategy: that is, he intended that his 'epic', political theatre on the one hand would replace the Aristotelian 'theatre of illusion', and on the other, and more importantly for Brecht, would have an immediate social and political effect. However, his performances fail to work in one important way: that is, the audience misses the ideological structure that underlies the play, and therefore Brecht's plays can only be understood, in the sense he intended, by the theoretically informed, and then can only work for a limited time and locality. Moreover, 'the theatre of illusion' (especially in Hollywood) thrives as never before. This is discussed further in Chapter 1.

Antonin Artaud's theorization of the 'theatre of cruelty' lists several aesthetic features that seem close to the liminal, but he differs in an important way, namely in his pursuit of an 'essentialism'. Artaud (1958, p. 70), in writing that the object of theatre is 'not to resolve social and psychological conflicts ... but to express objectively certain secret truths', emphasizes a certain essentialism together with an unchanging, fixed nature of relations (see Chapter 1).

Aristotle's linear 'theatre of illusion', Brecht's political didactic theorization and Artaud's fixed essentialism cannot satisfactorily relate to the (syn)aesthetics of liminal performance.[6] Other contemporary performance theorists have pointed to discrepancies between current performative practices and theatrical conceptualization. For instance, Philip Auslander, writing on the acting theories of Stanislavski, Brecht and Grotowski, believes they depend on 'logo-centrism and certain concepts of self and presence'. However, ultimately Auslander believes that performance based on 'a gratuitous demonstration of pure signification' is unlikely to create a 'satisfying performance' (Auslander, 1986, p. 12). Since the object of the liminal is not to produce satisfaction, in the sense of immediate satisfaction – the opposite is sought – Auslander's theorization, in this instance, proves to be inappropriate.

Bonnie Marranca, writing on the 'fetishization of the body' in anthropology and performance studies, links the 'writing of the body' to the interculturalist infatuation with rituals and body techniques. She believes that 'Artaud not Brecht has triumphed in our century as myth and ritual grow more attractive than history and its possibility of adversary cultures' (Marranca, 1985, p. 38). However, as Johannes Birringer (1991, p. 47) states, 'the irony is, of course, that Artaud and Brecht, as well as anthropology and deconstruction, belong to the same tradition and history of the dialectic of enlightenment and that enlightenment's self-deconstruction'. Birringer believes that the initial focus on the body-in-performance of recent performative theory has been superseded by a more 'reflexive formalist exploration' and a more 'commercially orientated' adoption of multiple hybridizations between the visual media and the new possibilities of 'technological intervention'. However, Birringer sees this as a 'fetishization of the contentless aesthetic surface' of the 'theatre of images', and nostalgically wants to retain a theatre of 'experience' which cannot be absorbed by the 'spectacle of a technological culture' (Birringer, 1991, pp. 221–8).

This seems to me to miss the point of the magnification in creative possibilities that results from such a 'technological culture', a potentiality which is highly relevant to liminal performance and conversely understated in performance theory. Furthermore, although the link between digitized technology and international commodification is undeniable and similarly mirrored in the liminal, I believe that the performances can nevertheless potentiate resistance strategies: for instance, their perceived complicity masks a critical deconstruction and their promotion of a diverse range of 'perceptive strategies' can lead to a challenging of traditional institutions of authority.

Discussions on film theory and practice until the early 1970s were the preserve of film-makers and theorists such as André Bazin and Jean Mitry. Such intellectual voices incorporated film-makers' perspectives into their views of how new technologies control change in film history (Mitry was himself a film-maker). This position is expounded in both Mitry's *Esthétique et psychologie du cinéma* and Bazin's essay 'The Myth of Total Cinema'. It presupposes an 'Idealist' and 'technologically determinist' appraisal of history, with film technology allowing film-makers ever greater means to manipulate images of reality (Mitry, 1965; Bazin, 1967). However, when Althusserian Marxism explored the relation between ideology and technology (Althusser, 1971, pp. 170–7), an attack on this position was inevitable. This attack was led by Stephen Heath, among others, who attempted to critique technology within a 'materialist' approach to cinema. He was joined by feminist film theorists such as Teresa de Lauretis and Annette Kuhn.

These writers spoke from the 'position of the spectator', from what can be seen and heard on screen, rather than from 'tainted' histories generated by film producers (Heath, 1981, pp. 226–69). For instance, according to Heath, it is this 'filmic construction of space, of achieving a coherence of place and positioning the spectator as the unified and unifying subject of its vision ... which is often regarded as the power of cinema and as defining the overall reality as ... "trick effect"' (Heath, 1981, p. 39). And Kuhn (1985, p. 33) believes that 'The spectator's gaze is masculine and the image addresses him as part of the action, constructing his sexuality as masculine.' However, their focus on historical change proved to be largely ineffectual, since they theorized only from the 'spectator's position', and new production practices are often made deliberately 'invisible and inaudible' to general film audiences (Eidsvik, 1988/9, p. 19).

Liminal film too, concentrates on subject positions, but no position is fixed and unalterable; rather, it is a *vacant* place that may be filled by different individuals at varying times: for instance, the 'viewing subject' or the 'questioning subject' (Foucault, 1972, pp. 54–5). Neither is the liminal concerned with historical change through technical means; instead, it celebrates the multiplicity of codes produced by these means. It is metacinematic, questioning and self-reflexive, its formation processes are not hidden but foregrounded. There seems to be little discussion among contemporary film theorists regarding these characteristics. Similarly, there is little analysis of the sensations produced by films, such as the feelings of unease and disquiet produced by these works.

Contemporary music theory seems equally unsatisfactory for analysing liminal music. For instance, Pierre Boulez, in defending the integrity of the musical avant-garde against the option of pluralism, appears to be clinging to a nostalgic, elitist position when he writes, 'there are musics which bring in money and exist for commercial profit, there are musics that cost something whose very concept has nothing to do with profit' (Foucault, 1990, p. 317). This position is recognizable in Robert Schumann's criticism of what he perceived as the vulgar virtuosity of Liszt, in contrast to the intellectual constructs of composers such as Brahms (Schumann, 1883). Schumann's writing was motivated by a desire to instil in the non-discriminatory middle classes what he regarded as the liberating thought articulated in the complex music of 'serious composers'. Similarly, Adorno's interpretation of Arnold Schoenberg argues that his private-language games are motivated by social critique, even if Schoenberg's conclusions resulted in inscribing the very contradictions he sought to transcend (Adorno, 1981, pp. 141–72). This presumed separation of the aesthetic from 'actuality' found in traditional theorization of the avant-garde is antithetic to liminal performance, since one of its central objectives is to merge art with everyday life.[7]

Simon Frith, an academic writer on styles of popular music, ties the development of rock to four different periods stretching from the 1950s to the late 1980s: a 'traditional' period, which consists mainly of white rock musicians appropriating black musical forms; a 'modernist' period, in which acid rock, hard rock etc. supplanted its own musical roots; a 'new traditionalist' period of reggae, ska and punk rock; and finally a 'postmodern' era of pastiche and mutation of previous forms (Frith, 1987). According to Frith, there is no longer a 'metanarrative' of rock music but a series of decentred, fragmented forms which sometimes correspond to a particular youth and ethnic subculture; 'a culture of margins around a collapsed centre' (Frith, 1988a, p. 5). Although Frith's theorization does go some way to providing a description of liminal music, it omits a discussion of the overtly theatrical, disruptive nature of such performances as those of Nick Cave and The Bad Seeds and the experimentation, immediacy and excess inherent in the *Gesamtkunstwerk* (collective work of art) of Einstürzende Neubauten. A further omission is any discussion of the unsettling sensations invoked by their neo-gothic performances, which strive to present the 'unpresentable' or 'play to the edge of what is possible'.[8] As Foucault (1990, p. 321) argues: 'Music today ... is willed. It is not a music that tries to be familiar; it is fashioned to preserve its cutting edge. One may repeat it, but it does not repeat itself.'

The digitized performance of sampled music has become a focal point of popular performance in a decentred process of instant recycling. It is a process with strong parallels to the collaged writings of William Burroughs, which are composed of cut-up, juxtaposed samples of randomly selected authors. For Burroughs (1982, p. 265), 'the Aristotelian construct is one of the great shackles of Western civilization. Cut ups are the movement towards breaking this down.' Several music theorists have written on this latest technology, some quite optimistically. For example, Iain Chambers (1987, p. 199) writes, 'pop's past stops being a mausoleum of picturesque relics and turns back into a contemporary reservoir of musical possibilities'. Other writers are perplexed by the art of sampling. Frank Owens (1988, p. 82) believes 'There's something strangely indecent about this music it denies the deferred gratification traditional pop is based on – the pop song as a narrative structure.' However, not very much has been written on the accompanying destabilization of originary identity foregrounded by sampling's deliberate and flagrant plagiarism or the delegitimation of authorial authority produced by this practice. Similarly, there seems to be a lack of theorization on its modes of signification, which suggest that an intersemiotic significatory practice is sorely needed.

Julia Kristeva's psychoanalytical writings have gone some way to providing theorization on the corporeal as a significatory practice. For Kristeva, the 'speaking subject', as a process, is crucial. She distinguishes between two modalities of signification, the 'semiotic' and the 'symbolic'. The semiotic is the primary organization of drives by rhythms, intonations and primary processes. The symbolic is formed beginning with the mirror phase, with its resultant capacities for absence, representation or abstraction; it is a matter of language as a system of meaning (Kristeva, 1985, pp. 214, 217). However, unlike Jacques Lacan, who posits the 'Real', 'Symbolic' and 'Imaginary' as abstract entities, Kristeva links each domain to actual processes. Lacan's subject is linguistic: that is, it is formed in and through every speech act; 'the end of the symbolic process is that non-being comes to be, that he is because he has spoken' (Lacan, 1985, p. 209). However, for Kristeva, the subject is a result of 'the play of signs . . . which is the basis for all creation and the artist knows it well' (Meisel, 1984, pp. 131–2).

By exploiting the semiotic dimension of the signifying process, she has given rise to a theory of a subject equally constituted by symbolic and semiotic elements. However, the semiotic, usually described in terms of musicality, gesture, colour and rhythm,[9] cannot be grasped by conceptual thought, yet it is the basis of 'all avant-garde experience since the late nineteenth century'

(Kristeva, 1984, p. 185). If the avant-garde is disruptive, it is not because it transgresses traditional artistic practices; rather, it is disruptive because it violates the closed rationality of the thetic, which is taken in Kristeva's work to refer to that symbolic moment which corresponds to acts of judgement or intention and also to the process of linguistic signification.[10]

However, although Kristeva's work constitutes a sustained critique of structural linguistic practice, it nevertheless depends on the absolute centrality of language. Kristeva, in seeking to establish the political dimension of language as the constitutive medium of a society, writes, 'La commune mesure de base c'est le langage' ('The fundamental common measure is language') (Kristeva, 1977, p. 13). Furthermore, if the relationship between the semiotic and the symbolic is a dialectical one, it would seem inevitable that the semiotic would be appropriated by the symbolic. Rather than displacing the symbolic, the semiotic would merely prove to be a confirmation and extension of it. In other words, following the logic of speculative dialectic, an emphasis on interpretation necessarily favours the symbolic.[11] Consequently, Kristeva's method of reading texts becomes difficult to distinguish from the psycho-analytical interpretation of themes. Therefore, Kristeva's theorization, with its centrality of both language and themic interpretation, would prove untenable if applied to the liminal, given its mainly intersemiotic modes of signification and the rejection of any thematic closure in much of its performance.

Since present critical theory appears to be somewhat deficient in providing a thorough description of what is indicated by the liminal, I believe it is necessary to undertake a selective review of aesthetic theorization. Immanuel Kant's work is central to this issue, largely because we cannot escape the structure of complex judgements. In undertaking such a review of aesthetic theorization, I am arguing that the aesthetic is not an autonomous sphere. Even Kant, contrary to popular belief, points to this when he writes, 'the concept never stands within safe limits' and, therefore, 'the completeness of the analysis of my concept must always remain doubtful' (Kant, 1911, pp. 584–5). Therefore, it is difficult to argue in any rigorous sense that the aesthetic concept is some closed finality, or that any other concept is, for that matter. In other words, in theorizing the aesthetic, I am arguing against a certain restricted reading of Kant. In doing this, I am suggesting that the aesthetic is a perspective which encompasses the whole of actuality.

Kant claims that aesthetic judgements are the result not of '*determinant*' but of '*reflective*' reason, which has exciting repercussions for liminal performance. In other words, when it comes to making aesthetic judgements every example must precede the rule: that is, rules are created on each occasion, and can in no way be determined beforehand (Kant, 1978a, pp. 5–36). This means that judgements need to be continually revised and no set judgement can be sustained. And, by implication, aesthetic judgement serves as a prototype for all judgements which must operate in the absence of closure as in the purely formal. Following Kant, reflective reason permits us to make up the rules for judging as we go along.[12] Jean-François Lyotard has noted this relevance: 'if the third *Critique*, fulfills its mission of unifying the field of philosophy, it does so ... by making manifest, in the name of the aesthetic, the reflective manner of thinking that is at work in the critical text as a whole' (Lyotard, 1991, pp. 6–8).

In a review of aesthetic theorization, the *sublime* is crucial to an analysis of liminal performance. The feeling of disquiet produced by certain aesthetic features of the liminal, especially in its experimental aspects, is closely allied to Kant's description of the sublime as a 'negative pleasure'. Kant argued that the sublime appears 'to be ill-adapted to our faculty of presentation' (Kant, 1978a, pp. 90–1). Lyotard, following on from Kant, believes that the task of a critical politics is, nevertheless, to present the unpresentable, to present the fact that the unpresentable exists and that it concerns our future. Therefore, ' "our" destination ... is to supply a presentation for the unpresentable, and therefore, in regard to Ideas, to exceed everything that can be presented'. For Lyotard, the sublime centres on a linguistic model, an incommensurability of phrase regimes: 'symbolization, then, does not occur here through a substitution of object, but through permutations of instances in the respective phrase universes, and without recourse to a direct presentation' (Lyotard, 1988, pp. 132–66). In contrast, I am arguing that it is possible to present the 'unpresentable' in some liminal performance as a result of a mode of signification not restricted to the merely linguistic, but also taking from aspects of the intersemiotic, in other words from *beyond* but also including language.

Kant is important in a review of aesthetic thought, because his *Critique of Judgement* first led to a belief in a separate aesthetic sphere. I review other writers who have dealt with this issue. Of special importance is Friedrich Nietzsche, due to his concern with the 'Dionysian' impulse (1956), the 'will to art' (1924b) and 'perspectival attitudes' (1990). Additional aesthetic writings include: Martin Heidegger's theorization on the 'work of art' as the 'becoming' or 'happening' of 'truth', by means of the 'hermeneutic circle' (1971b, pp. 17–87); Michel Foucault's focus on *énonciation*, i.e. the positioning of the subject, and 'discursive formations', which demonstrate how objects of discourse surface and are delimited and specified (1972); Jacques Derrida's 'deconstructive' analysis of pure origin and identity generated by such prelogical, strategic devices as the 'undecidables',[13] his problematization of aesthetic 'framing' (1987a, pp. 15–147) and his speculation on metaphor and metaphoricity (1982, pp. 209–71); Jean Baudrillard's 'seductive', 'simulated' universe of the 'spectacle' (1979, 1983a); and Lyotard's theorization on phrasal 'differends' (1988).

My main purpose in reviewing aesthetic theorization is not to provide a critique of any aesthetic writer; rather, it is an attempt, by selecting certain criteria from their work, to provide a new aesthetic form of theorization which would be capable of addressing such performances as the liminal. Although much traditional and current aesthetic theorization cannot be used as it stands, with considerable amendment and review and as part of a more sophisticated theoretical apparatus, it can still have value. For instance, the 'beautiful' is not an appropriate description of a liminal feature or of the aesthetic; rather, the 'exciting' would be more appropriate, and any 'delight' in such a performance is certainly not a universal issue (Kant, 1978a, p. 60), or necessarily a symbol of the 'morally good' (Kant, 1978a, p. 223). Moreover, given the importance of *corporeality* in liminal performance, Lyotard's phrasal 'differend' needs to be rethought. From the perspective of liminal performance, the 'linguistic turn' needs to be adjusted to allow for an intersemiotic analysis and hence for the prominence of the 'body'.

Chapter 1 provides a preliminary view of and signals what is indicated by liminal performance. I argue that Kant is central to an analysis of this performance due to his theorization in the third *Critique*, emphasizing the importance of the aesthetic. Kantian aesthetic theory is juxtaposed against contemporary and traditional performative theories.

In Chapter 2, I survey the writings of Kant, Nietzsche and Heidegger. For Kant, the aesthetic is important since it stands as a prototype for any complex judgement that must operate in the absence of closure. This has important consequences for such performances as the liminal. Nietzsche is important because of his postulation on the Dionysian aspect of art. Many Dionysian features – for example, immediacy, disruption and excess (Nietzsche, 1956, pp. 22–3) correspond to features of the liminal. Similarly, his embrace of a perspectival attitude that produces a certain practice of *parole de fragment* is reflected in this performance.[14] Heidegger provides a hermeneutic perspective on the aesthetic. The work of art does not merely reveal things; more importantly, 'it lets things be', it is the 'becoming' or 'happening' of 'truth' (Heidegger, 1971, pp. 44–57). I argue that Heidegger's conjecture is relevant to the liminal, given that each performance can be seen as a 'happening' or an 'event'.

In Chapter 3, I discuss the writings of Foucault, Derrida, Baudrillard and Lyotard. Foucault's theorization of the formation of discursive objects is important, as it indicates how new alternative discursive formations, such as liminal performance, emerge, are delimited and specified.[15] His emphasis on *énonciation*, the positioning of subjectivity, is also central, since in the liminal these positions are mostly 'vacant' sites up for grabs (Foucault, 1972, pp. 51–5). I argue that Derrida's deconstructive premise is likewise indispensable, since much of this performance reveals a complicity with what it seeks to critique (Derrida, 1978c, p. 281). In addition, his supposition of 'undecidables', such as 'différance' and 'iterability', is crucial, as they show the formation process of and, therefore, destabilize notions of pure identity and origin (Derrida, 1978c, 1981a). Derrida's writings on metaphor are similarly valuable, owing to audience expectations being repeatedly frustrated as a result of the use of wide, jarring metaphors (Derrida, 1982b).

Baudrillard argues for an 'aesthetic determinacy', but this is viewed in a negative light. Due to the 'hyperreality' of art, all targets of oppositional art have been destroyed, and therefore art has lost its critical effectivity (Baudrillard, 1984b, p. 22). Although Baudrillard's writings on 'seduction' by technology are illuminating (1988, p. 192), there are certain problems with his theorization, which I discuss in Chapter 3. Finally, I argue that Lyotard's work is crucial to the theorization of liminal performance, since he has attempted to provide a theory of the sublime. However, Lyotard's sublime (*differend*) is premised mainly on a linguistic perspective and when tested against the liminal demonstrates a certain deficiency.

Chapter 4 provides detailed case histories of performances that I believe are exemplary of liminal theatre. These hybrid performances share certain aesthetic features, such as innovation, indeterminacy, marginality and an emphasis on the intersemiotic. In addition, they continually challenge traditional theatrical concepts. In Chapter 5, liminal film is foregrounded. The works I examine are all typically parodic, metacinematic and questioning. A further distinctive feature of these films is their utilization of digitized media technology, which has led to a prodigious expansion of creative possibilities. Liminal music, which emphasizes heterogeneity, innovation, the experimental and the marginalized, is surveyed in Chapter 6. Digital sampling creates exciting new hybrid styles of music, which previous technologies have been unable to do, and neo-gothic performances are similarly innovative in their attempt literally to present the sublime through disruptive sounds, tropical lyrics and primordial visual imagery.

In Chapter 7, I conclude that liminal performance exhibits certain quasi-generic features and that there is an absence of effective critical tools with which to interpret such works. Principal areas of theoretical deficiency include a lack of critical efficacy in the area of non-linguistic signification. I have suggested that this can be remedied by a retheorization from an intersemiotic perspective, a theorization which can deal with linguistic but also non-linguistic modes of signification. And although traditional and current theorization, as it stands, is unable to address this deficiency, with some amendment and as a part of a collective 'toolkit', much of it still has value. Finally, I argue that liminal performance does have a political dimension, in as much as it is a site of immediate aesthetic intervention that has an *indirect* effect on the political, and it is, therefore, an experimental extension of our contemporary culture and times.

Notes

1. According to Walter Benjamin (1969a), the 'aura' of the work of art lies in its 'unique existence', which 'determines the history to which it was subject throughout the time of its existence'. It also points to a separation from the social, giving rise to 'a negative theology in the form of "pure" art' (p. 224). Liminal performance is not unique or separate from the social; in fact, it can be seen as an experimental extension of that sphere.
2. 'Shift-shape' is a term taken from popular science fiction. It indicates a shape that has no fixed form: that is, it is capable of continual transformation and mutation.
3. See Craig Owens (1980b, pp. 79–80) and Derrida (1978c, p. 281) on deconstruction and complicity.
4. Robert Corrigan (1984, p. 158) is using 'teleology' in the determinant sense of the term, not the revised Kantian sense (see Kant, 1978b, pp. 35–9).
5. See Brecht (1964, p. 37) for a description of 'epic' theatre.
6. 'Synaesthesia' is the subjective sensation of a sense other than the one being stimulated. For example, a sound may invoke sensations of colour.
7. See Susan McClary (1989, pp. 57–81) for a more detailed discussion on this issue.
8. Blixa Bargeld, quoted by Don Watson (1985, p. 34).
9. For example, Kristeva (1974, p. 402) writes: 'music in letters is the counterpart of the parliamentary *oratio*'.
10. According to Kristeva, phenomenology fails to account for the movement which creates *both* subject and object: the 'thetic moment' – 'practice' as movement. This omission leaves consciousness and therefore 'experience' in a prominent position. For Kristeva, art is constitutive of both subject and object. Therefore, she accentuates 'practice' over 'experience', which presupposes an object (Kristeva, 1984, pp. 195–7).
11. See Leslie Hill (1990, p. 148) for a more detailed discussion on this.
12. See Kant (1978b, p. 35): 'the *reflective* judgement has to subsume under a law that is not yet given ... the reflective judgement must in such cases be a principle to itself.'
13. See Derrida (1977, pp. 162–254; 1978c, pp. 278–93; 1980, pp. 202–32; 1981a).
14. Blanchot quoted by Geoffrey Hartman (1970, pp. 97–103).
15. See Foucault on 'Discursive Formation' (1972, pp. 31–9) and 'The Formation of Objects' (1972, pp. 40–9).

1

The liminal: a preliminary view

My aim is to provide a theorization of the aesthetics of 'liminal performance'. The term *limen* (Latin, threshold) or *liminal* was used by Victor Turner in his work on anthropology and performance to describe a certain marginalized space which holds a possibility of potential forms, structures, conjectures and desires, a space that the performance works of my study can also be said to occupy. Since the limen is central to this particular genre of performance, I think it is important to quote fairly extensively from Turner. The 'limen',

> A term ... from van Gennep's second of three stages in rites of passage, is a no-man's-land betwixt-and-between ... ritualized in many ways ... symbols often expressive of ambiguous identity ... [the] liminal phase being dominantly in the 'subjunctive mood' of culture, the mood of maybe, might-be, as-if, hypothesis, fantasy, conjecture, desire ... depending on which ... cognition, affect and conation (thought, feeling, or intention) is situationally dominant ... Liminality can perhaps be described as a fructile chaos, a fertile nothingness, a storehouse of possibilities, not by any means a random assemblage but a striving after new forms and structure. (Turner, 1990, pp. 11–12)

Following on from Turner, my own use of the term liminal includes the above but puts greater emphasis on the corporeal, technological and chthonic. Other quintessential features are heterogeneity, the experimental and the marginalized. Therefore, firstly and most importantly, liminal performance can be described as being located at the edge of what is possible.

An important trait of the liminal is the centrality of non-linguistic modes of signification. In much of the liminal, significatory modes are visual, kinetic, gravitational, proximic, aural and so on. Since there is an absence of any effective critical tools with which to interpret such modes of non-verbal signification, an 'intersemiotic' significatory practice is indicated: that is, one which includes but also goes beyond language.[1] It is only through such an intersemiotic significatory practice that a satisfactory description and interpretation of such practices as the liminal can be achieved.

Other traits that are central to the liminal are indeterminacy, fragmentation, a loss of the auratic and the collapse of the hierarchical distinction between high and mass/popular culture. For instance, central to many of the works is a mixing of popular knowledge with 'elitist' knowledge; this is amply demonstrated by Robert Wilson's *Einstein on the Beach*, discussed in Chapter 4. Again, there is a definite blurring of set boundaries; in other words a certain hybridization is evident. An example of this, among others, would be Pina Bausch's *Tanztheater*, where dance and theatre can be seen to coexist.

Liminal performance can be said to emphasize a certain 'shift-shape' style; content is pointed to only indirectly. A certain sense of excitement is generated in many of the works, a feeling almost of awe somewhat akin to discomfort is created. There is an accentuation on recent technologies: for instance, the 'paintbox' employment of digitized 'high definition television' creates a kaleidoscope of colour and a montage of imagery. The utilization of such technology is also apparent in some forms of liminal music created from digitized 'samples' of sound. In much liminal performance, there is evidence of certain Dionysian qualities, such as, 'disruption', 'immediacy' and 'excess', creating the sense of a pursuit of the almost chthonic. In fact, Turner, writing on theatre, could be describing liminal performance when he claims that 'true theatre is an experience of heightened vitality, and at its height signifies complete interpenetration of self and the world of objects and events' (1990, p. 13).

Further characteristics of liminal performance include a stylistic promiscuity favouring eclecticism and the mixing of codes (especially the juxtaposition of nostalgia with novelty), pastiche, parody,[2] immanence (Hassan, 1978, pp. 51–85), cynicism, irony, playfulness and the celebration of the surface 'depthlessness of culture',[3] the decline in the genius and authority of the artistic producer and the assumption that art can only be repetitious, a repetitiveness which foregrounds not sameness but difference (Jameson, 1984, p. 60). Additional traits are self-consciousness and reflexiveness, montage and collage, an exploration of the paradoxical, ambiguous and open-ended nature of reality, and a rejection of the notion of an integrated personality in favour of the destructured, dehumanized subject. It can be seen that the features of liminal performance display a close affiliation to the aesthetics of postmodernism.

The above qualities appear in different ways in liminal theatre, music and film. In her hybridized *Tanztheater*, Pina Bausch combines a visually rich production style with techniques drawn from both Brecht's 'epic theatre' and Artaud's 'theatre of cruelty'. Her performers employ 'method' principles, complete with emotional intensity, at the same time applying 'defamiliarizing' techniques, which undermine the spectator's empathetic identification by presenting their role-playing as self-consciously theatrical, to the point of parody. The result is a performance that simultaneously distances and engages the spectator. Especially unresolved are the images of gender roles and sexual relations. Bausch shows men and women locked into power plays and obsessive patterns of physical and emotional violence with no sense of resolution.

In Bausch's work, *Café Müller*, one of the male performers spends the entire performance moving tables and chairs out of the path of the other performers. This role was initially played by the theatre's stage and costume designer, who, in perpetually clearing the stage, literally creates a continually changing set, translating his behind-the-scenes preparation into performed, physical action. Therefore, this choreographed realization of his function contradicts the traditional belief that the physical setting for theatre and dance is essentially only decorative, and points to a total integration of sets and properties.

Several dramatic threads parallel one another throughout the piece. Loneliness, compulsive behaviour and the search for contact determine one level; the examination of the dance medium determines another. There is a degeneration of traditional theatrical barriers between various genres demonstrated by the blurring within the performance of the 'stage designer'. Within its composition, *Café Müller* contains the essential instruments of Bausch's dance theatre: the fragmented gestures, defamiliarization techniques, repetition at varying speeds and the disjunction of processes into separate sequences. Bausch's theatre proceeds from internalized norms and conventions. Her performance derives everything from the *gestus*, which, in this instance, is strongly related to the actions of the body. It is not secondary to something spoken; rather it speaks itself.

In liminal film, there is an emphasis on the use of new technologies that can produce both a visual and oral multiplicity of special effects. For instance, Peter Greenaway's work *Prospero's Books*, an adaptation of Shakespeare's *Tempest*, is almost operatic in its use of visual imagery, music and song. The spectacle is further enhanced by the density of the images. Greenaway uses both conventional film techniques and the resources of digitized high definition television to layer image upon image, superimposing a further frame within his frame. At the same time, the text of the film is highly literary and self-referential in its constant reminders that *The Tempest* is the text.

The film, throughout, continues to draw attention to its own artifice. The 24 books that punctuate the narrative and create the structure of the film include books of architecture with buildings that spring out fully formed and anatomy texts with organs that throb and bleed and even illustrate graphically the processes of giving birth. *Prospero's Books* is a self-consciously filmic film that paradoxically wants to challenge the outer peripheries of film. At the same time, it questions both subject and identity formation. For any 'past' can be known in the present only through its 'traces': that is, through its texts or, in this case, through 'Prospero's books'.

Showing the formation process, not just of subjectivity but also of narrativity and visual representation, has become fundamental to contemporary metacinema. This self-reflexivity calls attention to the acts of production and reception of the film itself. In *Prospero's Books* the audience is placed in the same position as Prospero, as the conventions of movie-making are bared in a self-conscious way. This focus on *énonciation* is typical of contemporary art and liminal performance in general, with its overt awareness of both the production and reception of art within a social, ideological and aesthetic context (Hutcheon, 1990, p. 127).

An example of liminal music in its neo-gothic form is provided by a group of Berlin-based performers who collectively form *Einstürzende Neubauten* (Collapsing New Buildings). Blixa Bargeld, frontsman and self-styled visionary, creates lyrics abounding with the sort of dreamscapes associated with the German painter Albrecht Dürer, whose woodcuts and canvases are peopled with goat gods, apocalyptic horsemen and crucified messiahs. On stage or in the studio, Einstürzende Neubauten, a quintet including bassist Mark Chung, electronicist F. M. Einheit, percussionist N. U. Unruh and guitarist Alexander Hacke, are equal parts 'Teutonic ritual, Gothic rock, medieval flagellation and noise pollution' (Dery, 1990, p. 10).

Einstürzende Neubauten's early performances are highly evocative of the ritualistic aspects of the 'Viennese Actionist' movement (discussed in Chapter 4). These performances, involving ritual and blood, were described as an 'aesthetic way of praying'. Actionism was not only a form of art, but above all an existential attitude. Not surprisingly, psychology, especially the studies of Freud and Wilhelm Reich, featured heavily in this movement and led to performances dealing specifically with art as therapy. Neubauten claim to have been heavily influenced by this particular hardcore art group, and traces can be seen in the disruption and destruction demonstrated in their performances: for instance, the rhythm track on the band's *Durstiges Tier* (*Thirsty Animal*) (1982) was created by punching Bargeld's amplified chest then looping the resultant smacks and gasps. On another track, pork bones, hearts and meat were used as percussion instruments.

Originally labelled an 'industrial band' (now preferring the generic description of 'crossover' or even 'hardcore new age'), Neubauten used unconventional instruments to create their sound. Their performances included destroying their surroundings with power drills, sledgehammers and Molotov cocktails in an attempt literally to break down the barriers separating music from life. Einstürzende Neubauten have never seen music as an end in itself, and from their inception have searched for ways of breaking with traditional rock music, gaining a reputation for providing apocalyptic yet affirmative endings, seemingly gleeful in their destructive character. It would seem that the central idea behind the 'collapsing of new buildings' is to destroy what has been newly created in order continually to disrupt expectations of their music: 'Neubau means "new built" – the official designation for postwar' (Laddish and Dippé, 1993, p. 94). Bargeld claims that, following the 'interruption of the Third Reich', writing German songs is analogous to 'planting trees without roots'. Therefore, he argues that songs are not necessarily the first choice in sounds in the creation of German contemporary music (Maeck and Schenkel, 1993). Bargeld has stated that although Neubauten started off outside pop culture, they came to realize that it is more effective to play from inside, 'even if you play to the edge of what is possible' (Watson, 1985, p. 34). Therefore, he maintains that the band are now working in the discipline of pop music: 'we're now trying to work with song structures in order to dissolve them' (Owen, 1985, p. 37).

Craig Owens could almost be describing this impulse of liminal performance when he considers 'allegory' to be not representation but a deconstructive rhetorical trope which involves an 'impossible complicity' with what it seeks to deconstruct. He writes: 'The deconstructive impulse is characteristic of postmodernist art in general and must be distinguished from the self-critical tendency of modernism ... Postmodernism neither brackets nor suspends the referent but works instead to problematize the activity of reference' (Owens, 1980b, pp. 79–80).

I believe that in order to be able to give a thorough description of what is indicated by such liminal performances, it is necessary to undertake a selective review of aesthetic theorization. Kant's work is central to this issue, largely because we cannot escape the structure of complex judgements. In such a review of aesthetic theorization, it is important to state that although aestheticism usually denotes an enclosed space and separation of aesthetic objects and sensations from the 'real world' of the non-aesthetic, I am using it in this study to refer to almost the opposite: that is, I am using it as an attempt to expand the aesthetic perspective to encompass the whole of actuality. In other words, I am using it to refer to a tendency to see 'art' as constituting the primary realm of human experience.

When Nietzsche refers to 'the world' as a 'self-generating work of art'

(1924b, p. 239), or when Heidegger writes 'towering up within itself, the work opens up a *world* and keeps it abidingly in force' (1971b, p. 44), when Foucault concludes the *History of Madness* with the statement that from now on 'the world ... becomes culpable (for the first time in the Western world) in relation to the work' (1965, p. 228), or when Derrida argues that 'there is nothing outside of the text' (1976, p. 158), they are delineating an aestheticist position and they are also responding to Kant, or more specifically to a certain Kantian tradition, yet at the same time using Kant's intellectual resources. Nietzsche, of course, stands as the founder of what became the aesthetic metacritique of 'truth', wherein 'the work of art' or 'text' is seen as establishing the grounds for truth's possibility.

Kant, in his *Critique of Judgement*, has been read by many as maintaining the autonomy of aesthetic judgement, appearing to suggest there is a rigorously independent realm of the aesthetic, a realm distinct from the realms of morality and nature, and therefore crucial to a study of the aesthetic. In one sense this is the case – the emphasis is on Kant's conceptualization of the 'finality apart from an end' of art – but in another sense it needs to be qualified from two perspectives: first, Kant's own warning as to a falsely assumed stability of conceptualization (see below); second, Lyotard's recent reading of the third *Critique*, in which the 'aesthetic' takes on a broader scope (for a detailed discussion see Chapter 3). On the one hand, Kant seems to oppose any assimilation between aesthetic and moral judgements, in other words denying that they are matters of sentiment or feeling; on the other hand, he opposes any tendency to assimilate art to physiology or psychology, thereby also denying sensual pleasure in aesthetic judgement. This is reflected in his definition of aesthetic pleasure as 'disinterested delight' and in his conception of form in art as 'purposiveness without purpose' (1978a, pp. 42–69). Although Kant does deny that there exists a third realm of being, distinct from the realms of nature and freedom,[4] he was read as insisting on the existence of an autonomous sphere of the aesthetic, a sphere whose function was primarily to mediate between the other two (Megill, 1985, p. 12). Something of this idea of art as mediator underlies Nietzsche's claim that in the aesthetic 'the whole opposition between the subjective and objective ... is altogether irrelevant'.[5]

Kant contends that aesthetic judgements make a claim to universal validity: therefore, a beautiful object is one that excites delight that is not only disinterested but also necessary and universal (1978a, p. 60). By establishing this point, Kant touches on issues of morality. He argues that underlying the judgement of aesthetic taste is the concept of the purposiveness of nature. He writes: 'the judgement of taste does depend upon a concept ... its determining ground lies perhaps in the concept of that which may be regarded as the supersensible substrate of humanity.' Beauty is viewed as 'the symbol of the morally good' (1978a, pp. 207–23); there lies its claim to universal acceptance. Beauty therefore points towards the sphere of morality, of which it gives sensual intimations.

However, it is my belief that certain of these aesthetic features need to be rephrased with regard to liminal performance. For instance, here the 'beautiful' is now no longer an appropriate description of an aesthetic feature – it has been replaced by the 'exciting', 'the edge of what can be said' – and 'delight' is certainly not, in this instance, a 'universal' issue, or a symbol of the 'morally good', in so much as it lacks any purposiveness of nature; rather, it can be seen only in a localized context, as I will discuss below. As for the question of ethics and morality, I would argue that liminal forms of aesthetics can affect, though *indirectly*, the ethical and political.

Following on from this, a further issue is whether art, in any way, conveys a truth. Here Kant becomes somewhat ambiguous. While he insists that art 'is a mode of representation which is intrinsically final ... although devoid of an end' (1978a, p. 166), and therefore a matter of pleasure rather than knowledge (1978a, p. 42), some of Kant's additional statements in the *Critique of Judgement* appear to contradict this view. Here, he infers that while art cannot supply us with knowledge in any logical sense, it can put us into contact with something that cannot be fully presented in experience or grasped through concepts (1978a, p. 119). Kant's 'aesthetic idea' as a 'representation of the imagination which occasions much thought', but for which 'an adequate concept can never be found', and which therefore 'cannot be completely encompassed and made intelligible by language', indicates a view of art as expressing the inexpressible, in which case art, for Kant, is more than a mere purveyor of pleasure (1978a, pp. 175–6).

Although the Kantian apparatus cannot be used as it stands in an aesthetic theorization of liminal performance, there is certainly much of it that can be reviewed with considerable amendment and, importantly, his heuristic insights are often directly applicable. Especially valid is the transcendental procedural, a method without which we would be unable to make any cogent judgement at all.

In his *Critique of Pure Reason*, Kant writes, 'I will call all knowledge *transcendental* which is occupied not so much with objects, as with our *a priori* concepts of objects', and 'these representations', although not being empirical, can yet refer to '*a priori* objects of experience' (1911, pp. 9–45). For Kant, then, the *transcendental schema* is a mediating representation which is free from everything that is empirical, 'yet intelligible on the one side, and sensuous on the other'. According to Kant, the schemata are the only means of relating concepts or ideas to objects, or, in other words, of producing signification. This can occur only because of an *a priori* necessary unity which subjects all phenomena to general rules of synthesis and therefore enables them to make a general connection in experience (1911, pp. 113–19).

Many readings of Kant have assumed that his transcendental schema points to a transcendental signified or some closed finality, yet Kant himself denies this when he claims that 'no *a priori* given concept can be defined. ... For I can never be sure that the clear representation of a given but still confused concept has been completely analysed. ... As its concept, however, such as it is given, may contain many obscure representations ... the completeness of the analysis of my concept must always remain doubtful.' Hence, his transcendental is a *procedural* issue rather than a matter of content. Kant further critiques any notion of a fixed and closed concept when he states that 'the concept never stands within safe limits' (1911, pp. 584–5). This of course has consequences when applied to the accepted reading of Kant, which claims that the aesthetic sphere is autonomous, for since no concept can stand within safe limits and the completeness of an analysis must always remain doubtful, it is difficult to argue that the aesthetic concept is some closed finality, or that any other concept is for that matter, in any rigorous sense.

A further reassessment of Kant would be indicated in his analysis of teleological judgement, where he distinguishes between 'determining' and 'reflective' reason. Art and nature, according to Kant, belong to reflective reason. This has exciting repercussions for constituting aesthetic judgements, especially in the study of liminal performance, and by implication this applies to all complex judgements in which neither the ingredients to be judged nor the toolkit of analyis are given from the outset, but elaborate one another in a progressive dynamic. '*Determinant* judgement', according to Kant, is not an 'autonomy'; it '*subsumes* merely under given laws', as principles. 'But the *reflective* judgement has to subsume under a law that is not yet given. ... Now as there is no permissible employment of the cognitive faculties apart from principles, the reflective judgement must in such cases be a principle to itself' (1978b, p. 35).

In other words, when it comes to making aesthetic judgements, every example must precede the rule: that is, rules are created on each occasion, and can in no way be determined beforehand. Kant follows this by claiming that reflective judgement has maxims that are necessary for gaining knowledge of natural laws through experience, and between these maxims a conflict may arise, leading to an antinomy which affords the basis of a dialectic. The consequences of this for liminal performance are that judgements need to be revised on every occasion and no set judgement can exist, and following this, the universal, in that instant, is negated and replaced by the local. Kant, still retaining the universal as an overall structure, is aware of this when he writes: 'The particular cannot be derived from the universal alone. Yet ... this particular has to accord with the universal in order to be capable of being subsumed under it ... this accord must be very contingent and must exist without any determinate principle to guide our judgement' (1978a, pp. 62–3).

Therefore, although Kant's reflective teleology is important for an analyis of liminal aesthetics, his emphasis on universality proves untenable in the face of liminal performance. How is it possible to reconcile the Kantian universality with the heterogeneity and local so characteristic of liminal performance? However, it is not possible to discard all features of universality, since even the stipulation of an 'open genre' makes demands which neither heterogeneity nor the emphasis on the local is able to meet.

It is important to compare Kant's aesthetic theory in the context of performance to Brecht's performance theory, since both theories contain important aesthetic criteria but in themselves fall short of a sustained practice. Since Kant believed that aesthetic judgement is a practical activity and has no hidden agenda or other self-interest when applied to performance, this, too, can only be described as being essentially clear or transparent: that is, a 'finality without end'. However, for Brecht, aesthetic activity is located at a second remove; his performance takes a political detour. In other words, a certain polarity exists between Kant and Brecht, with Kant concentrating on the purely aesthetic and Brecht accentuating the political.

When Brecht first defined his theories in the 1920s he had already experimented with a variety of techniques. His plays had shown the influence of the expressionist trend and he had worked with Erwin Piscator, the exponent of the 'political theatre', whose stage was ultimately a forum for political affairs. Another of Brecht's sources was Asian theatre, he was especially impressed with Chinese theatre, where the performance demonstrates not only the behaviour of the characters but also the behaviour of the actors. This prevents any false identification or empathy with the performance. Brecht's theories demonstrated the influence of these experiments, and he was convinced that the theatre must become a tool of social change. In 1931, he wrote: 'Today when human character must be understood as the "totality of all social conditions" the epic form is the only one that can comprehend all the processes, which could serve the drama as materials for a fully representative picture of the world.' In conceiving his 'epic' theatre, Brecht was reacting against a certain German classical theory of drama formulated in the theories of Goethe and Schiller, which were presented in an essay called 'On Epic and Dramatic Poetry'. Epic poetry presents the drama as totally past, while dramatic poetry presents it as totally present, and, in contrast to the audience of epic poetry, 'the spectator [of dramatic poetry] must not be allowed to rise to thoughtful contemplation; he must passionately follow the action; his imagination is completely silenced' (Esslin, 1980, p. 113).

Goethe and Schiller had based their theory on Aristotle's *Poetics*. The Aristotelian concept of drama is a drama of catharsis by terror and pity, a drama of spectator-identification with actors, a drama of illusion that creates events which are represented as 'totally present' while they are, in fact, absent. This theatre, then, for Brecht was a deception. He wanted, instead, a theatre of calm contemplation and detachment, a theatre of critical thoughtfulness, and he wanted a theatre that produced active participation; in other words, appropriating Goethe and Schiller's concept of epic poetry, he wanted to create an 'epic' theatre (Brecht, 1964, p. 37). For Brecht, then, while the theatre of illusion tries to re-create a dubious present by pretending that the events of the play are actually taking place at the time of each performance, the epic theatre is strictly historical, it constantly reminds the audience that it is merely representing past events, thereby distancing the audience from what is seen and allowing them to change distance into critique.

Many of Brecht's critics have claimed that Brecht's theatre works despite his theory.[6] To claim this is to say that his plays make sense but only as 'gestures' or 'actions' performed on a stage, they do not make the sense that Brecht would have wished. One of the reasons for this popular misunderstanding is that it fails to distinguish between two senses of theory: that is, theory as a general political philosophical conviction underpinning all of Brecht's work and theory as a set of epic-dialectic structural principles which inform all the essential aspects of Brecht's performances. In fact, in my opinion, it is quite impossible to read and view Brecht's plays carefully as he intended without understanding antithetic structures, effects or epic-dialectic (as against causal) arrangements of scenes in their interaction, and that is a problem with both his practice and theory.

With regard to Brecht's philosophical political convictions, it is important to understand that he believed that poets should not only produce art but contribute to progressive change, and theatre should not merely show something, it should also offer a critical interpretation (Brecht, 1964, p. 35). The kind of social realism that Brecht had in mind allows the audience to go beyond mere recognition and identify the laws which determine social processes. According to Brecht, seeing is not enough, it is necessary to be critical. This is why Brecht is highly derisive of empathy and identification with performers. For Brecht, feelings during a performance are allowed only as long they do not interfere with or obscure social issues. Instead, Brecht argued, respectable art should always entertain while leaving the viewer's intellect intact, giving him or her the option to agree or disagree.

In order to achieve this 'philosophical wakefulness' during a performance, Brecht developed a number of techniques which he called *Verfremdungseffekt*. This term is commonly mistranslated in English to mean alienation

(*Entfremdung*), but the correct English translation of *Verfremdung* is 'defamiliarization' or the making strange or unfamiliar. Brecht appropriated the expression from the Russian formalist term *Ostranenie*, which is literally the 'making strange'. *Verfremdung* can operate on many different levels and differing aspects of the theatre. The narrative of the play, for instance, unfolds in a number of separate situations, each episode complete in itself; the effect of the play is built up through the juxtaposition and 'montage' of these contrasting episodes. Each of these isolated episodes retains its significance even if taken out of context of the play as a whole, as do the non-literary elements — lighting, décor, music and choreography — which remain autonomous and instead of acting as mere appendages to the text enter into a dialectical relationship with it. For instance, musical numbers are introduced as entirely different ingredients of the performance and interrupt its flow, breaking the illusion and therefore presenting the action as 'strange'. This is demonstrated in a scene from *Mother Courage and Her Children* (Brecht, 1966), a cautionary tale about the inevitable consequences of battening on war, where a war-ruined village is presented complete with soldiers, a destroyed farm, a crying baby, an amputee and Mother Courage, who is trying to sell her merchandise. This is juxtaposed with the sound of military music, indicative of a victory march. Therefore, the *mise-en-scène* provides a contradiction between, on the one hand, the obvious despair of the visual scene and, on the other, the celebratory and triumphant nature of the music. This antithetical situation is intended to prevent viewers from establishing empathy or simple identification with the performance, at the same time awakening their social critical faculties.

However, epic distance does not alone produce social critique. Brecht's concept of the dialectic becomes important in structuring audience response into a coherent moral philosophical stance. Brecht's dialectic structures operate at the level of language, projected world ideas and overall narrative-dramatic structure. In *Mother Courage*, all twelve scenes form a complex chain of antithetical structures, all of which propose a summary synthesis. However, the synthesis is not given in the play itself, but must be deduced by the audience on an abstract level of meaning. For instance, in one scene Mother Courage's son Eilif is commended for his bravery after killing some peasants, yet in another he is executed for the same act. In another scene Mother Courage has a chance to save Eilif's life by selling her wagon, but she haggles for too long and her son is shot. Throughout the play moral and commercial values are forcefully juxtaposed to point out that in war the two are incompatible. Mother Courage does not get this message, but according to Brecht the audience should.

When the play was first performed at the Zurich Schauspielhaus, the audience was moved to tears by the sufferings of a poor woman who, having lost everything including her three children in war, heroically continued her brave struggle. Brecht was furious at this response and rewrote the play to emphasize the corrupt nature of Mother Courage's character. Brecht supervised the Berlin production of the play, which was a triumph, but yet again Mother Courage was seen as a 'humanist saint'. Again, hardly anyone had noticed the depravity of Mother Courage. Brecht eventually admitted that the play was not working as he had intended, but claimed it was a fault not on his part but on the part of the audience, who were still enslaved to entrenched habits of emotion.[7]

It would seem that Brecht believed that he could achieve what amounts to a double political strategy: that is, he intended that his intertextual, political theatre would replace the Aristotelian 'theatre of illusion' on the one hand, and on the other, and more importantly, his theatre would have an immediate social and political effect. However, no matter how well Brecht incorporated his theory into his performances, when performed before a non-Brechtian audience — that is, an audience which has little or no prior realization of Brecht's theory or is unfamiliar with his *Little Organon for the Theatre* — his performances fail to work in one important way: that is, the audience misses the ideological structure that underlies the play, and therefore Brecht's plays can only be understood, in the sense he intended, by the theoretically informed. Furthermore, for the minority who are theoretically aware, Brecht's performances can only work for a limited time and locality, which is certainly not what Brecht intended when he devised his epic-dialectic theatre. Moreover, Brecht's intertextual politics failed to replace the 'theatre of illusion'; in fact, it thrives as never before.

It is clear that neither Kant's nor Brecht's theorization can adequately encompass liminal performance, certainly not on a narrow reading of Kant. As I have already stated, Kant's theory presents a 'disinterested' aesthetics, in contrast to Brecht, who stresses the political; neither is adequate in phrasing the aesthetics of liminal performance. Nor is Artaud's concept of the 'theatre of cruelty' any closer to the mark, for while he does list aesthetic features which seem close to the liminal, he differs in an important way, namely in his pursuit of an 'essentialism' which he believed could be realized through performance.

Artaud claimed that theatre is 'a kind of organized anarchy'. He wrote that the object of theatre is 'to express objectively certain secret truths'. Artaud's stage was a theatre of dreams crowded with objects and bodies seen as signs, open to interpretation and without a narrative text (Artaud, 1958, pp. 51–90). Artaud's actors were 'animated hieroglyphs', bodies that moved about like living ciphers in a type of choreographed cryptography (Price, 1990, p. 327). As Derrida writes, Artaud's theatrical writing is a 'writing of the body itself' (1978a, p. 191), and also a critique of the logocentrism of Western society.

Therefore, although Artaud's aesthetic theory can in many ways relate to liminal performance, his theory, too, ultimately proves to be deficient. When he writes, 'We are not free. And the sky can still fall on our heads. And the theater has been created to teach us this first of all' (Artaud, 1958, p. 79), he emphasizes a certain essentialism together with an unchanging, fixed nature of relations that is not compatible with the aesthetic features of liminal performance. Hence, neither Brecht nor Artaud will feature in any major sense in my analysis of liminal performance, while Kant is less easily jettisoned.

In formulating an aesthetic theorization that can address liminal performance, I believe that traditional critical equipment is inadequate in its present form. Kant's concept of a 'pure' aesthetic judgement is now no longer valid (as he, himself, would seem to indicate); neither is Brecht's political theatre, borne out by the fact that the Brechtian project has largely been discarded; nor is Artaud's 'theatre of cruelty'. In addition, unlike Brecht, I would argue that every work of art constitutes a scene of intervention, though not, as Artaud believed, to present certain secret truths. Rather, I believe that the experimental, intertextual nature of liminal performance produces an immediate effect which has *indirect* results on the political, though perhaps a redefinition of this term, and the social in as much it questions the very nature of our accepted ideas and belief systems. In this sense, liminal performance does what all avant-garde art does: it is an experimental extension of the socio-political and cultural of an epoch.

Following on from Kant, writers as diverse as Nietzsche, Heidegger, Foucault, Derrida, Baudrillard and Lyotard have responded to and continued in a certain Kantian tradition. In the following chapters I will discuss their aesthetic theorization in more detail. However, I would like to state that my main purpose in reviewing aesthetic thought is not to provide a critique of Kant, or of any other aesthetic writer for that matter, it is instead an attempt, by choosing selective criteria from these particular theorists, to provide a new aesthetic form of theorization which would be capable of addressing liminal performance or, in other words, as Baudrillard writes of postmodernism, would be able to survive 'among the remnants' and play 'with the pieces' (1984c, pp. 24–5).

Notes

1.   For Horst Ruthrof, 'language cannot mean by itself but can do so only semiotically, i.e. in relation to and through corroboration by non-verbal systems' (1992, p. 6), and, 'far from language constituting a replacement of non-verbal forms of signification, language and non-linguistic sign

systems develop side by side toward ever more complex formations. Moreover ... they interact with one another to constitute "reality" ' (1992, p. 102). See especially Chapter 6, 'The Limits of Langue' (pp. 102–19), for a more detailed discussion on the constraints of language, and his more recent account of intersemiotic semantics (Ruthrof, 1995, 1997).

2. Jochen Schulte-Sasse argues that the historical avant-garde was the first movement to understand fully the modern differentiation of art, and responded to that discovery with an unsuccessful attempt to lead art back to life (see Peter Bürger, 1984). Postmodernism, according to Schulte-Sasse, does not attempt to overcome this separation, but accepts the fact that this functional differentiation of society is irreversible by allowing this insight to shape art's contents. Schulte-Sasse argues that this may well be the reason why parody has become such a characteristic feature of postmodernism (1986/7, pp. 5–22). Although I believe that Schulte-Sasse is correct in his analysis of parody to a certain extent, I would argue that liminal performance, in particular, does still strive to overcome this separation, and parody seems to be a useful tool in this attempt.

3. According to Frederic Jameson, 'the first and most evident [postmodern feature] is the emergence of a new kind of flatness or depthlessness, a new kind of superficiality in the literal sense' (1984, p. 60).

4. Kant, in his introduction to *The Critique of Judgement*, writes, 'our entire faculty of cognition has two realms, that of natural concepts and that of the concepts of freedom. ... In accordance with this distinction, then, Philosophy is divisible into theoretical and practical' (1978a, p. 12).

5. See Nietzsche (1956, Chapter 5).

6. According to Martin Esslin, 'the primary factor was always his creative work: the theories he put forward were postscripts to plays or poems rather than *a priori* principles on which these had been based' (1980, p. 111).

7. See Esslin (1980, pp. 211–13) for a more detailed account of the reception of *Mother Courage*. Esslin argues that Brecht refused to consider the presence of subconscious or emotional factors in his work. His denial of emotional factors was an indication of his constant preoccupation with them, and although Brecht was convinced he was arguing on strictly logical and rational grounds, his arguments are nothing but the rationalizations of instinctive impulses. For Esslin, this is particularly demonstrated by Brecht's unwillingness to change the ending of *Mother Courage*, which would have 'spoiled his play'.

2

The problem of aestheticization: Kant, Nietzsche and Heidegger

In a selective review of aesthetic theorization, Kant is central, since he devoted a major part of his third *Critique* to the problems of the aesthetic, making complex judgements a central part of his philosophical system. Kant's theorization of the 'sublime' is equally relevant, since its features prefigure and correspond to those of the liminal.

Nietzsche responded but also continued in the Kantian tradition. In his theorization on 'perspectival attitudes' he proposed an aesthetic metacritique of 'truth', replacing it with a practice of *écriture fragmentaire*, which is mirrored in the fragmented performance of the liminal. His postulations on the Dionysian are of equal value, since their features are reflected in the immediacy, experimentation and excess of this performance.

For Heidegger, the 'work of art' does not merely reveal things, 'it lets things be'. It is not a purveyor of truth; rather, it is a 'becoming' or 'happening' of 'truth' and it 'opens up a world'. Heidegger is prominent in the theorizing of liminal performance, since his hermeneutic perspective attempts to cancel out the distance between the aesthetic and the non-aesthetic.

Kant

In his 'Preface to the First Edition' (1790) of *The Critique of Judgement*, Kant provides the following 'explanation' for beginning with aesthetic judgement and, by implication, for making all judgements in terms of it. It concerns the difficulties involved in discovering the particular principle belonging to this faculty. Kant writes:

> We may readily gather, however, from the nature of the faculty of judgement ... that the discovery of a peculiar principle belonging to it ... must be a task involving considerable difficulties. For this principle is one which must not be derived from *a priori* concepts.

For Kant, 'it is chiefly in those estimates that are called aesthetic, and which relate to the beautiful and sublime, whether of nature or of art, that one meets with the above difficulty about a principle'. Aesthetic judgement is therefore a form of judgement for which the difficulties in discovering a principle are the most exacting, yet in which the search for the principle is the 'most important item'. The aesthetic is chosen as the context in which to investigate critically the problem of *reflective* judgement in general, because it is where the antinomies basic to judgement are the most extreme, as its concept cannot be derived from the *a priori* principles of understanding (Kant, 1978a, pp. 5–35). Aesthetic judgement is therefore central and fundamental. Moreover, for these reasons aesthetic judgement serves as a prototype for all judgements that must operate in the absence of models as in the purely formal. This has important consequences, especially in the study of liminal performance.

By allocating the major part of his third *Critique* to the problems of aesthetic judgement, Kant became the first modern philosopher to make his aesthetic theory an integral part of a philosophic system. Although it needs to be remembered that under rigorous and close scrutiny the strict notion of an autonomous sphere of the aesthetic does not hold, for as Kant (1911, pp. 584–5) himself stated, 'the concept never stands within safe limits' and 'the completeness of the analysis of my concept must always remain doubtful', still he has been read by many as suggesting just this. So what are the preconditions for aesthetic judgements in general?

According to Kant, aesthetic judgements, just like theoretical judgements are divided into the empirical and pure. So there is a division between judgements, which depend on pleasure or displeasure and those which are actually aesthetic. The former are judgements of sense (material aesthetic judgements) while the latter (as formal) are disinterested judgements of taste proper.[1]

Judgements of beauty (also called 'judgements of taste') are analysed in terms of the four 'moments' of the table of categories: *quality, quantity, relation* and *modality*. First, according to Kant, aesthetic satisfaction is evoked by an object that is purposive in its form, though in fact it has no purpose or function ('purposiveness without purpose'). The second moment lays claim to universal acceptance: 'The *beautiful* is that which, apart from a concept, pleases universally.' We would now perhaps say 'socially' or 'culturally'. Third, the judgement of taste does not (like ordinary judgements) subsume a representation under a concept, but states a relation between the representation and a special disinterested satisfaction: that is, a satisfaction independent of desire and 'apart from any interest'. The fourth moment deals with modality: that is, the beautiful is claimed by the judgement of taste to have a necessary reference to aesthetic satisfaction. 'The beautiful is that which, apart from a concept, is cognized as object of a *necessary* delight' (Kant, 1978a, pp. 50–85).

It is the above four moments in the judgement of beauty that give rise to the philosophical problem of validation which Kant formulates. How can their claim to necessity and subjective universality be legitimized? According to Kant, this can only be done if it can be shown that the conditions presupposed in such a judgement are not confined to the individual who makes it, but may be imputed to all rational beings. In arguing for the disinterestedness of aesthetic satisfaction, Kant is saying that our satisfaction is in no way dependent on individual interests: it takes on a kind of intersubjectivity.[2] However, the validation of the synthetic *a priori* judgement of taste requires something more, namely a transcendental deduction.[3]

In the *Critique of Pure Reason*, all knowledge which is occupied not so much with objects but with our *a priori* concepts of objects is called *transcendental* and 'these representations', although not being empirical, can still refer to *a priori* objects of experience (1911, pp. 9–45). The *transcendental schemata* are therefore mediating representations, free from any empiricism, which produce signification (1911, p. 113). The transcendental schema has been read by many as denoting a transcendental signified. Yet Kant denies this when he claims that no concept can be defined because a concept may contain many obscure representations and its analysis must always remain in doubt (1911, p. 585). Therefore, Kant's transcendental is a *procedural* issue rather than a matter of content. Not the attainment of specific transcendental signifieds but rather a heuristics, or the *conditions* of the possibility of knowledge.

The main tenets of Kant's validatory argument are as follows: empirical knowledge is possible because the faculty of judgement can bring together general concepts and particular sense-intuitions prepared for it in the imagination. These cases of *determinate* judgement presuppose, however, a general harmony between the imagination in its freedom as synthesizer of representations and the understanding, in its *a priori* lawfulness. The formal purposiveness of an object as experienced can induce what Kant calls 'the free play of imagination', an intense disinterested pleasure that depends not on any particular knowledge but just on consciousness of the harmony of the two cognitive powers imagination and understanding (1978a, pp. 58–60). This is the pleasure we affirm in the judgement of taste. The general possibility of sharing knowledge with each other presupposes that in each of us there is a cooperation of imagination and understanding, which means that every rational being has the *capacity* to feel under appropriate discernible conditions this harmony of those cognitive powers. Therefore, a true judgement of taste can be said to be true for all in a given culture, and taste is seen as 'a *kind* of sensus communis' (Kant, 1978a, p. 150).

However, since the Kantian structure, based on principles of critical philosophy, requires that there be a dialectic of taste with an antinomy to be dissolved, a contradiction arises in the judgement of taste. For if the judgement involves concepts, it must be rationally disputable and provable by reason (which it is not), and if it does not involve concepts, it cannot even be the subject of disagreement (which it is). The solution, therefore, is that no determinate concept is involved in such a judgement, but only the indeterminate concept of what Kant calls the 'supersensible', which underlies the object as well as the judging subject.[4] Therefore, the judgement of aesthetic taste is based on the concept of the purposiveness of nature and, consequently, beauty is viewed as 'the symbol of the morally good'; there lies its claim to universal acceptance and its sensual intimations (Kant, 1978a, p. 223).

So what are the preconditions for the aesthetic judgement of liminal performance? It would seem that certain of the above aesthetic properties need to be rephrased with regard to the liminal. Certainly, the 'beautiful' is now no longer an appropriate description of a quintessential liminal feature. It may have to be rephrased as the 'exciting' or 'the edge of the possible'. Nor is it any longer an object of '*necessary* delight', since liminal features have little to do with delight in the harmonious sense of the term. In fact, self-conscious harmony between the 'imagination and understanding', which causes pleasure and which is a prerequisite for a judgement of taste in Kant's analysis, does not occur in liminal performance at all. Nor in this instance is the judgement of taste a 'universal' issue, since the performance lacks any purposiveness of nature and for this reason is now no longer a symbol of the 'morally good'. Rather, it can be viewed only in a localized context. Furthermore, heterogeneity and the local, which are integral characteristics of the liminal, cannot be integrated with universality. Yet, as I have already indicated, it has not been possible to dispose of all features of Kantian universality, since even the qualification of an 'open genre' has certain requirements which neither heterogeneity nor the accentuation on the local is able to fulfil. As for the question of ethics and morality, I believe that liminal forms of aesthetics can affect, though *indirectly*, the ethical and the political.

Kant's analysis of the sublime proceeds on quite different grounds. Kant claims that the beautiful and the sublime, though agreeing on the point of pleasing on their own accord and sharing a presupposition of a reflective judgement, also present 'important and striking differences between the two'. He writes, 'the most important and vital distinction between the sublime and the beautiful is certainly this: whereas natural beauty (such as is self-subsisting) conveys a finality in its form ... the sublime, may appear ... to be ill-adapted to our faculty of presentation, and to be, as it were, an outrage on the imagination' (1978a, pp. 90–1).

Essentially, Kant explains this type of (dis)satisfaction as a feeling of awe in the face of reason itself and of human moral destiny. This occurs in two ways: first, when we are confronted in nature with the extremely vast (the mathematical sublime), our imagination hesitates in the task of comprehending it and we become aware of the supremacy of reason, whose ideas reach towards infinite totality; second, when we are confronted with the overwhelmingly powerful (dynamical sublime), the weakness of our empirical selves makes us aware, again by contrast, of our worth as moral beings.[5]

The sublime is another instance of the problem of attempting to read an aesthetic perspective as an autonomous object. A paradox must exist if the experience of beauty rests upon seeing natural objects as though they were somehow the artefacts of a cosmic reason, yet at the same time the experience of the sublime makes use of natural formlessness and fearfulness to celebrate reason itself. Kant writes, 'The sublime ... is an object (of nature) the _representation of which determines the mind to regard the elevation of nature beyond our reach as equivalent to a presentation of ideas_' (1978a, p. 119).

Therefore, the sublime is the tension between joy and sorrow: the delight of having a feeling of totality inseparable from the pain of not being able to present an object equal to this idea of totality. Spectators are not simply engaged in passive contemplation but are called to do what, according to Kant, cannot be done, to present the unpresentable, to surpass what is possible for something else, to strive continually towards a judgement that can never be guaranteed. The sublime indicates that there can never be security in mere contemplation, for the signs presented demand more than this.

The sublime is crucial in the analysis of liminal performance, especially in its experimental aspects, with its concomitant feelings of disquiet: that is, in this striving to present the unpresentable. Furthermore, the feelings of disquiet produced by certain aesthetic features of liminal performance are closely allied to Kant's notion of 'negative pleasure'. In discussing the sublime, he writes, 'the sublime does not so much involve positive pleasure as admiration or respect, i.e. merits the name of a _negative pleasure_' (1978a, p. 91, emphasis added).

Kant argued that the sublime could not be presented at all. Lyotard, following on from Kant, agrees with this but believes that there must still be a constant striving to present the unpresentable because, for Lyotard, the sublime is 'that which, in the modern puts forward the unpresentable in presentation itself. ... A Postmodern artist or writer ... is in the position of a philosopher working without rules in order to formulate the rules of what will have been done. Hence the fact that work and text have the characters of an event ... they always come too late for their author' (1984, p. 81).

However, it is my belief that the unpresentable is presentable and is demonstrable in liminal performance, not, as Lyotard strongly argues in *The Differend*, dependent on a linguistic perspective, which in my opinion ultimately prevents this event from occurring, but from aspects of the intersemiotic, in other words from beyond and including language. This would bear a closer affinity to the Kantian sublime, which is reviewed further within Lyotard's theorization in Chapter 3.

Nietzsche

Certain aspects of Nietzsche have proven important in the theorization of liminal aesthetics. Especially so are his emphasis on the world as an aesthetically self-creating entity, and his concept of the *Dionysian*, a symbol of Nietzsche's commitment to immediacy: that is, a knowledge that does not proceed from analysis or concepts. For Nietzsche, art is not a vehicle of truth; rather, it is a purveyor of a necessary illusion. He writes, 'take care philosophers and friends of knowledge, and beware of martyrdom. ... Flee away and conceal yourselves! And have your masks and subtlety, so that you may be misunderstood' (1973, pp. 37–8). Nietzsche links the 'will to art' to 'falsehood, to a flight from "truth", to a denial of "truth"' (1924b, p. 289).

In *The Birth of Tragedy*, Nietzsche provides an example of his early aesthetic theorization in his revaluation of the classical Greeks, 'who developed their mystical doctrines of art through plausible *embodiments*, not through conceptual means' (1956, p. 19). *The Birth of Tragedy* is essentially a discussion of the relationship between Apollonian and Dionysian influences on art and culture. The Apollonian and Dionysian, for Nietzsche, were symbols rather than concepts, and his theorization of the aesthetic was based on their opposition. However, despite their apparent radical opposition, they have in common a shared rejection of any mediated understanding provided by concepts or analysis.[6]

Apollo is associated with form and structure; the pure artistic expression of the Apollonian principle is sculpture. By contrast, Dionysus is associated with energy, sexuality, fertility and nature; the pure Dionysian art is music. While the Apollonian experience is found in the 'dream' which has form (image), the Dionysian experience is characteristically that of 'intoxication', which is by definition formless. Nietzsche describes the Dionysian as 'The tremendous awe which seizes man when he suddenly begins to doubt the cognitive modes of experience ... whose closest analogy is furnished by physical intoxication.'

Apollo, in contrast, is 'the god of illusion', wrapping man in 'the veil of maya' and protecting him from the harsh realities of his existence.[7] Dionysus 'annihilates' the veil of maya and opens the way for a direct and unmediated participation in reality. Nietzsche argues that Dionysian art 'does not ... represent appearance, but the will directly' (1956, p. 97).

The Nietzschean Dionysian can be argued to be central to the liminal in its expression of immediacy, disruption and excess. In addition, it demonstrates an exploration of the ambiguous and open-ended nature of reality, together with an emphasis on the destructured, dehumanized subject which is also fundamental. In this performance there is an accentuation on a certain 'shift-shape' style, pointing only indirectly to content, creating the sense of a pursuit of the almost chthonic.

Nietzsche refers to 'the world' as a 'a self-generating work of art', thereby expounding his aestheticist position. The most important element in Nietzsche's concept of the aesthetic is the notion of creativity. Again and again, he glorifies the artist who transforms the brute material of existence into something made after his own image. Artists should not 'see things as they are; they should see them fuller, simpler, stronger'. Nietzsche's conception of art is important, because he extends it to his own activity, conceiving himself ultimately to be an *artist-philosopher* (1924b, pp. 239–43). He envisages a joining together of the 'artistic energies and the practical wisdom of life' with 'scientific thinking' (1974, p. 193). In *Thus Spoke Zarathustra*, philosophy turns into art, with Nietzsche becoming an artist-philosopher.[8] Therefore, Nietzsche himself saw his own thought as essentially aesthetic in character, and viewed that aesthetic factor as crucial to his own significance as a thinker.

Nietzsche, in providing a theorization of the aesthetic, can be seen on one level to be reacting to what he believes is the anthropomorphic permeation within the Kantian aesthetic. He writes, 'like all philosophers, Kant, instead of viewing the esthetic issue from the side of the artist, envisaged art and beauty solely from the "spectator's"' (1956, p. 238). However, Nietzsche seems to (deliberately) misunderstand the Kantian project, since Kant is talking of the conditions that make complex judgements possible, of which the aesthetic judgement is a special case, and if the emphasis is on judgement then it follows that the spectator or the act of viewing is at the centre of the argument.

In arguing that there are no grounds for choosing one mode of behaviour over another (morality is not a question of 'the nature of things' because 'there are no moral phenomena at all, but only a moral interpretation of phenomena' (1973, p. 108)), Nietzsche presents the dilemma of choosing between competing modes of behaviour. He resolves this by arguing that the choice ultimately has to be made on aesthetic grounds. The idea of the free creativity of the artist is decisive in this choice. For Nietzsche, 'man', in order to enhance his species, had to develop his unconditional will to power by, among other things, 'his powers of invention and dissimulation' and 'the art of experiment' (1973, p. 54). This idea of free creativity, invention and experimentation is crucial for liminal performance, given its emphasis on heterogeneity and indeterminacy.

Nietzsche argues that the state was created by conquerors having the egotism of artists who imposed on a formless 'reality' their own image of how the world ought to be ordered.[9] Nietzsche is therefore ascribing to art an ontogenetic — that is, a world-making — significance. What comes into being does so as a result of artistic will; the 'given', 'natural' materials of this creation have no more significance than the blank emptiness of the artist's bare canvas. Nietzsche writes, 'a man is an artist to the extent to which he regards everything that inartistic people call "form" as the actual substance ... his own life included' (1924b, p. 61).

Even though the emphasis is on the creative, for Nietzsche all authorship is excluded. The idea of the world as aesthetically self-creating constitutes an absolutely remarkable innovation in thought, providing the basis for much of the theorization which follows Nietzsche. He stands as the founder of what became the aesthetic metacritique of 'truth', where 'the work of art' is seen as establishing the grounds for truth's possibility.

The question of authority and its legitimation is a critical issue in Nietzsche's writing. Whether he is deconstructing the authority of the moral theological tradition, excising the metaphysical authority within language or even questioning his own authority, his refusal to legitimate any figure of authority remains consistent. Authority demands obedience; therefore, a philosophy of the future will require a critique of authority to transcend and undermine previous values. The whole Nietzschean project of *genealogy* directs itself to deconstructing the dominant foundations of modernity, which presupposes a delegitimation of existing (moral) authority. This notion is analogous to the decline of the genius and the authority of the artistic producer, which is a quintessential characteristic of the liminal.

Fundamental to Nietzsche's theorization is his conviction of the 'death of God', which embraces a condemnation of the present world as null. The recognition of this nullity is what we know as nihilism. According to Nietzsche, there are two kinds of nihilism. First, there is a nihilism that fails to respond to what Nietzsche sees as the opportunity offered by the world's nullity; a passive and anaesthetic attitude is adopted. Second, and more importantly, there is an active, aesthetic nihilism. Instead of drawing back from the void we dance upon it, instead of lamenting the absence of a world suited to our own being we invent one. We become the artists of our own existence, free from natural constraints and limitations. In one sense at least, the active aesthetic response to nihilism is therefore one dimension of a broader affirmative approach to the 'little things',[10] against the revenge of reason as represented by the 'theoretical man' (Stauth and Turner, 1988, p. 233).

It is this belief in the aesthetic that leads Nietzsche to write that 'the extremest form of Nihilism' is the view that there is 'no real world at hand' and therefore everything is 'only an *appearance seen in perspective*, whose origin must be found in us' (1924a, p. 16). This is a Kantian view without noumenal constraints. Throughout his critique of morality, philosophy and religion, Nietzsche attempts to dismantle or deconstruct such oppositional hierarchies as truth/error, good/evil and being/becoming. In genealogically investigating the origin of the positive valuation of truth, Nietzsche finds it is simply a moral prejudice to affirm truth over error. To this he suggests that error might be more valuable than truth and that error might be a necessary condition of life. However, his analysis does not stop there, as Heidegger assumes when he accuses Nietzsche of 'completing' the history of metaphysics through an 'inversion' of Platonism,[11] for by adopting a perspectival attitude and denying the possibility of an unmediated interpretive apprehension of 'reality', Nietzsche, in effect, displaces the truth/falsity opposition altogether. The question is now no longer whether a perspective is 'true' or 'false'. The sole question that interests the genealogist is whether or not a perspective enhances life: 'The true world we have abolished: what world then remains? The apparent one perhaps? ... But no! *with the real world we have also abolished the apparent world!*' (Nietzsche, 1990, p. 51). Therefore, in the deciphering of one pole of the binary opposition – the 'true world' – as an illusion, the opposition itself loses its critical force.

Nietzsche demonstrates that a certain faith in binary thinking is at the centre of philosophical discourse. In rejecting the binary structure of moral evaluation, Nietzsche's transvaluation calls forth a playful experimentation with values and a plurality of perspectives that he labels *'the interpretation of action*, and not merely the *transvaluation* of concepts' (1924b, p. 103).

As we shall see, liminal performance similarly presents a deconstruction of binary oppositions, which is demonstrated in the collapse of hierarchical distinctions such as those between high and mass/popular culture. Central to the liminal is a mixing of popular knowledge with 'elitist' knowledge, together with a definite blurring of set boundaries; in other words a certain intertextuality is presented. Other aesthetic features that are present in the liminal and parallel Nietzsche's 'active interpretation' are playfulness and the celebration of the surface 'depthlessness of culture', together with a stylistic *bricolage* and the mixing of codes.

In answering the question 'What is truth?', Nietzsche writes: 'A mobile army of metaphors, metonymies, and anthropomorphisms ... truths are illusions of which one has forgotten they are illusions; worn out metaphors which have become powerless to affect the senses' (1964, p. 180).

Nietzsche insists that language distorts: 'there must be something that thinks when we think, is merely a formulation of a grammatical custom which sets an agent to every action' (1924b, p. 14). He writes: 'I fear we are not getting rid of God because we still believe in grammar' (1990, p. 48). For Nietzsche, God is a product of a grammatical habit, he is the thinker who thinks, the doer of the deed, and as long as we continue to believe in grammar, in the metaphysical and epistemological presuppositions hidden within language, we will continue to believe in God. The death of God and the deconstruction of divine authority are prerequisites for the *Übermensch*'s (superman's) transvaluation of all values and therefore; our faith in the authority of language must also be suspended if a transvaluation is to be possible.

Therefore, for Nietzsche, language is itself a work of art. This leads to accepting the necessity of 'distortions' and a 'plurality of perspectives', and hence a 'divine' or creative way of thinking. According to Maurice Blanchot, Nietzsche's style of writing is a practice of *parole de fragment,* an *écriture fragmentaire* which says nothing outside itself but delights in a play of language for its own sake, subverting the 'spirit of gravity' in his own 'philosophical discourse' (Hartman, 1970, pp. 97–103). It would appear that liminal performance, especially in its emphasis on pastiche and fragmentation, parallels this creative way of being.

Heidegger

In a discussion of Heidegger's *hermeneutic* aesthetic perspective, most lucidly and accessibly expressed in 'The Origin of the Work of Art', it is important to remember that, for Heidegger, the work of art is in no way tied to an 'empirical' or 'ordinary' actuality. Nor is it subject to the demands of mimetic or representational truth. Instead it creates 'truth', but more than that it creates worlds, as Heidegger writes, 'towering up within itself, the work opens up a *world* and keeps it abidingly in force'; therefore, 'to be a work means to set up a world' (1971b, p. 44).

The concept of setting up worlds can be interpreted in two senses. In a weaker sense, Heidegger is asserting that art serves to sensitize us to realities that we may be unaware of: for example, when a painting helps to open us up to the play of colours. The world is not immediately present to us but requires an astonishing receptivity. Heidegger points to this when he claims that the work of art 'holds open the Open of the world'. In the second and stronger sense of setting up worlds, Heidegger, instead of accepting a view of art that points to the 'world of the work of art' as an imaginary space which provides an aesthetic distance from the 'real world', cancels out the distance between the aesthetic and the non-aesthetic. He argues that the work of art does not merely reveal things, but more importantly it lets things be, 'it lets the earth be an earth'. For Heidegger, the work of art is not seen as a purveyor of truth; rather, he sees it as the 'becoming' or 'happening' of 'truth' (1971b, pp. 44–57), which is important for liminal performance in so much as each performance can be seen as a becoming or a happening, with all the potentiality this implies. Heidegger's belief in this world creating potential of the work of art evokes Nietzsche's assertion in *The Birth of Tragedy* that 'the Dionysiac element ... calls into being the entire world of phenomena' (1956, p. 145).

For an understanding of Heidegger's theorization of the aesthetic, it is important to examine his preoccupation with alienation. In *Being and Time*, Heidegger presents an ontological situation in which *Dasein* (literally 'there-being', more loosely translated as 'human existence') is constantly being threatened by an alienation from its 'ownmost potentiality-for-being' (1971b, p. 188). According to Heidegger, the 'everyday publicness of the "they" ' conceals from us the knowledge that we are alienated beings and makes us feel 'at home' within the world (1978, p. 233). However, this feeling is deceptive and Dasein's true condition manifests itself more clearly when it finds itself in a state of anxiety where it feels *Unheimlich* (literally unhomelike): that is, uncomfortable or uncanny (1978, p. 322).

Dasein as a 'falling away' from its 'authentic potentiality for Being itself' and into the 'world' should not be interpreted in historical terms; rather, every Dasein, at all times, demonstrates such a fallenness (Heidegger, 1978, p. 220). Therefore, there is no belief in a particular 'age of anxiety'. Nevertheless, Heidegger does introduce a temporal element, since much of his work is pervaded by a metaphoric of 'going back' or of a 'return to origins'. Nowhere is this more evident than in 'The Origin of the Work of Art', where he asks about the source of the nature of art. But what then is art? Can 'art as such' be spoken about meaningfully? 'Can art be an origin at all? Where and how does art occur? Art – this is nothing but a word.' It would appear that as long as it remains an open question as to whether or how art comes-to-presence, the only way to find the essence of art is to examine the work of art itself. For Heidegger, 'What art should be is inferable from the work. What the work of art *is* we can come to know only from the nature of art. Anyone can easily see that we are moving in a circle' (1971b, pp. 17–18).

In trying to explain the individual's 'primordial' way of knowing, that which is inherent in Dasein's concern, Heidegger portrays Being as a structural unity which implies three different elements; mood (*Beflindlichkeit*), understanding (*Verstehen*) and *logos*.[12] Not only do individuals possess an existential possibility of being always in a mood, but their modes of Being are determined equiprimordially by their understanding. For Heidegger, understanding is not a concrete mode of knowing, but what makes all modes of knowing possible.

In primordial understanding, the mode of Being manifests itself as 'Being able to ...', and constantly moves in a range of possibilities because it possesses in itself the existential structure of a 'project'. For this reason, primordial understanding entails essentially an antecedent view of the world as a whole and also of our own modes of Being.[13]

Primordial understanding, which is irrevocably connected with mood, always has the character of an anticipating, interpretive conception, in which individuals disclose themselves as Being-able-to-be in the different modalities that are available to them, modalities to which different possibilities correspond with respect to their things, works, equipment or the world. But this interpretive conception is as such not yet articulated in understanding. It can only develop in that direction by means of *Auslegung*, a term which means explanation as well as interpretation (Heidegger, 1978, p. 188).

Therefore, in Heidegger's opinion *all understanding is interpretation*. Interpretation may be implicit, as in our dealings with things, or explicit, as in our interpretive explanation and enunciation. For Heidegger, the profoundest root of the hermeneutic character of all human understanding is to found in the fact that all understanding necessarily takes place in the *'hermeneutical situation'*. To understand a phenomenon necessarily presupposes a totality of meaning within which this phenomenon can appear as meaningful ('fore-having'). A certain point of view is also assumed, which fixes how that which is to be understood is to be interpreted ('fore-sight'), and finally, due to the help of concepts which are extracted from the phenomenon itself or are forced upon it and to 'which it is opposed in its manner of Being', the interpretive understanding has already decided for a definite way of interpretation ('fore-conception') (1978, pp. 190–1). Thus, without already participating in things and without being able to anticipate, we could not understand (1978, p. 275).

It could be argued that using this type of circular interpretation implies that there is a presupposition of the idea of Being. And Heidegger does not deny this. Indeed, he shows that all arguments are circular in a certain sense. Yet he denies that the process of interpretation implies positing any proposition from which further propositions about Being can be deduced. He writes: 'In the projecting of the understanding, entities are disclosed in their possibility. The character of the possibility corresponds, on each occasion, with the kind of Being of the entity which is understood.'

Therefore, the fundamental existence which constitutes the disclosedness of Being or Being-there are states of mind and understanding, where lies the possibility of both being understood and interpreted. For Heidegger, language also has it roots in the existential constitution of Dasein's disclosedness (1978, pp. 192–203). According to Heidegger, the intelligibility of something has always been articulated, even before there is any appropriate interpretation of it, and that which can be articulated in interpretation is what we call meaning. Heidegger, in writing 'everyday language is a forgotten and therefore a used-up poem', points to poetic speaking as the richest form of language used, distinguishing it not only from 'idle talk' but also from the merely technical of the *apophantic* (1971a, p. 208). According to Heidegger, 'in "poetical" discourse, the communication of the existential possibilities of one's state-of-mind can become an aim in itself, and this amounts to a disclosing of existence' (1978, p. 205).

'Poetry', for Heidegger, 'is the saying of the unconcealedness of what is' and 'art, as the setting-into-work of truth, is poetry' (1971b, p. 74). In contrast to technical language, which never questions its 'identity' ('mathematics is not more rigorous than historiology, but only narrower' (1978, p. 195)), poetic language is continually questioning human destiny and human being. Therefore, in interpreting a poem or a work of art we are dealing with something that could be seen as an interpretive spiral or a 'hermeneutic helix' rather than a circle (Ruthrof, 1992, p. 141). It begins with our entering interpretive – that is, thoughtful – reading; however, the ending is never clearly defined. Heidegger too points to this when he writes, 'What is decisive is not to get out of the circle but to come into it in the right way. ... In the circle is hidden a positive possibility of the most primordial kind of knowing' (1978, p. 195).

Therefore, the 'hermeneutic circle', for Heidegger, refers to an interpretive movement at the end of which we know more than we did before, without having left that circle in any analytical sense. For we already bring with us a rich resource that thoughtful attention can bring to bear on language itself. In this sense there is no real or simple repetition in viewing a work of art or, for that matter, in observing a performance, for each turn of the circle produces new insights. This is particularly relevant for liminal performance, with its abundant array of such aesthetic features as eclecticism, pastiche, parody, reflexiveness, montage and collage, and a repetitiveness which foregrounds not sameness but difference.

In 'The Origin of the Work of Art', Heidegger argues for a distinctive 'truth value' of art. Commenting on a painting by van Gogh of a pair of peasant shoes,[14] Heidegger argues that through the painting the Being of the shoes comes to light.[15] How does this occur? According to Heidegger, it is through our normal propositional, conceptual, representational thinking that we view the world. In seeking to understand 'the thing', we apply fixed definitions to it.[16] According to Heidegger, the history of Western metaphysics has seen three attempts to answer the question: 'what is the thingness of the thing?' One interpretation presents the thing as the subject, Latin *subiectum* (substance) from the Greek *hypokeimenon* (what is). However, beneath this seemingly innocent translation from Greek to Roman-Latin there is concealed a *translation* of Greek experience into a different way of thinking. Being in general becomes being in the particular and, for Heidegger, the rootlessness ('fall') of Western thought originates from this (mis)translation. The second interpretation of the thing is the *aistheton*, that which is conceived as a collection of sense perceptions. In this 'thing-concept' there is an attempt to bring it into the closest proximity to us. But a thing never reaches that position as long as its thingly features are assigned by what is perceived by the senses. The final interpretation is of the thing as a unity of matter with form. This distinction of matter and form 'is *the conceptual schema which is used ... generally for all art theory and aesthetics.* This incontestable fact, however, proves neither that the distinction of matter and form is adequately founded, nor that it belongs originally to the domain of art and the art work' (Heidegger, 1971b, p. 27).

Therefore, all three interpretations miss the thingness of the thing. In other words, conceptual thought fails. It falsifies reality, it does not let reality be. But in art we have a different approach to the world and to the things and tools and works that occupy that world.

For Heidegger, van Gogh's painting of the peasant shoes lets the shoes be. In a similar way, we 'let the painting be', approaching it in the same way that it approaches the world. Consequently, there is a speaking and hearing that would not otherwise occur. In the vicinity of the artwork, we are suddenly 'somewhere else than we usually tend to be. The art work lets us know what shoes are in truth.' Yet 'it would be the worse self-deception to think that our description, as a subjective action, had first depicted everything thus and then projected it into the painting'. Instead, what is portrayed 'first genuinely arrives at its appearance through the work and only in the work' (1971b, pp. 23–36).

According to Heidegger, specialized and systematic thinking about art and the artist is of relatively late origin, and so is the name for this kind of thinking: that is, aesthetics. Aesthetics treats the work as an object, 'the object of *aisthesis*, of sensuous apprehension in the wide sense'. This apprehension, known as 'experience', is supposed to give information about art's nature. However, although 'experience is the source that is standard not only for art appreciation and enjoyment, but also for artistic creation', it is perhaps the element in which art dies.

Heidegger's intention, following Hegel, is to question whether 'art is still an essential and necessary way in which that truth happens which is decisive for our historical existence' (1971b, p. 80). For Heidegger, 'truth' is the 'unconcealment of that which is as something that is'; above all, truth is the truth of beauty. When truth is at work, it appears. The beautiful belongs to the coming-to-pass of the truth. Therefore, beauty is not merely relative to pleasure, nor is it purely an object. The beautiful, for Heidegger, lies in form but only because the form, *forma*, once took its light from Being as the 'isness' of what is, at the time Being made its advent as *eidos*. Being eventually became 'objectivity' and then 'experience'. Therefore, in the way in which, for the world determined by the West, that which 'is as the real', conceals a peculiar (post-Keatsian) confluence of beauty with truth, and the history of Western art corresponds to a change in the conception of the essence of truth. For Heidegger, this means that art cannot really be understood in terms of either beauty or experience (1971b, pp. 79–81). This is also true of liminal performance, since beauty can no longer be seen as its feature and no previous experience can wholly prepare an audience for this event.

Notes

1. In *The Critique of Judgement*, Kant writes: 'aesthetic, just like theoretical (logical) judgements, are divisible into empirical and pure. . . . The former are judgements of sense (material aesthetic judgements), the latter (as formal) alone judgements of taste proper' (1978a, p. 65).
2. According to Kant (1978a, p. 51), 'the judgement of taste . . . must involve a claim to validity of all men, and must do so apart from universality attached to Objects, i.e. there must be coupled with it a claim to subjective universality.'
3. Kant argues: 'Judgements of taste are synthetic', yet 'a priori . . . what is represented a priori as a universal rule for the judgement . . . is not the pleasure but the universal validity of this pleasure perceived' (1978a, pp. 145–6).
4. For Kant, the antinomy presented by the 'principle of taste' is therefore 'Thesis . . . not based upon concepts' and 'Antithesis . . . based on concepts'. Kant resolves this dialectic by claiming: 'The judgement of taste does rest upon a concept, although an indeterminate one (that, namely, of the supersensible substrate of phenomena)' (1978a, pp. 206–8).
5. According to Kant, the sublime involves 'as its characteristic feature a

mental movement combined with the estimate of the object', this movement has to be estimated as 'subjectively final'. Therefore, 'it is referred through the imagination either to the faculty of cognition or to that of desire ... the first is attributed to the Object as a mathematical, the second as a dynamical, affection of the imagination' (1978a, p. 94).

6. For Nietzsche (1956, p. 109), Socrates provided Western culture with a new hero: 'theoretical man'. However, 'modern man has begun to be aware of the limit of Socratic curiosity and to long in the wide waste ocean of knowledge for shore'.

7. Nietzsche describes Apollo as 'at once the god of all plastic powers and the soothsaying god' and 'it is by those two art-sponsoring deities, Apollo and Dionysos, that we are made to recognize the tremendous split ... between the plastic, Apollonian arts and the non-visual art of music inspired by Dionysos' (1956, pp. 19–22).

8. Nietzsche writes, 'within my writings my Zarathustra stands by itself ... it is not only the most exalted book that exists ... it is also the profoundest' (1979, p. 35).

9. According to Nietzsche, 'Such natures come like destiny ... their work is an instinctive imposing of forms. They are the most spontaneous ... artists that exist' (1956, pp. 219–20).

10. Nietzsche expounds his life-affirming view when he writes, 'contempt has been taught for the "little things" which is to say for the fundamental affairs of life ... my formula for greatness in a human being is amor fati: that one wants nothing to be other that it is' (1979, pp. 67–8).

11. Heidegger claims that despite his revaluations of metaphysics, Nietzsche remains 'in the unbroken path of the tradition'. However, this reading can be challenged. For although Heidegger's metaphysical reading of Nietzsche dictates a univocal determination for such concepts as the 'will to power' and the 'eternal recurrence', he asserts the absolute 'primacy of the practical' (1967, p. 267). Karl Jaspers (1979) analyses Nietzsche's 'philosophical activity' in terms of infinite reflection, self-dissembling writing and groundless thought. Heidegger, by emphasizing the ethical intention of Nietzsche's thought, fails to grasp the multiplicity in use, meaning and origin which such concepts reveal in their practical aspect.

12. According to Heidegger, 'state-of-mind and understanding are characterized equiprimordially by discourse' (1978, p. 172).

13. 'In understanding the world, Being-in is always understood along with it, while understanding of existence as such is always an understanding of the world' (Heidegger, 1978, p. 186).

14. Derrida (1987b, p. 381) provides an important critique of Heidegger. Heidegger has situated himself 'in the nearness of the work', but, Derrida

argues, there are 'pathetico-fantasmico-ideologico-political investments' tied up with the world that Heidegger invokes in the painting. Why should the shoes belong to peasants? Why this truth? Indeed, why should there be any truth at all, from the work of art, from poetry, from language?

15. For Heidegger, 'van Gogh's painting is the disclosure of what the equipment, the pair of shoes, is in truth. This entity emerges into the unconcealedness of its being ... there is here an occurring, a happening of truth at work' (1971b, p. 36).

16. According to Heidegger, 'We are bound to meet with the definition of thingness of things already in the traditional interpretations of being' (1971b, p. 22).

3

Contemporary aesthetics

Foucault, Derrida, Baudrillard and Lyotard, despite the diversity of their writings, have a great deal to contribute to the theorization of contemporary culture. In this respect, their work continues the European and especially Kantian Philosophical tradition.

In a retheorization of the aesthetic in relation to liminal performance, Foucault's notion of 'discourse formation' is central, since it indicates how new discursive formations such as the liminal emerge, are delimited and specified. Derrida's writings on deconstruction and identity formation are of equal value. His 'undecidables', such as 'différance' and 'iterability', problematize and destabilize notions of origin. This has implications for generic formation within the liminal, as the boundaries within this performance are continually being stretched and transgressed. Baudrillard's conjectures on technology, 'seduction' and simulacra are similarly important. One of the quintessential features of the liminal is the prominence of state-of-the-art technologies. Finally, Lyotard's work is crucial, since he attempts to provide a redefinition of the 'sublime'. However, his theorization, as I argue, falls short in one important way: it is premised primarily on a linguistic model. This proves ultimately untenable in the face of such intersemiotic practices as the liminal.

Foucault

In *The Archaeology of Knowledge*, Michel Foucault suggests that 'what is discovered in the analysis of formations is not the bubbling source of life itself. ... One remains within the dimension of discourse' (1972, p. 76). Foucault's discursive, analytical, aesthetic underpinnings can be made fruitful when we apply them to art as a largely self-referential entity and not to a representation of something exterior to the text. For Foucault, discourse is always a perspectival process, as he declares in his intention to 'dispense with "things"... To substitute for the enigmatic treasure of "things" anterior to discourse, the regular formation of objects, that emerge only in discourse' (1972, p. 47). This recalls Nietzsche's claim that 'facts are precisely what is lacking, all that exists consists of *interpretation*' (1924b, p. 12).

We can look at liminal performance using a Foucauldian analysis, but only in a very limited sense for what is relevant to this work, since Foucault, in his analysis, ultimately and perhaps not surprisingly ends up totalizing the discursive diversity he seeks to defend.[1] Nevertheless, in situating and positioning liminal performance, Foucault's notion of 'discursive formations' provides a promising critical perspective.

Foucault, in discussing the basis of the unity of large statements such as *'medicine, economics,* or *grammar'*, argues first that what appears as a well defined field of objects is no more than a series full of gaps, interplays of differences, distances and transformations. Second, a definite normative type of statement is much too different and heterogeneous to form 'a sort of great uninterrupted text'. Third, well defined notions on closer inspection present concepts that differ too much in structure and in the rules governing their use to enter the union of a 'logical architecture'. Finally, in relation to the permanence of a thematic, what are found are various strategic possibilities that lead to the activation of incompatible themes. Therefore, Foucault concludes that the unity of these large statements is not based on 'an order in their successive appearance' or 'linked and hierarchized transformations'. Consequently, an analysis, 'instead of reconstituting *chains of inference* ... instead of drawing up *tables of differences* ... would describe the *systems of dispersion'*. According to Foucault, when such a system of dispersion can be described and whenever regularity can be defined between objects, types of statements, concepts and thematic choices, 'we are dealing with a *discursive formation* ... and the condition to which the elements of this division ... are subjected we shall call the *rules of formation'*.

In analysing these 'rules of formation', Foucault begins by examining the formation of objects. For Foucault, it is necessary first to map the *surfaces* of their *emergence*, to show where individual differences which will be accorded the status of alienation, deviation and *liminality* may emerge and then be denoted and analysed. These surfaces of emergence are different for different societies, at different periods and in different forms of discourse. In these 'fields of initial differentiation', in the 'distances' and 'discontinuities', and the 'thresholds that appear within it', discourse finds a way of 'limiting' and 'defining what it is talking about ... and therefore making it manifest, nameable, and describable'. Therefore, in the mapping of the surfaces of emergence of the liminal, the 'fields of initial differentiation' and 'discontinuities' that define and delimit it are demonstrated in its aesthetic features and its emphasis on heterogeneity, the experimental and the marginalized.

Second, according to Foucault, the *authorities of delimitation* must be described. This can be as an institution possessing its own rules and as an authority recognized by public opinion, the law and government. For instance, medicine became the major authority in society that delimited, designated and established madness as an object, together with the law, religious authority and literary and art criticism. Liminal performance takes issue with its own 'authorities of delimitation': that is, certain traditional performative conventions which are reflected in the notion of completion, the need to exhibit something and the audience's attitude of passive anticipation.

Finally, Foucault insists that the *'grids of specification'* must be analysed. These are systems according to which different kinds of knowledge are divided, contrasted, related, regrouped, classified and derived from one another as objects of discourse. The 'grids of specification' of liminal performance refer to two phenomena: verbal text and body. The text is heterogeneous and demonstrates either a non-narrative or a multinarrative, open-ended nature. The body in performance emphasizes the *gestus,* which is not a representation of something spoken, but rather speaks itself. Again the intention is not to produce a performance that is finite and closed in the accepted sense but a work that demonstrates new and different aspects of existence.

However, according to Foucault, a 'system of formation' is made possible only by a group of relations established between authorities of emergence, delimitation and specification. The conditions necessary for the appearance of an object of discourse are many. Therefore, the object exists under the positive conditions of a complex group of relations. These relations are established between institutions, economic and social processes, behavioural patterns and systems of norms. They are not present in the object and they do not define its internal constitution, but what enables it to appear, to situate itself, to define its difference, 'in short, to be placed in a field of exteriority'. Foucault's endeavour, then, is to define objects without reference to the *ground,* the *foundation of things,* but by relating them to the body of rules that enable them 'to form as objects of a discourse' and therefore constitute the conditions of their 'historical appearance' (Foucault, 1972, pp. 37–48).

This is not to return to the linguistic analysis of meaning. Foucault rejects the idealized analysis of lexical contents at the disposal of the speaking subject in a given period or the semantic structure that appears on the surface of discourse. His emphasis is on discursive practice in which objects appear and disappear. In his discussion of statements, Foucault writes, 'an equation of the nth degree, or the algebraic formula of the law of refraction ... a graph, a growth curve, an age pyramid, a distribution cloud are all statements. ... It would not appear to be possible therefore, to define a statement by the grammatical characteristics of the sentence' (1972, p. 82). This is important for liminal performance because of its emphasis on the 'intersemiotic'. Whatever statement is made by liminal performance is composed fundamentally of narratives inscribed by the body, with its emphasis on *gestus*, which is strongly related to the actions of the body, presenting the free association of themes rather than a linear narrative or verbal message.

Therefore, for Foucault, in analysing discourses themselves, there is a loosening of words and things and the emergence of a group of rules proper to discursive practice. These rules define 'not the dumb existence of a reality, nor the canonical use of vocabulary, but the ordering of objects': a task that consists of practices, which systematically form the objects of which they speak. In attempting to discover the law operating behind and the origin of assorted statements, Foucault questions: '*Who is speaking*?' Who has the right to use this sort of language (*langage*)? What is the status of the individuals who, sanctioned by law or tradition, proffer such a discourse. In traditional theatrical performance the authority of the 'speaking' subject lies in the author or director. However, in the liminal, there is a loss of authority together with the decline of the genius of the artistic producer, though not their disappearance.

'*Institutional sites*', from where the 'speaking' subject speaks, also need to be described. In contrast to traditional performances which play in mainstream theatres and venues, the liminal emits from alternative sites depending on the particular performance. For instance, liminal film tends to be shown in arthouse theatres rather than central city theatres, and therefore plays to a smaller audience. Liminal music performances also take place in fairly unconventional settings: for example, digitized sampled music is usually played at rave parties, which normally take place in disused warehouses or other such buildings. Similarly, literature on such liminal events tends to be found in selective, underground (rather than popular, widely read) publications.

According to Foucault, the '*position of the subject*' is defined by the possibility of his situation in relation to various groups of objects. He can be the 'questioning' subject or, according to certain programmes of information, the 'listening subject'. He may also be the 'seeing' subject and, according to a descriptive type, the 'observing' subject. He is situated at an optimal perceptual distance, whose boundaries delimit and define relevant information. To these perceptual situations should be added the position that the subject can occupy in the information networks. Foucault writes: 'In the proposed analysis, instead of referring back to *the* synthesis or *the* unifying function of *a* subject, the various enunciative modalities manifest his dispersion.' Therefore, 'discourse is not the majestically unfolding manifestation of a thinking, knowing, speaking subject' but 'a space of exteriority in which a network of distinct sites is deployed' (1972, pp. 49–55).

According to Foucault, the subject's position is a *'vacant'* place that may in fact be filled by different individuals. However, instead of being defined and maintained once and for all throughout a text or work, this position varies, either unchanging through several statements or altering with each one. This is one of the characteristics proper to the enunciative function, and allows it to be described. Therefore, if a group of signs can be called a 'statement', it is not because someone happens to speak them or put them into some concrete form of writing, it is because the position of the subject can be assigned. To describe a formulation *qua* statement consists not in analysing the relations between the author and what he says but in determining what position can and must be occupied by any individual if he is to be the subject of it.

Foucault's 'exteriorities' help us in situating liminal performance, which precludes closure and resolution, thereby allowing several possibilities of subject positioning. Showing the formation process of subjectivity is fundamental to this performance. This focus on *énonciation* is typical of postmodern art and the liminal in general.

Derrida

Writing (*écriture*) and textuality, terms associated with the work of Jacques Derrida, create more misunderstanding than the term deconstruction itself. However, Derrida insists that his position on writing is not a defence of that term in the traditional sense. He argues: 'What is being pursued ... is a certain displacement of writing. ... The old opposition between speech and writing no longer has any pertinence as a way of testing a text ... that deliberately deconstructs that opposition' (1981a, p. 181).

Much of the debate surrounding Derrida's work remains polemical and often consists of misreadings.[2] The polemic is most heated when it comes to the relation of literature to such terms as writing, textuality and dissemination, and to Derrida's position on the 'outside' or the *'de hors texte'*. Typically, Derrida is attacked for neglecting the world, society, politics and so on. This attack rests largely on the misunderstanding that text for Derrida is merely linguistic. I will resume this discussion below. It is apparent that literature, which according to Derrida is viewed primarily from a mimetological perspective rather than as a system of signification, has an important strategic function in his critical project. But it is debatable if this implies that he is either a formalist or an aestheticist. However, regardless of this, certain 'tools' of analysis central to Derrida's notion of deconstruction are important in the theorization of liminal performance.

Deconstruction has been accused by many of being a self-defeating method since it can transgress metaphysics only by continuing to speak the language of that tradition. Derrida raises this issue when he claims that 'all these destructive discourses ... are trapped in a kind of circle. ... There is no sense in doing without the concepts of metaphysics in order to shake metaphysics ... we can pronounce not a single destructive proposition which has not already had to slip into the form, the logic, and the implicit postulations of precisely what it seeks to contest.'

This 'kind of circle' is not merely a circle for Derrida, since the very meaning of deconstruction is linked to this circularity. This recalls Heidegger's hermeneutic circle, which, far from being a *circulus vitiosus* to be avoided at all costs, is a circle that has to be entered in the right way if we are to think at all. Therefore, the necessity of utilizing the resources from what is to be deconstructed is the very condition in which deconstruction can successfully intervene in the discourse of metaphysics. As Derrida so succinctly argues, 'we cannot give up this metaphysical complicity without also giving up the critique we are directing against this complicity' (1978c, pp. 280–1). This is important for liminal performance, since much of it appears to be complicit with what it seeks to deconstruct.

Deconstruction does not engage in the annulment or neutralization of opposites; rather, it aims at foregrounding the asymmetrical nature of its object of enquiry, such as philosophy. Derrida insists that, 'in classical philosophical opposition we are not dealing with peaceful coexistence of a *vis à vis*, but rather with a violent hierarchy' (1981b, p. 41). Rudolphe Gasché stresses the double nature of Derrida's deconstruction in order to distinguish it from 'deconstruction-as-criticism', and to differentiate between Derrida's notion of writing and the normal 'everyday sense' of the term. He writes: 'Two moments are thus characteristic of deconstruction: a *reversal* of the traditional hierarchy between conceptual oppositions ... and a *reinscription* of the newly privileged term. ... The deconstructed term ... is no longer identical with the inferior term of the initial dyad' (Gasché, 1979, pp. 192–3).

Dissemination is a key term for Derrida and can be seen as an anti-dialectic; it opposes the dialectical rule of three and the 'ternary rhythm' of Hegelian philosophy: 'Dissemination *displaces* the three of onto-theology along the angle of a certain re-folding ... these marks can no longer be summed up or "decided" according to the two binary opposition, nor sublated in to the three of speculative dialectic ... they cannot be pinned down at any one *point* by the concept or the tenor of a signified' (1981a, p. 25).

These 'marks', 'undecidables' or 'infrastructures' are what 'ground' philosophical contradictions, aporias and inconsistencies. Derrida, in arguing that 'to know why one says "structure", is to know why one no longer wishes to say *eidos*, "essence", "form", *Gestalt*, "ensemble"' (1978, p. 301), points at the same time to what 'structure' owes to other concepts, namely 'closure'. By contrast, undecidables are plural and constitute a 'connection, *ratio, rapport'*, which can account for 'the differences, contradictions, *aporias*, or inconsistencies between concepts, levels, argumentative and textual arrangements' (Gasché, 1986, p. 147). They can be seen as prelogical, synthetic and strategic devices. However, it would be a misrepresentation of Derrida if we were to assume that undecidables can act as a new grounding for philosophy. The idea of ground from which concepts are generated or produced is replaced in deconstruction by that of 'inscription', which contextualizes and therefore heteroglizes unitary concepts. Therefore, inscription is seen as a strategy of 'accounting', with the aim of 'overturning and displacing the conceptual order' (Derrida, 1982a, p. 329).

Undecidables (following Gödel's theorem regarding undecidable propositions within logical systems) are philosophical 'quasi-synthetic constructs', critical tools which overlap, in contrast to traditional analytical concepts which do not and are categories separated from one another.[3]

Différance is probably the most important quasi-concept used by Derrida to provide a critique of the notion of differentiation. It is also the non-unitary ground for all possible kinds of differentiation, differing and deferring. Derrida argues that différance is not simply deferring, because an act of delay does not necessarily entail a movement of difference. Therefore, together with deferring, différance implies difference: 'As distinct from difference, différance thus points out the irreducibility of temporalizing. ... Différance is not simply active. ... With its *a*, différance more properly refers to what in classical language would be called the origin or production of differences and the difference between differences, the *play* [*jeu*] of differences' (Derrida, 1982a, pp. 130–1). Therefore, by insisting on the difference among differences, Derrida avoids resolving them in a logical unity, thereby promoting the plurality of difference, of a conflictuality that does not culminate in contradiction but remains a contradiction without eventual dissolution.

Supplementarity is 'another name for différance', and like différance it both fissures and retards presence, but, unlike the former, supplementarity stresses the function of substitutive supplementation as a principle; it displaces and deforms the unity of the signified and the signifier. These displacements and deformations are regulated by the contradictory unity of a concept itself. As Derrida remarks, 'the supplement occupies the middle point between total absence and total presence' (1976, pp. 150–7). The structure of supplementarity makes origins dependent on an originary substitution of an absent 'other'. Supplementarity can therefore assume this role of origin because supplements are supposedly full origins. The supplementation is therefore also a compensation. In its positivity, an origin compensates for the lack of another origin, but is inhabited by this lack; because of this it can supplement itself and can serve as a supplement. Moreover, by indicating what structurally exceeds any totality, supplementarity is the *essential nothing* from which this whole originates; but as 'the excess of a signifier which, in its own inside, makes up (for) space and repeats the fact of opening' (Derrida, 1981a, p. 235).

'*Trace*' is a further example of Derrida's undecidables, which can be summed up as a structure of referral, in that it allows us to inscribe differences between terms and entities. Difference cannot be thought of without trace. The trace is not a difference with respect to an already constituted presence; rather, it is 'an originary synthesis not preceded by any absolute simplicity', it is 'the *pure* movement which produces difference. . . . It does not depend on any sensible plenitude, audible or visible, phonic or graphic. It is, on the contrary, the condition of such a plenitude.' Derrida's usage of trace is an adaptation of Heidegger's *die frühe Spur*; therefore, 'trace' is a metaphysical (quasi-)concept which names an originary tracing and effacement. Within metaphysics, the difference between two terms is perceived from the perspective of one of the terms, the term of plenitude, from which the second term is held to derive. According to Derrida, the fictions of plenitude and oppositions can only be thought because they both contain traces of the other and thus are always already contaminated. Therefore, the purity of concept is merely a fiction. The general structure of reference as trace accounts for the fact that all concepts appear in opposition to other concepts and are formed by the difference in which they appear.[4]

Other undecidables are '*iterability*' and '*re-mark*'. Iterability marks the relation between repetition and alteration and so acts as a critique of pure identity. It 'supposes a minimal remainder . . . in order that the identity of the *selfsame* be repeatable and identifiable *in, through*, and even *in view of* its alteration', and displacement is implied, as it 'alters, something new takes place' (Derrida, 1977, pp. 175–90). Re-mark suggests that everything is marked, forever leaving new traces and supplements on signification. Re-marks cut across other infrastructures. This prevents diacritically constituted series of terms, concepts, traces or marks from achieving closure. This accounts both for the necessary illusion of totalization and for its simultaneous displacement. It also refers to the totality of objects which function as marks in their semantic fields. Re-mark is a mark that contains the necessity of repetition. Every concept always carries a mark with it that can be followed and that also identifies it as belonging to something else.[5] This is a theme that goes through much of Derrida's work; any search for an ultimate origin is frustrated. Instead of an origin there are only edges, such as supplement, margin and trace. In fact, the origin merely reveals itself as yet another signifier for a further chain of signification, a signification which always involves dispersion and dissemination, and is an infinite regress without origin and without end. Further undecidables are the 'margin', the 'pharmakon', the 'hymen', as well as 'syncategoremata', function words of a certain kind, such as 'and', 'or', 'not', 'if', 'every' and 'some' (Gasché, 1986, p. 244).

Undecidables are important in a theorization of liminal performance, since they help to explain how identity can never be fully established, how new genres are formed and how unstable these formations are. This is because, in any rigorous analysis of an origin, there are found only 'différance', 'supplement', 'margin', 'trace' and so on. Derrida points to this when he argues that generic distinctions, in particular the law that dictates that genres are not be mixed, are more an impediment to the critical investigation of writing than an aid. 'What', Derrida asks, 'if it were impossible not to mix genres. What if there were, lodged within the heart of the law itself, a law of impurity or a principle of contamination?' Such an opposition to the law of genre within the law itself would indicate that all texts are hybrid and heterogeneous: 'Can one identify a work of art ... especially a work of discursive art, if it does not bear the mark of a genre?'

Derrida clarifies this by suggesting that, first, it is possible to have several genres, an intermixing of genres or a total genre, and, second, the re-mark can take on a diverse number of forms and can itself pertain to highly diverse types. It need not be a designation of the type found beneath the title of certain books: for example, 'novel, drama, *récit*'. Nor does the belonging need to pass through the consciousness of the author or reader. It can refute this consciousness. Finally, this re-marking trait does not need to be a theme. According to Derrida, then, 'every text participates in one or several genres, there is no genreless text ... yet such participation never amounts to belonging' (1980, pp. 211–12). This, of course, has correlations with the liminal, since the boundaries of this performance are continually stretched and transgressed.

The inside and the outside of a text, what is included and excluded, is another critical assumption put under scrutiny in Derrida's theorization. He writes, *'there is nothing outside of the text [there is no outside-text; il n'y a pas de hors-texte]'* (1976, p. 156). In other words, text, in a broad sense and including the non-linguistic, is all there is.[6] This has often been read as indicating a defence of the interiority of the text to the exclusion of the outside, indicating Derrida's lack of political or social concern. However, Derrida responds to this by stating: 'If there is nothing outside the text, this implies, with the transformation of the concept of text in general, that the text is no longer the snug airtight inside of an interiority or an identity-to-itself ... but rather a different placement of the effects of opening and closing' (1981a, pp. 35–6). For Derrida, then, the text does not open to the outside because the outside is not completely outside. More generally, whatever humans are able to think is some sort of text. Hence, text is all there is.

Derrida's essays on art have as their principle critical goal the displacement of the established borders of art and theory. Art is questioned in terms of its borders and the effects on it of forces coming from 'outside' its borders that interfere with its integrity, self-knowledge and representation. These essays are not so much on art as on the difficulties that major philosophies of art have in fixing the border between theory and art. Since Derrida considers the notion of a fixed border to be a sign of critical dogmatism, his questioning of art, together with the theory of art, takes the form of a critical dialogue with the major philosophies of art, basically those of Kant, Hegel and Heidegger.

In 'Parergon', Derrida focuses on the difficulties of resolving the problem of inside and outside by problematizing the notion of the frame. He argues that, in the examples of *parerga* given by Kant (the frames of paintings, the clothing of statues, the columns around an edifice), their exteriority defines them less than does the necessity that links them to the internal structure of the work; in other words, no *ergon* without *parergon* (1987a, pp. 59–60). The problem for Derrida becomes, then, how to take a position in terms of an exteriority which is necessary to the interior integrity of the work, necessary because the interior lacks something in its interior and needs to be set off from an outside it cannot really do without. How is it possible to determine in such a situation what truly belongs to the inside and what does not? And is it possible to delineate a purely aesthetic space? The major thrust of Derrida's reading of the *Third Critique* is to argue that this is not possible and to suggest that there are insurmountable difficulties in realizing the project of aesthetic purity or autonomy in general. This does not mean that the aesthetic does not push against or exceed the limitations theory imposes on it. It suggests instead that the aesthetic resists theoretical closure from within a space that is not entirely aesthetic in nature. In fact, for Derrida even the attempt to grant the aesthetic the privilege of autonomy or integrity constitutes a way of limiting and framing it. The issue of aesthetic specificity is central to Derrida's investigation of Kant and the focal point of his attempt to rethink the relation between the exterior and the interior, across each side of the frame. The aesthetic and the theoretical are, for him, too interconnected to be effectively separated by any frame or border drawn arbitrarily between them. Yet, as Derrida points out, neither can effectively do without the notion of the frame. In order to break this notion of the frame, fundamental to the aesthetic, a form of judgement is needed that functions without any border whatsoever. This is central to the theorization of the liminal, since in this performance the barriers between the aesthetic and everyday life are continually being eroded.

Finally, Derrida's theory of metaphor is important because it presents a critique of philosophy, rather than merely a rhetorical game. Derrida describes the irreducible metaphor as 'A classical philosopheme, a metaphysical concept. ... If one wished to conceive and to class all the metaphorical possibilities of philosophy, one metaphor, at least, always would remain excluded ... the metaphor ... without which the concept of metaphor could not be constructed ... the metaphor of metaphor' (1982b, pp. 219–20). Because Derrida deconstructs metaphor, he is able not only to broach its opposite, the proper or literal, but also to move to the more general level of metaphoricity as a structure that accounts for the deep metaphoric nature of all signification. I would argue that Derrida's treatment of metaphor is an extension of Heidegger's 'as-structure' ('as-what', 'as-such'), which underlies all forms of understanding. Derrida claims that, 'since everything becomes metaphorical, there is no longer any literal meaning and, hence, no longer any metaphor either' (1981a, p. 258). When everything turns out to be metaphorical, both metaphor and the proper disappear, and for this reason Derrida introduces the notion of quasi-metaphoricity or the source of the universality of concepts. In this sense, there appears to be a double displacement of the Heideggerian Being, since it is inscribed in a system of differences and so becomes merely a function of quasi-metaphoricity. According to Derrida, then, 'the determination of the truth of Being in presence passes through the detour of ... [a] tropic system, ... supposing that we might reach it ... this tropic and prephilosophical resource could not have the archaeological simplicity of a proper origin, the virginity of a history of beginnings, ... [and] metaphors. The word is written only in the plural. If there were only one possible metaphor ... there would be no more true metaphor' (1982b, pp. 229–68).

For Derrida, metaphor is a structure of referral for the possibility and impossibility of philosophical discourse in general. He points to Western philosophies as our mythologies – that is, our unacknowledged metaphorical texts – yet metaphor cannot be regarded as a substitute for the concept either, in the sense of supplanting it as a ground principle. For there is no ground, only signification, with metaphoricity as a general condition of all textuality. This is amply demonstrated in liminal performance, where there is an endless flow of verbal as well as non-verbal signification grounded largely in its own (inter)textuality. This liminal signification produces wide and jarring metaphoric effects which continually frustrate the expectations of any simple closure and thus promote active spectatorial participation.

Baudrillard

With regard to Jean Baudrillard's position in relation to postmodernism and liminal performance, it is important to realize that he has endeavoured to develop a theory that makes intelligible one of the most fascinating and perplexing aspects of industrial society, namely the proliferation of communications throughout the media. For Baudrillard, the world is understood only in relation to sign systems, and nothing exists outside the sign (which is always an empty entity; no original referent exists, only a simulation), providing him with what could be termed a purely 'textualist view' of the world.[7] According to Baudrillard, contemporary language exchange differs from both face-to-face symbolic exchange and print. The new media employ the montage principle of film (unlike print) and time-distancing (unlike face-to-face conversation), to organize a unique linguistic reality: 'space is what prevents everything from being in the same place. Language is what prevents everything from meaning the same' (Baudrillard, 1990, p. 191). Baudrillard theorizes from this perspective to argue that a new culture has emerged, one that is impervious to the old forms of resistance and impenetrable by theories based on traditional metaphysical assumptions. For Baudrillard, culture is now dominated by simulations, objects and discourses that have no firm origin, no referent, no ground or foundation. In fact, for Baudrillard, as for Walter Benjamin, 'the age of mechanical reproduction'[8] applies now to all realms of everyday life. Baudrillard argues for 'an aesthetic determinacy of things. ... Everything is sexual. Everything is political. Everything is aesthetic'. However, when everything is aesthetic, 'art itself disappears' (1992a, pp. 9–10). He writes: 'Art did not succeed in negating itself as such in order to actualize itself as world, as ideal form of life. ... It abolished itself in a general aestheticizing of daily life' (1992b, p. 238).

For Baudrillard, our contemporary values 'have no value in relation to any human purpose whatever. ... We are to some extent the equivalent of the nineteenth-century *"sublimes"* ... virtue, the daemon of philosophy, the daemon of critical craftwork, a regal indifference to industrial development' (1990, p. 226). This 'aesthetic determinacy' is a central issue for liminal performance. I will resume this discussion below.

Baudrillard grounds his thoughts in a historical sketch of the transition from modernity to postmodernity. Modernity was the era of the primacy of the bourgeoisie, where production determined social life. Following the technological revolution, reproduction replaced production as the centre of social life; and models, codes, simulacra, 'spectacles' and the 'hyperrealism' of simulation replaced the use-value of commodities, the forces of production, class struggle and therefore the hope of liberation through revolution.

Baudrillard's universe of simulacra without referents in the traditional sense can be seen as a result of French post-structuralist critiques of meaning and reference taken to their extreme, where the effluence of simulacra replaces the play of textuality in a world with no stable structures or fixed meanings in which to anchor theory or politics. He claims to be part of a 'second revolution, that of the twentieth century, of postmodernity which is the immense process of the destruction of meaning, equal to the earlier destruction of appearances, whoever lives by meaning, dies by meaning' (1984c, pp. 38–9).

Phenomena in the contemporary condition are themselves seen as effects generated by the structural code, rather than interpreted in terms of structuralism: that is, abstracts of a structure. Simulation is universalized both historically and socially, and implicitly in a historical process where each order of value is superseded and absorbed as illusion by the next. In Baudrillard's schema, the image draws increasingly away from reality until it bears no relation to reality whatsoever. As he writes,

This would be the successive phases of the image:

- it is the reflection of a basic reality
- it masks and perverts a basic reality
- it bears no relation to any reality whatever: it is its own pure simulation. (1983a: 11)

This last development is where the image becomes postmodern and where production is superseded by simulation: 'every century throws the reality principle into question as it closes but it's over today, finished, done' (1990, p. 183).

Although in much of Baudrillard's writing his universe appears to be without boundaries, all the old distinctions of traditional philosophy, politics, social theory and bourgeois capitalist society are imploded into an undifferentiated flow of simulacra. Yet he suggests that there are quite precise and important lines between modernity and postmodernity. Indeed, his claim to originality is based on his belief that he is moving rapidly beyond previous thinking and politics. His crucial tool of analysis is '*seduction*' which, he argues, replaces symbolic exchange as the privileged oppositional term to production and utility. Baudrillard's argument, then, is concerned with the opposition of seduction and production. Seduction is the 'strategy of appearances' which opposes relations of power (1979, p. 19). Baudrillard's 'seductive' analysis of technology, derived from his almost Heideggerian nostalgia for a pre-technological age, has implications for an analysis of liminal performance, since much of that performance employs the latest forms of technology and 'artifice' to create its special effects.

According to Baudrillard, seduction is a transformation of the body and sexuality in postmodern society. This analysis of the body also focuses on the notion of cloning. Cloning makes possible an extension and multiplication of the body and 'human being' itself. There is 'no more subject either, since self identical duplication puts an end to its division'.[9] This analysis is exemplary of Baudrillard's postmodern theory, which aims to bring to an end previous problematics of sexuality, reproduction and the body. As he writes, 'The digital Narcissus replaces the triangular Oedipus. . . . "Love your neighbour as yourself" this old problem of Christianity is resolved − your neighbour it's yourself' (1979, p. 235).

Baudrillard's most interesting analyses of seduction concern what he describes as 'cool seduction' in the society of media, simulations and information. Collapsing McLuhan's distinction between 'hot and cold', he claims that we have been seduced by the 'cool' medium of objects. By 'objects', Baudrillard is referring to a system of commodities − advertising, different modes of consumption and so on − which structure our lives, leading to new values and different modes of behaviour (1979, p. 32). Baudrillard claims that the society of simulation exerts a ludic and cool seduction throughout all domains of social experience.[10]

In a society saturated with media messages, information and meaning 'implode' into meaningless noise, pure effect without content or meaning.[11] Baudrillard's model of the media, 'a black hole of signs and information', absorbs all contents into cybernetic noise, which no longer communicates meaningful messages in a process in which all contents implode into forms. Therefore, the claim that 'the medium is the message signifies not only the end of the message but also the end of the medium' (Baudrillard, 1983b, p. 102). A new fascination emerges with the universe of media and communication, together with a new form of subjectivity which is saturated with information, images, events and ecstasies. Without defence or distance, individuals become 'a pure screen, a switching centre for all networks of influence' (Baudrillard, 1983c, pp. 131−3).

Baudrillard suggests that in the face of media simulation the masses respond with a simulation of meaning. It is important not that we believe in specific messages from the media but that we plug into various communications. In this way we become terminals in the communication matrices and are seduced by pleasure and play into participating within these networks. He warns that unless we understand seduction properly we will be unable to grasp the ubiquity and superiority of objects in our lives. Even such a recognition may be too late, for the objects which have been mastered for far too long are now rebelling and taking their revenge (Baudrillard, 1988, p. 203).

In the late seventies and early eighties, Baudrillard suggested that the fascination exhibited by the masses with both media and spectacle, together with their silence and apathy and the absence of any meaning, might well be seen as a 'resistance strategy'.[12] In other words, the masses by their very apathy are offering a resistance to the media. However, Baudrillard's very notion of simulation and his critique of all politics and denial of political change would rule out in advance any revolution of liberation, except perhaps by default.

As society is saturated to its limit it implodes and winds down into inertia and entropy. This process leads to 'catastrophe' for the subject.[13] Catastrophe represents the rebellion of the object world against the subject's laws, desires and expectations. It also represents the objects' tendencies to exceed themselves: that is, spontaneously to produce spectacles which delight and entrance the masses. The exhausted subject's fascination with the play of objects turns into apathy, stupification and an entropic inertia. Liminal performance, likewise, produces 'spectacles' which delight and entrance, but far from leading to lethargy and inertia, suggest an active interaction. The liminal indicates that there can never be security in mere contemplation, for the signs presented demand much more than this.

For Baudrillard, the media society signals the end of the era of interiority, subjectivity, meaning, privacy and the inner life; a new era of obscenity, fascination, vertigo, instaneity, transparency and overexposure begins. And while production was the key to modern, industrial society, 'simulations' dominate postmodern society as models precede the 'real' and constitute society as a 'hyperreal'. The social organization of capitalist societies is 'hyperreal' in as much as increasing areas of social life are reproductions of models organized into a system of models and codes. Such a hyperreal society of simulations includes fashion, architecture and housing developments.[14] This gives rise to the notion that all behaviour and thought are likewise determined by codes and models. In such a world there is no opposition and no critique because everything is designed and controlled.

The triumph of the object in its simulated form is connected with the end of the political and the emergence of the transpolitical *'figures du transpolitique'*. This 'is the transparency and obscenity of all structures in a destructured universe of information', yet suffused with media networks and messages. The transpolitical is also a mode of disappearance of history, politics, sexuality and subjectivity. For instance, in relation to history, Baudrillard claims, 'history isn't over, it is a state of simulation ... there is no end in the sense God is dead, or history is dead. Suddenly, there is a curve in the road, a turning point' (1987, p. 69).

It is the mode of disappearance and not the mode of production that should be of interest to social theory. Baudrillard's method is to point to the transformation of all modes of life in postmodern society. This transformation, exemplified in his analysis of cloning, leads to hyperrealization of the body and the social, redoubling and extensive growth, speed, size and quantity; even more to the hyperreality of simulation, which produces a new hybridized reality. Baudrillard believes that there is a way to preserve the subject, and that is by 'one fatal strategy: theory' (1988, p. 198). A 'fatal theory' must renounce subject positions and the projection of subjective passions, preferences and fantasies on to objects;[15] instead, it must take the position of the object and conceptualize the world from this point of view (1988, p. 204). The true revolution of modernity was 'the radical destruction of appearances and the disenchantment of the world together with its abandonment to the violence of interpretation and history' (1984c, p. 38). Just as the revolution of modernity was grounded in the dialectics of history, in the postmodern theories float around as if in a void. Everything is visible, explicit and transparent; for Baudrillard, this means 'obscene'.

Baudrillard claims that even art has lost its critical function: 'truly art can no longer operate as a radical critique or destructive metaphor' (1984b, p. 22). All targets of oppositional art have been destroyed and therefore art has lost its critical effectivity. Referring to the hyperreality of art, he observes that 'The anti-theatre is the ecstatic form of theatre: no more stage, no more content; . . . theatre for everyone by everyone. . . . The more art tries to realize itself, the more it hyperrealizes itself, the more it transcends itself to find its own empty essence' (1988, p. 187). Baudrillard argues that 'works of art' can no longer be exchanged since they have no relation to any referential value. Nor do they have any secret complicity and they cannot be read; rather, they can only be decoded according to 'more and more contradictory criteria'. Therefore, 'One can even say that the blazing fire of advertising and media in art is directly proportional to the impossibility of any aesthetic Judgement' (Baudrillard, 1982a, pp. 11–14). All that art and presumably politics, theory and individuals can do is play with forms already produced, 'all that remains to be done is to play with the pieces'. Postmodernism 'is more a survival among the remnants than anything else' (Baudrillard, 1984b, pp. 24–5).

Baudrillard's theory of 'aesthetic determinacy' is important for liminal performance in as much as he believes that everyday life has become aestheticized and much of this performance encourages the blurring of borders. However, this need not necessarily point to the disappearance of art, as Baudrillard claims; it could just as well point to its universal pervasiveness; not to a 'scene of nihilism' but to a redefinition of 'meaning'. Nor is aesthetic judgement impossible; on the contrary, if the aesthetic is ubiquitous, so are aesthetic judgements. Since in making those judgements every example must precede the rule, rules are created on each occasion, which can in no way be determined beforehand. Therefore, as already discussed, aesthetic judgement serves as a prototype for all judgements that must operate in the absence of models. This has important consequences, not only in the study of liminal performance but in all areas of life. Far from being impossible, aesthetic judgement is both integral and necessary, since we cannot escape the structure of complex judgements.

In contrast to Baudrillard, I believe that 'playing with the pieces' is an innovative project in itself, since it can lead to the creation of new artistic forms, not necessarily to inertia or apathy. In fact, this *bricolage* or pastiche is an important component of liminal performance. Similarly, 'complicity', which Baudrillard refutes in the contemporary work of art, is a central strategy in this performance. And rather than possessing no critical function, as Baudrillard claims, the experimental, intertextual nature of liminal performance produces an immediate effect which has indirect results on the political and the social, since it questions the very nature of our accepted ideas and belief systems.

Lyotard

Jean-François Lyotard's work is important in the theorization of liminal performance because he has delineated a contemporary theory of the postmodern which displays aesthetic features similar to those of the liminal. Lyotard, following on from Kant, has attempted to provide a political theory of the sublime. Unfortunately, Lyotard's sublime is premised mainly on a linguistic perspective. Given the importance of *corporeality* in liminal performance, Lyotard's 'linguistic turn' needs to be adjusted to allow for an intersemiotic analysis and hence for the prominence of the 'body' (I discuss this below).

For Lyotard, a crisis of 'legitimation' in science occurred with the dissolution of the positivist dream of a unified totality of knowledge built on observation. In the words of Werner Heisenberg, natural science does not explain and describe 'nature in itself but nature exposed to our method of questioning' (Heisenberg, 1971, p. 57). There is, therefore, no singular 'reality' to provide common ground upon which all scientifically rational demands of the people can be met or in which all instances of 'pure research' in the pursuit of a 'unified knowledge' can abide. Both major narratives have therefore entered a terminal crisis. Lyotard's response to this crisis of legitimation is through linguistics, particularly through a modified appropriation of Wittgenstein's notion of language-games. Elaborating on Wittgenstein's 'use' (Wittgenstein, 1968, p. 109), Lyotard offers a model of a postmodern society in which various language-games struggle with one another in an agonistic environment characterized by diversity, conflict and difficulty. Postmodern knowledge involves knowledge of local terrain and tolerance of variety and diversity. It also involves the search for 'paralogisms', for new discoveries that disturb and destabilize existing forms of knowledge (Lyotard, 1984a). Lyotard goes on to distinguish between 'different regimes of phrases and different genres of discourse' (1993, p. 20). This idea is developed further in Lyotard's *The Differend*, discussed below.

Lyotard, in a paper given at an Institute of Contemporary Arts conference in London, argues that the 'modern project' has failed, and 'we can no longer call this development [of techno-science] by the old name of progress'. Instead, development is taking place by an autonomous force or 'motricity'. No more is art viewed with the presuppositions of modernity. Instead, this has been replaced by 'analysing' and 'anamnesis' (the recollection of past events) (1986a, p. 6): 'the anamnesis of a patient in analysis is at least a matter of language; that of the working painter remains ... in the realm of vision. ... The sentimental *we* demanded and promised by aesthetics is an Idea. It cannot be shown. It marks the limits of an anamnesis of the visible, of the sensible' (1989, pp. 231–8).

Lyotard observes that 'a work of art can only become modern if it is first postmodern'. The postmodern 'would be that in which the modern puts forward the unrepresentable in presentation itself'; in other words, 'the sublime' (1984b, pp. 79–81). The 'sublime', for Lyotard, is seen as a response to art deprived of rules and limits, and therefore analogous to the 'postmodern situation' where, in a similar fashion, artistic rules have been 'dissolved' (1986b, p. 8). This can also be said to correspond to the liminal, where rules are likewise disseminated. This 'joyful sublime', not 'a nostalgic one',[16] as 'a contradictory feeling ... of both pleasure and displeasure', allows us to confront the new techno sciences and their 'complexity' by concerning itself with such things as the unrepresentability of technology and the ineffability of the multinational corporation (Lyotard, 1986c, p. 10).

Lyotard claims that a certain form of art, because it is not formed in terms of established social organizations, practises a critical politics that no other political activity has succeeded in practising. He writes:

> The reconstitution of traditional political organizations is bound to fail, for this kind of reconstitution settles precisely into the order of the social surface where its organizations are 'appropriated' ... deconstruction, which might appear as an aesthetic formalism ... actually constitutes the only type of activity that is effective and this is because it is ontologically ... located outside the system. (Lyotard, 1984c, p. 29)

However, if Lyotard believes that art is ontologically outside the socio-political, he also warns against attempts to institute art as an ideal or pseudo-religion. It would seem that art, being ontologically 'outside', does not lead to an aesthetic idealism but instead points to an 'extra-linguistic permanence' or a 'given':[17] that is, a reality which cannot be spoken about without already being presupposed.[18] However, 'what art does – what it ought to do – is always to unmask all attempts to reconstitute a pseudo-religion' (1984c, p. 72). According to Lyotard, it appears that the privilege of being 'outside' is not given to all art but just to those forms of art that do what art 'ought to do': that is, deconstruct ontology, religion and even itself. Aesthetic ideals do not replace political ideals, but a certain form of art serves to deconstruct certain kinds of traditional thinking. Liminal performance, in a similar way, deconstructs certain traditional assumptions. Art, then, has a double status; in order to fulfil its critical function as art, Lyotard demands that it must be art and anti-art at the same time. Hence the equation 'aesthetics = the work shop for the forging of the most discriminating critical concepts' (1984c, p. 16). Critical discourse is a derivative of art and must consequently develop the tools and concepts which have originated in art. Therefore, the aesthetic precedes the critical. This critical activity, together with a continual search for and reinvention of the rules of all games, and the possibility of an approach to the political that resists all attempts to reduce, resolve, regulate or repress heterogeneity, is further attested to by what Lyotard calls the '*differend*'.

The 'differend' (*différend*) is described as 'distinguished from a litigation. . . . [It] would be a case of conflict, between (at least) two parties, that cannot be equitably resolved for lack of a rule of judgement applicable to both arguments. . . . A wrong results from the fact that the rules of the genre of discourse by which one judges are not those of the judged genre or genres of discourse' (Lyotard, 1988, p. xi).

Lyotard's objective in *The Differend*, which 'has the form of a labyrinth with many digressions that lead into blind alleys' (van Reijan, 1992, p. 19), is the uncovering of differends where they have been repressed or supposedly resolved. However, his intention is not to reverse the injustice and replace the acceptable 'phrase' with the silenced one, which would eventually lead to a further injustice, but rather to formulate a political strategy and to practise a justice in terms of the non-resolution of differends. His purpose, therefore, is to emphasize what traditional historical validation cannot account for: that is, the irresolutions and undecidables of history. For Lyotard, following on from Adorno, Auschwitz marks the limitations of rational history. 'Everything that is real is rational, everything that is rational is real: "Auschwitz" refutes the speculative doctrine. This crime at least, which is real . . . is not rational' (1988, p. 179). Or, as Adorno writes, 'after Auschwitz there is no word tinged from on high, not even a theological one, that has any rights unless it underwent a transformation' (1983, p. 367). For Lyotard, 'the silence imposed on knowledge does not impose the silence of forgetting, it imposes a feeling' (1988, p. 56). This 'silence' is interpreted as a 'sign' in the Kantian sense, a sign that something that should be phrased cannot be phrased.[19]

As central as Kant's theorization is, what ultimately differentiates Lyotard's thinking is his notion of the subject. And what causes Lyotard eventually to jettison Wittgenstein's concept of language-games and replace it with a 'philosophy of phrases' (though not an ontology[20]) is the difficulty, if not the impossibility, of orchestrating 'games' without a subject who is external to those games. Therefore, a philosophy of phrases is crucial to Lyotard's theorization, in as much as it situates the subject within the universe of phrases and therefore makes the notion of a prior or external subject redundant (Lyotard, 1993, p. 27).

Therefore, in opposition to a historical-political model founded on speculative, dialectical totalizations, Lyotard practises a radical critical politics of heterogeneity based on a 'philosophy of phrases', which affirms the 'differend' rather than suppressing or resolving it. For Lyotard, the phrase is 'presupposed', more so than anything else, not because it is presupposed in some particular instance,[21] but because it exists when it says it does not: 'there is no phrase is a phrase' (1988, p. 65). Therefore, when you say something exists before it is phrased, 'your phrase presents it. It presents it as being there before all phrase' (1988, p. 28). Lyotard does not define a phrase, for to do so would lead to 'the concept of a well-formed totality' (Carroll, 1987, p. 314).

Therefore, the problem posed is, 'given 1) the impossibility of avoiding conflicts (the impossibility of indifference) and 2) the absence of a universal genre of discourse to regulate them (... the inevitable partiality of the judge): to find, if not what can legitimate judgment (the "good" linkage), then at least to save the honour of thinking' (Lyotard, 1988, p. xii). From this position, Lyotard attempts to rephrase the political without the traditional limits which generally preform it. Linkage is a political question in the form of the differend. The dispute of possible linkages underlies all linkage and reveals that no linkage can ever be determined before the fact. What is determined is only that there must be another phrase: 'for there to be no phrase is impossible, for there to be *And a phrase* is necessary. ... To link is necessary, but how to link is not' (1988, p. 66). For Lyotard, the question of the political, on the most fundamental level, is the linkage of phrases, and therefore the political is everywhere; yet at the same time it is not totally determining, for 'Everything is political if politics is the possibility of the differend on the occasion of the slightest linkage. Politics is not everything, though, if by that one believes it to be the genre that contains all the genres. It is not *a* genre' (1988, p. 139).

Lyotard, in analysing the selection of various phrase linkages, foregrounds Kant's *Critique of Judgement*.[22] For the faculty of judgement is in question not only in the third *Critique* and in terms of the aesthetic, but 'each time a phrase has to be validated by a presentation'; therefore, it 'appears as a force of "passages" between the faculties, to the point that it is accorded a major privilege in the area of unifying capacity. At the same time, a major flaw is recognised ... *it has no determined object'* (1988, p. 130, emphasis added). For Lyotard, following Kant, the aesthetic is privileged because it is here that the problem of judgement is most radically articulated, due to its demand for a form of judgement that in the absence of determined rules judges without knowing or presuming to know its object.[23] According to Lyotard, 'in matters of taste ... our power to judge is not *determinate*, but *reflective*. ... The activity resulting from this ... is that of the artist, the critical philosopher ... any inventive step which, on the path of the unknown, of the unacceptable, breaks with constituted norms, shatters consensus and revives the meaning of the *differend'* (Lyotard and Rogozinski, 1987, p. 26).

The aesthetic, then, is an uncharted sea where a particular form of judgement is necessary, given that 'beauty' is not a quality of the object and thus cannot be determined. The aesthetic 'object' is not 'an object of experience. ... Its aesthetic properties are not in itself, as givens, but in the feeling of taste. ... What is felt ... in the ethical phrase is not the object, but the law. ... Symbolization, then, does not occur here through a substitution of object, but through permutations of instances in the respective phrase universes, and without recourse to a direct presentation' (Lyotard, 1988, p. 132).

Lyotard opposes any attempt to posit the ethical ideal of community as a concrete, empirical and therefore knowable entity, or any attempt to impose a form of society as an ideal. The notion that an ethical-political community cannot be presented as an object achieves its most extreme and therefore most powerful manifestation in the sublime: 'The sublime feeling is neither moral universality nor aesthetic universalization, but is, rather, the destruction of one by the other in the violence of their differend. This differend cannot demand, even subjectively, to be communicated to all thought' (1991, p. 239). Given the limitation of and in presentation, Lyotard believes that the task of a critical politics is, nevertheless, to present the unpresentable, to present the fact that the unpresentable exists and that it concerns our future. Therefore, '"our" destination ... is to supply a presentation for the unpresentable, and therefore, in regard to Ideas, to exceed everything that can be presented' (1988, p. 166).

Lyotard's strategy in *The Differend* remains analytical in his categorization of phrases and rules of linkage. He derives his theorization from such writers as Kant and Wittgenstein, who distinguish between genres of discourse, families of phrases and so on. He writes, 'the free examination of phrases leads to the (critical) dissociation of their regimens (the separation of the faculties and their conflict in Kant; the disentanglement of language games in Wittgenstein). They lay the ground for the thought of dispersion ... which ... shapes our context' (1988, p. xiii). Lyotard could perhaps be criticized for accepting such distinctions and categories; yet such distinctions are necessary for his strategy,

for the phrase, regardless of its conceptual limitations, is an example *par
excellence* of the heterogeneity within the unresolvable plurality and conflict of
language. And while Lyotard criticizes 'the cumbersome debt to anthro-
pomorphism' of Kant and Wittgenstein, this does not stop him from utilizing
their analytical tools. Lyotard's strategy is not to challenge formalist categories
on the level of the distinctions they make, but rather to challenge them only
when those distinctions become unified in terms of a specific system. In that
instance, Lyotard's intervention consists of an attempt to maintain dispersion
at all costs against any determination imposed by that system.

Although Lyotard's differends arise from the problematic relation between
language and social reality, his theorization remains tied primarily to a
linguistic model. According to Lyotard, what we call 'reality' is neither a
function of simple ostension nor an idealist construct of meaning. Ostensive
phrases contain deictic expressions such as 'I-here-now', which 'designate their
object as an extra-linguistic permanence. ... Far from constituting a
permanence, ... however ... this "origin" ... appears and disappears ... with
this phrase' and such phrases are alone insufficient to establish the fixity of
reference: ' "before" knowing whether what one says or will say about it is true
or false, it is necessary to know what one is talking about' (1988, pp. 33–5).
Therefore, it is necessary to have recourse to proper and relational names, or
what Lyotard following Kripke calls 'rigid designators' (Kripke, 1980, p. 48). In
order to avoid confusion with idealism or essentialism, Lyotard emphasizes
that names meaningless in themselves are relationally determined within
nominal systems and networks of descriptions.

Differends arise from the fact that ambiguity is an essential feature of
ordinary language. The addressee is free to classify a phrase under a regime
different from that intended by the addresser, therefore subsuming the phrase
in question under a different genre of discourse. Because each genre of
discourse is determined by a specific idea that serves to impose unity over the
disparate regimes of phrases that occur within it, the subsumption of one and
the same phrase under two different genres of discourse will have the effect of
silencing whichever one is prior; 'the greater probability of one of them will be
provided by refuting the other's and this by means of new ostensions and
nominations' (Lyotard, 1988, p. 55).

In *The Differend*, Lyotard makes what seems like some explicit semiotic
reference only in a brief sentence where he argues that 'a wink, a shrugging of
the shoulder ... can be phrases' (1988, p. 70). Other than that, he makes no
mention of the semiotics of gesture. In order to move from phrases to an
'extra-linguistic permanence', Lyotard 'not only eliminates the phenomenolo-
gical pre-predicative cogito, but also any possible non-predicative semiotic',
which involves a rewriting of one of his main sources, Kripke, whose linguistic

and non-linguistic items, such as 'birth and meetings', are levelled by Lyotard solely on to the plane of linguistics (Ruthrof, 1992, p. 122). What therefore appears to be lacking in Lyotard's analysis is a theory of non-linguistic signification. For instance, his 'universe of phrases' does not allow for the modes of signification found in such practices as the liminal. Many of these performances are fundamentally narratives inscribed by the body, the use of *gestus* being closely related to bodily actions which neither support nor represent something spoken; rather, they speak themselves, leading to a free association of themes rather than a linear narrative which can provide no answers in manifest or rational (or linguistic) terms.

I would argue that liminal performance is a deliberate and creative differend, with its intersemiotic practices and aesthetic features provoking sensations of disquiet and discomfort. Since the genre of performance discourse is determined by a specific idea that serves to impose unity over the disparate regimes of its phrases, the subsumption of liminal performance under two different genres of discourse, such as the traditional mainstream and the experimental liminal, leads to its enforced silence in the face of dominant theatrical practices. This is demonstrated in its marginalized status and its concurrent expulsion to the edges of mainstream performance. Lyotard could be prefiguring the liminal when he writes:

> Is postmodernity the pastime of an old man who scrounges in the garbage-heap of finality looking for leftovers, who brandishes unconsciousness, lapses, limits, confines, goulags, parataxes, non-senses, or paradoxes, and who turns this into the glory of his novelty, into his promise of change? But this too is a goal for a certain humanity. A genre. (Lyotard, 1988, p. 136)

Finally, in contrast to Lyotard's differend, I believe that an intersemiotic analysis is needed. In this way the 'unpresentable', which exceeds the sign and is more in keeping with the Kantian sublime, can be presented in and through such practices as the liminal.

From the above spectrum of theoretical perspectives, which I have gleaned from Kant through to Lyotard, I will in the following chapters view liminal performance. In Chapters 4, 5 and 6, I provide detailed case histories of works which I believe are exemplary of this emerging 'genre', together with a new aesthetic form of theorization that is capable of addressing such practices.

Notes

1. Dreyfus and Rabinow write: 'the archaeologist stands outside all discursive formations. Or, to be more exact, the archaeologist, like Husserl's transcendental phenomenologist, must perform an "ego split" in order to look on as a detached spectator at the very phenomena in which ... one can't help being involved' (1982, p. 87). Therefore, 'the archaeologist who claims to have emerged in history only to have stepped outside it ... tells a seamless story' (1982, p. 97).

2. If American 'deconstructionists', as Rodolphe Gasché argues, have turned Derridean deconstructionism into another form of 'new criticism', then anti-deconstructionists have accepted this in order to attack his work for being a literary formalism (Gasché, 1986, 3). However, it is only when writing is equated with literature and textuality with specific literary texts that deconstruction is open to such attacks.

3. Derrida argues that 'an undecidable proposition, as Gödel demonstrated in 1931, is a proposition which given a system of axioms governing a multiplicity, is neither an analytical nor deductive consequence of those axioms, nor in contradiction with them, neither true nor false with respect to these axioms. *Tertium datur*, without synthesis' (Derrida, 1981a, p. 219).

4. Derrida states: 'It is not the question of a constituted difference here, but rather, before all determination of the content, of the *pure* movement which produces difference' (1976, p. 62).

5. 'In the recoiling of the blank upon the blank, the blank colors itself, becomes-for itself ... ever more invisible, ground. Not that it is out of reach ... but that, in the act of inscribing itself on itself indefinitely ... it multiples and complicates its text, a text within a text ... the one indefinitely repeated within the other an abyss' (Derrida, 1981a, p. 265).

6. According to Derrida, 'there is such a general text everywhere that ... this discourse and its order ... are *overflowed*. ... This general text is not limited of course ... to writings on the page' (1981b, pp. 59–60).

7. Ruthrof (1992, pp. 8–14) provides an illuminating discussion on 'textualist' positions.

8. According to Benjamin, 'that which whithers in the age of mechanical reproduction is the aura of the work of art' (1969a, p. 221).

9. Jean Baudrillard (1984a, pp. 16–17): 'Still no longer a question of the phantasm of self generation. The father and mother have disappeared not in the interest of a risky freedom of the subject but in the interest of a matrix called the code.'

10. According to Baudrillard, 'the social contract has become a pact of simulation, sealed by the information and the media' (1979, pp. 221–2).

11. For Baudrillard, 'Information devours its own content, it ... dissolves meaning and the social into a sort of nebulous state leading not at all to a surfeit of innovation but to the very contrary, to total entropy' (1983b, pp. 96–100).
12. See Baudrillard (1983b, p. 11; 1985, p. 578).
13. Baudrillard writes, 'when light is harnessed and engulfed by its own source. There occurs a brutal involution of time into the event itself. This is a catastrophe' (1988, p. 192).
14. According to Baudrillard, 'today it is quotidian reality in its entirety – political, social, historic and economic – that from now on incorporates the simulatory dimension of hyperrealism' (1983a, p. 147).
15. For Baudrillard (1990, p. 215), 'theory does not derive its legitimacy from established facts, but from future events. ... It does not act upon consciousness, but directly on the course of things from which it draws its energy. It therefore has to be distinguished from the academic practice of philosophy and from all that is written with an eye to the history of ideas.'
16. Lyotard claims that 'examples of both forms of sublime can be found ... in the mode of inscription which ... will always dictate what cannot be expressed ... in no matter what epoch of the history of literature, or art, or of ideas' (van Reijen and Veerman, 1988, p. 291).
17. According to Lyotard, 'deictics are designators of reality. They designate their object as an extra-linguistic permanence, as a "given"' (1988, p. 33).
18. See Ruthrof's discussion on 'extra-linguistic permanence'. Unlike Baudrillard, who claims nothing exists outside the sign, Lyotard allows for an 'extralinguistic permanence', which provides him with a 'realist textualist' position, 'to which deictic reference points but for which we cannot argue without committing the ontological fallacy: "for nothing can be said about reality that does not presuppose it"' (Ruthrof, 1992, p. 186).
19. For Lyotard, 'Signs are not referents to which are attached significations validatable under the cognitive regimen, they indicate that something which should be able to be put into phrases cannot be phrased' (1993, p. 56).
20. 'Above all it is a question of withdrawing from the very possibility of an ontology' (van Reijen and Veerman, 1988, p. 285).
21. For Lyotard, 'the mode is that of metalanguage in the linguist's sense (phrases are its object) but not in the logician's sense (it does not constitute the grammar of an object-language)' (1988, p. xiv).
22. Lyotard writes: 'the principle of judgement can be found neither in the realm of theoretical understanding nor in the realm of practical reason. ... There can be no question, therefore, of reflection being summoned ...

merely in its heuristic capacity: it invents its own principle, finality, and
lets itself be guided by this principle in deciphering the empirical laws of
nature. ... It is proper, therefore, to introduce the faculty of reflection
between understanding and reason in order to provide the indispensable
supplement for this project' (1991, pp. 2–3).

23. According to Lyotard, 'if the third *Critique* fulfills its mission of unifying
the field of philosophy, it does so, not primarily by introducing the theme
of the regulative Idea of an objective finality of nature, but by making
manifest, in the name of the aesthetic, the reflective manner of thinking
that is at work in the critical text as a whole' (1991, pp. 6–8).

4

Liminal theatre

Hybridization appears to be one of the quintessential features of liminal theatre. Other quasi-generic traits are experimentation, innovation, marginality and an emphasis on the intersemiotic, a significatory practice which involves such non-linguistic modes as those provided by corporeal *gesta*. Analogous to all liminal performance, hybrid theatre strives to play to the edge of the possible, continually challenging traditional aesthetic concepts. Expositions of hybrid theatre are best exemplified in the *Tanztheater* of Pina Bausch, the 'theatre of images' of Robert Wilson and Philip Glass, the 'synthetic fragments' of Heiner Müller and the 'social sculptures' of the Viennese Actionists. Hybrid theatre creates a scene of immediate aesthetic intervention which has an *indirect* effect on the political. By providing 'perceptive strategies' it creates non-'docile bodies' of non-performance (Foucault, 1972, pp. 135–69). In this sense, liminal theatre can be said to have a political dimension, since it is an experimental extension of, while providing a challenge to, our accepted socio-cultural and political belief systems.

Tanztheater: a dancing across margins

On the evening of 20 June 1991, the Théàtre de la Ville was sold out: Pina Bausch's *Palermo, Palermo* was having its Paris premiere, a performance which I attended. If the then mayor of Palermo, who had urged Bausch to make the work, hoped for any reference to 'the country of orange trees', he would have been disappointed. The performance commenced with the terrifying collapse of a wall that had filled the stage and blocked the audience's view, producing an almost claustrophobic sensation. The performers were left to pick their way through the remnants of dust and cement. A female skilfully danced her way through the rubble, watched by a group of males. Another woman gripped an

Liminal Acts

open bottle between her thighs, the water escaping from it paralleling the woman's emptiness. Loose morsels of meat from overflowing pockets; revolvers pointing blindly; mad bombs exploding in large columns of white smoke which reached up to stormy skies; and rainfalls of red earth forming a menacing volcano provided the *mise-en-scène*. For the finale, a procession of hunched women passed by, legs bent and faces hidden in their breasts, tied together in a long collective sob.

Pina Bausch has said that she is not interested in 'how' people move, what she wants to know is 'what' moves them and what goes on inside (Servos and Weigelt, 1984, p. 16). Her work is separated from traditional ballet by her particular type of realism, which avoids seamless illusions and standardized ideas of beauty. Her distance from mainstream dance is measured by her lack of interest in the formalist concerns that have predominated in modernism.

Tanztheater (dance theatre), influenced by Bausch, has been supplanting traditional ballet in several regional opera houses in Germany. This contemporary art form grew out of the political and cultural traditions of the left. The often disruptive behaviour of new left activists was intended as a calculated affront to bourgeois sensibilities. Similarly, dance theatre, whose origin dates from approximately 1973, when Bausch became the director of the relatively obscure Wuppertal Dance Theatre, ridiculed what its proponents regarded as the illusions and irrelevance of 'ballet'; instead, dance theatre cultivated the expressive possibilities of realism. Suddenly the body served as a medium through which to talk about reality just as effectively as through the spoken word. The distinguishing feature of the new left movement was the attempt to relate the personal to the political. Bausch's dance theatre, which is manifestly concerned with the nature of private life, claims in this sense to reflect broader truths.

The Wuppertal Dance Theatre cannot be seen in isolation as an aesthetically avant-garde event. The cultural antecedents of dance theatre are in the German dance and theatrical traditions of the Weimar Republic years, to which postwar Germany restored fragile and isolated links despite the discontinuities of the Nazi period. In the late 1950s, Bausch studied under Kurt Jooss at the Folkwang School in Essen. Jooss had choreographed in and later taught the modern expressionist style known as *Ausdruckstanz* (literally form of expression, expressiveness).

Although Bausch spent a short period of time studying at the Juilliard in New York, the influence of American formalist modernism is limited in her most characteristic works — that is, the works following on from the mid-seventies — which 'can be seen as the conclusion of the period of choreography in its narrower sense and . . . the progressive emergence of what has since come to be familiar as the Wuppertal Dance Theatre concept' (Servos and Weigelt,

1984, p. 29); in Foucauldian terms, its 'surface of emergence' (Foucault, 1972, p. 41). Subsequently, dance itself became an object to be questioned, to the extent that some critics ask whether Bausch's work remains a form of dance. Of perhaps more influence was Bausch's interest in the work of the Living Theatre, widely known for its experiments in expressionistic psychodrama.

Different developments in the theatre − for instance, Robert Wilson's 'theatre of images', or the 'synthetic fragments' of Heiner Müller − have also shaped dance through problematizing the genres of dance and drama and producing what can be seen as a hybrid, dance theatre.[1] Müller, in writing about the dance theatre of Pina Bausch, points out that in her theatre, 'the image is a thorn in our eye' (Müller, 1984, p. 30), referring to the fact that she provokes and unsettles her audience. The sensations of disquiet produced by her performances are analogous to the 'negative pleasure' experienced by the Kantian sublime (Kant, 1978a, p. 91).

Paralleling her contemporaries in theatre, Bausch combines a visually rich production style with techniques drawn from both Brecht's 'epic theatre' and Artaud's concept of a 'theatre of cruelty'. Her performers apply 'method' principles, imbuing their interactions with the intensity and pain of remembered experience, at the same time employing 'defamiliarization' techniques, undermining the spectator's empathetic identification by presenting their role-playing as self-consciously theatrical, to the point of parody. The result is a heterogeneous performance that simultaneously distances and engages the spectator. This flux leaves many spectators exhausted by the end of a performance, overwhelmed by the emotional complexity of the experience. Especially unresolved are the images of gender roles and sexual relations. Bausch shows men and women locked into power plays and obsessive patterns of physical and emotional violence. Her particular 'shift-shape' style of the 'theatre of cruelty' leaves the audience depleted but with no sense of resolution. This lack of resolution or closure is a central trait of liminal performance.[2] Her response when asked about her pieces was: 'Basically one wants to say something which cannot be said, so we make a poem where one can feel what I meant. You see it, and you know it without being able to formulate it' (Birringer, 1991, p. 140).

In discussing Bausch's work it is useful to take a closer look at two of her performances which are exemplary of her style. The first, *Café Müller*, was originally part of a collective four-part evening under the same title. Bausch's piece lasted approximately thirty minutes and was videotaped at the Wuppertal Theatre (20 May 1978).

The set is a bare, greyish room cluttered with round coffee tables and dozens of chairs, with a large revolving glass door in the background. Two female dancers in thin, white slips (one of them Bausch) and three men in dark suits move among the tables and chairs; the furnishings block any attempts by the performers to create group formations. The performers are initially restricted to slow movements on the spot, focusing on their own bodies and on the limited routes within the room.

The chairs, perhaps symbols for absent persons, point to the emptiness and the impossibility of contact. They are obstacles for the dancers. Despite this, the performers are able to negotiate this tangle of chairs, able to ignore the obstructions placed in front of them. This is due to the efforts of one of the male performers, who spends the entire performance moving tables and chairs out of their path.

Initially, this role was performed by Rolf Borzik, Wuppertal's stage and costume designer, who, in perpetually clearing the stage, literally creating a continually changing set, translates his behind-the-scenes preparation into performed, physical action. This choreographed realization of his function contradicts the traditional belief that the physical setting for theatre and dance is essentially only decorative and points to a total integration of sets and properties, thus creating alternative 'institutional sites' (Foucault, 1972, p. 51) in the performance itself.

His agitation in removing obstacles from the paths of the performers, who move with closed eyes in a somnolent, trance-like state, transmits tangible tension to the audience. His job is to create a space in which the performers can move freely. For this he needs to observe their movements with intense concentration in order to be in the right place at the right time. The other performers move as though he does not exist and are completely unaware of his efforts.

The two female performers, one at the front of the stage and one almost invisible in the upstage gloom, are complementary but move in counter-time. They run their hands over their bodies, they hurl themselves against walls, slide down them and lean against them for support. Their bodily movements suggest isolation, alienation and despair, the more poignant as the performance is taking place in a social setting. One of the female performers, trance-like, comes into contact with a male. The couple cling to each other but their embrace is constantly broken. The search for someone to lean on is continued. Again and again, the couple attempt to cling to each other, another male repeatedly placing the female in the first male's grasp, who is unable to bear her weight. Each time, eight in all, he lets her fall to the ground. Failing to make contact, the first male steps over her. This time the second male tries by different means to reunite them, but the couple automatically lapse back into their previous ineffectual patterns of behaviour. They remain incapable of dealing with new demands and new situations or of learning from their unsuccessful actions. Even with guidance, or what could be seen as social intervention, the couple cannot maintain the correct position. Their frantic movements and repeated attempts suggest that behaviour between men and women is 'learned, culturally coded, determined' and 'inept' (Price, 1990, p. 324).

A red-haired woman wearing a fur coat bursts into the middle of this situation, tripping hurriedly through the revolving doors in her high-heeled shoes. She regards the proceedings with amazement. Her persistent, somewhat anxious, attempts to approach the others and make contact with them are repulsed by their self-absorption. Finally, she gives her coat and wig to the dancer hiding in the background, who dons them while continuing her trance-like dance, and she leaves the stage.

In *Café Müller*, Bausch deals with her recurring themes, the inability to communicate, the alienation between couples and the search for self-fulfilment and intimacy. According to Bausch, one of the central themes in her work relates to 'Wanting to be loved, or all the things we do to make somebody like us' (Hoghe, 1980, p. 67). Additionally, she deals with the dance environment. The dancers in *Café Müller* seem lost in their own worlds, barely conscious of their surroundings; their movement language is perhaps referring to the more formal *Ausdruckstanz* tradition. The red-haired woman, on the other hand, is very real; she is the only one to notice the frantic efforts of the 'stage designer'. She treads the same paths as the other dancers but also pursues her own way and makes her own use of the stage properties. With her vocabulary of movement drawn from everyday life and her attire so different from the other dancers, she embodies the more socially concrete and therefore more provocative theatre of movement. She proves more aware and more interested in her surroundings than the other dancers. The rhythm of her movement provides sharp contrast to that of the other performers. While the dancers move in slow motion, her tempo is rapid. The various time strata within the piece coincide at certain points, overlap and change, demonstrating another of Bausch's dramaturgical devices. However, the music of the performance is performed without modification and without defamiliarizing effects or contrasting montage. The two Henry Purcell compositions, arias from *The Fairy Queen* and *Dido and Aeneas*, are tonal songs evoking feelings of the pain of love and separation and of grief and despair. They complement the content of the piece.

Several dramatic threads parallel one another throughout the piece. Loneliness, compulsive behaviour and the search for contact determine one level, and the examination of the dance medium determines another. There is a certain degeneration of traditional theatrical barriers that exist between various genres, as demonstrated by the blurring within the performance of the 'stage designer'. Within its composition, *Café Müller* contains the essential instruments of Bausch's dance theatre, the fragmented gestures, 'defamiliarization' techniques, repetition at varying speeds and the disjunction of processes into separate sequences, all aesthetic features of liminal performance.

In contrast to *Café Müller*, *Arien* 'has a lot do with the things children do. The things we do sometimes you can actually do only when you are a child – splash around in the water, get greasy, paint yourself, play. That you can do this on stage once more as a grown-up is great, I think' (Hoghe, 1980, p. 68). One scene in this piece has the performers sitting on a circle of chairs, playing the choral game *Jetzt fahr'n wir über'n see*. Anyone who continues singing after the progressively short lines have finished is eliminated.

Arien (*Arias*) was originally created in 1979 but was one of the main attractions of the Brooklyn Academy of Music's (BAM) Next Wave Festival in 1985. Stephen Holden, writing in the *New York Times*, claims,

> Miss Bausch's appearance at the Next Wave festival is a triumphant return engagement to BAM. ... The bravura theatrics, provocative images and rigorous physical discipline of her work have made Miss Bausch internationally renowned as the godmother of Neo-Expressionist dance-theater. (Holden, 1985).

However, not all American critics were so generous. In fact, some were openly hostile in their defence of American choreography in the face of a perceived Germanic invasion.[3] With *Arien*, Bausch developed a new dance experiment. For the performance, the opera stage was opened as far back as the firewall and the stage was submerged ankle-deep with reflecting and purifying water, creating a counter-space to the synthetic stage. During the course of the two-hour performance, without intermission, numerous moods are evoked: melancholia, anger, despair and feelings of individuals confined in ritualized, prescribed patterns of behaviour. Bausch has described the point of departure for *Arien* as 'showing everything people do or have done to one another, at various times'.[4]

In *Arien*, Bausch's treatment of opera and classical ballet becomes quite comical. Fairy tale queens and divas, who are grotesquely decorated and dressed up by their partners, plunge into exaggerated movements and litanies. They look and sound nonsensical when juxtaposed with classical Italian bel canto arias. The music and the words seem incongruous together. In Bausch's performances, words are 'fragmentary and blurred' (Hoghe, 1980, p. 69); only very seldom do they serve as communication or provide mutual under-standing.[5] For Bausch, 'words ... are a means – a means to an end. But words are not the true aim' (Servos and Weigelt, 1984, p. 230).

Arien demonstrates how formal atmospheres can come together momenta-rily, only to disintegrate. A row of dressing tables with spotlights between them dominates one side of the front of the stage. To the accompaniment of slow jazz music, the dancers prepare for the performance, changing, making up, smoking and talking among themselves. The performance begins with this casual dressing room situation. Someone rehearses a boxer's pose in front of the mirror, while someone else examines the beginnings of a paunch. The water on the stage floor transforms the bare, unadorned room. During the course of the performance, the dancers' movements become heavy, laden with water. As the beautiful folds of an evening dress or the perfect fit of a suit become ruined, naked bodies become apparent. One of the performers becomes a photographer running through the scene with tripod and cameras. He photographs himself with a self-timer, joining groups that are strangers to him. Releasing the self-timer, he creates 'real' group pictures, 'simulacras', reproductions of something that never existed in the first place (Baudrillard, 1983a, p. 11).

In one of the opening scenes, the traditional theatre situation is reversed as the performers scrutinize the audience, shattering any expectations of passive spectatorship by telling absurd stories, making jokes and reading gutter press news items. A dress-up ritual follows to the accompaniment of Mozart's *Eine kleine Nachtmusik*. The women are led to the front of the stage, where a row of chairs is set up, close to the footlights. They sit on the chairs, while the men dress them up in an assortment of clothes, colourful wraps, girlie frocks and old dresses. The men paint the women's faces with gaudy colours. Ribbons, bows, rings, braids and wigs are added until each man has created his ideal woman. The result is a collection of grotesque doll-like creatures, seemingly making explicit both the stereotypical male view of women and the audience's attitude of expectation. This make-up and dressing scene appears to be a clear indication of a situation where women are forced into certain conventions and attitudes, forced to adapt to the dominant male view of them, and therefore both are 'inscribed' in a play of difference.[6] The exposed transformation of the performers destroys the illusionary character of the theatrical process.[7]

One of the 'impossible' (love) stories told in *Arien* is between a woman and a hippopotamus. When the huge hippopotamus rises out of the water, no one seems to notice the incongruity. The hippo is shy and sensitive. That a human can play the part of a hippopotamus, making the monster human, suggests that the relationship between men and women is just as difficult and impossible as the relationship between a woman and a hippopotamus. When the woman sees the hippopotamus approaching her for the first time, she laughs very loudly and forcedly and shies away from the impossible. Slowly and clumsily, the sensitive pachyderm moves back into the darkness of the stage, only to return later. The impossible remains a possibility against all odds (Hoghe, 1980, p. 70).

A large blond man carries a small black-haired woman stiffly across the pool, lifts her up, her feet reaching to his knees, their lips glued in a kiss. The woman is swept off and cannot stand on her own feet. When the male lets go of her she slides down and sinks into the water at his feet. The difficulties of togetherness are exposed in Bausch's performances as couples are shown attracting and repulsing, clinging to and rejecting each other.

Arien has many dark undertones that undercut the apparent humorous aspects. The antics of the photographer or the Titania-like love affair with the sad-looking hippo offer comic relief but are coupled with a sense of danger. It is almost as if pictures are being taken of a society drowning its destructive desires in a continuous masquerade of optimism. One of the dancers, as she puts thick make-up on her face, asks, 'What do you think of arias?' Somebody replies, 'I associate them with blood-red fingernails and torture' (Birringer, 1991, p. 140). These tropical and figurative juxtapositions, found in most liminal performance, create wide, jarring metaphors.[8] They unsettle the audience by frustrating their expectations of any simple interpretation; at the same time, they produce a synaesthetic-like effect.

During the performance the stage is awash with consumer objects that seem out of place or useless, but the performers cling to them. How life is deformed by such clinging is made explicit during a grand dinner party (Birringer, 1991, p. 140). The hostess of the dinner party welcomes her guests (friends with exaggerated attention, enemies with scarcely concealed dislike, both in perfect film cliché manner) and the company sit down at the table. One of guests, despite tactful hints from the hostess, remains standing, a foolish expression on his face. The company grows impatient. Standing on chairs, the women are carried to the mirror, where they continue their trivial conversation over the men's heads. A man models a series of evening dresses with effeminate poses. Gradually, the formal gathering develops into a 'Hollywood-style' social gathering with exaggerated make-up and costumes. Someone proudly announces, 'I was offered two film roles.' Someone else continually recites his class, graduation, assets and hygiene.

Bausch goes even further in disconcerting and disturbing her audience. In one of the scenes, as the group turn their backs on the audience and utter incomprehensible sounds over their shoulders, a figure appears in the auditorium and threatens to hurl himself from the balcony. Panic erupts on the stage as everyone cries, 'John! John, don't do it! Don't be mad! Come down!' After some hesitation, the suicide attempt is abandoned. However, the ensuing calm is short-lived. The group breaks into roars of tired, forced laughter, which culminates in piercing screams, losing all semblance of humour; instead, expressing only fear, despair and anger. The scene is reflective of the mood that prevails through the entire work.

In *Arien*, the apparently amusing is constantly revealed as merely theatrical, the repetition of conditioned patterns of behaviour; a self-deception, evoking the illusion of laughter and love. The individual in society habitually survives with the help of similar illusions, which likewise provide surrogate amusement and entertainment. Bausch's themes and aesthetics seek to expose these self-deceptions. In this work, all Bausch's instruments and motifs are present and appear in their full complexity. The intention is not to produce a performance which is finite and closed in the accepted sense, but a work which demonstrates new and different aspects of existence as presented through dance. Bausch's performances are fundamentally narratives inscribed by the body. Dance theatre that presents the free association of themes rather than a linear narrative can provide no answers in manifest or rational terms. Instead, the spectator, expecting some hidden meaning or essence, is required to turn to his or her own life experiences. This is precisely the advantage of dance theatre. The 'defamiliarization' effect of Bausch's performances goes beyond Brecht's didactic theatre, leading to a release of symbols that dismiss hierarchies of conventional narrative dramaturgy, at the same time retaining sense and meaning. These are created in the sensuousness of the physical activity, with its consequential liberation to a new self-awareness.

Tanztheater provides a certain merging of the aesthetic with everyday life.[9] If dance had previously been the domain of the 'beautiful appearance', then Bausch's dance theatre refers the spectator directly to reality. The distinctive aspect of dance, the transmission of body signals, opens the way to defining a reality determined by corporeal conventions. Following on from Brecht, Bausch employs 'epic' theatre techniques. Brecht wrote:

> Choreographers ... will reassume tasks of realistic nature. It is a mistake of recent time that it has nothing to do with the depiction of people as they really are. ... In any case a theatre that bases everything on the *Gestus* cannot do without choreography. The elegance of a movement and the charm of an arranged position, *verfremdet*, and the creativity of pantomime greatly assists the fable. (Servos, 1981, p. 438)

However, in Bausch's liminal dance theatre the contents are not transmitted in a didactic fashion, as in the Brechtian theatre, by fables and such like; instead, she employs other aesthetic devices, such as montage, an important component in her theatre which creates a similar feeling of *Verfremdung* (literally 'the making strange'). The use of montage is not new and has been at the centre of the artistic avant-garde since the early part of the twentieth century, either aesthetically manipulated, as in futurism, dadaism and surrealism, or politically translated, as in the work of the Russian film-maker Eisenstein. The specific features are the juxtaposition of various elements for a particular purpose. Bausch, in her use of montage, appropriates various media technology in order to make her statements. It is in this method, which emphasizes the functional value of expression above the purely theatrical, that a clear affinity can be seen to Brechtian theatre (Servos, 1981, p. 438).

Bausch also produces defamiliarization effects through repetition; this 'repetition' provides not sameness but 'difference' (Derrida, 1977, p. 175). Word patterns and fragments of sentences sound strange when they are monotonously and arbitrarily repeated. This repetitiveness is something Bausch defends, arguing, 'We must look again and again' (Birringer, 1991, p. 137). Therefore, in Bausch's theatre, basic concepts and traces of 'epic' theatre can be seen: the *gestus* of showing, the technique of *Verfremdung* and a particular application of the comic have increasingly been established as characteristic modes of performance, together with motifs taken from the everyday world of experience, leading to individuals being presented 'as they really are' (Servos, 1981, p. 438). The principle of presentation is the everyday process of understanding through body language, a process that is translated on stage by a distinctive corporeal language. Moreover, because bodily gestures on stage originate directly in everyday life, art and everyday life are no longer separated.[10] Therefore, actions on stage are removed from purely aesthetic abstraction and made analogous to the individual's concrete life experience. As formal barriers are shattered by the use of montage expropriated from various media sources – theatre, film and pantomime – subjectivity can be introduced (see Foucault, 1972, p. 52, on 'subject positions'). The lack of closure in Bausch's work, together with the inclusion of subjective fears, wants and needs of the writer, calls for active identification and therefore participation of the spectator.[11] However, this identification is not intended to produce an empathy for the characters; rather, it aims for an emotional involvement in the formation of problems (Servos, 1981, p. 439). For example, the use of comic elements and the tragicomic exaggeration of everyday situations lend general validity to the scene, while at the same time defamiliarization distances the spectator and prevents identification. The condition for this awareness is enhanced by the principle of montage, with its concurrent formation of a 'hyper-reality' (Baudrillard, 1983a, p. 147) based on the juxtaposition of separate situations.

Bausch's theatre is distinguished from conventional dramaturgy by its complex simultaneity of stage processes, leading to the impossibility of producing a single interpretation; rather, her work is open to many readings. In contrast to conventional theatre, which strives for a self-contained harmonious whole, an open structure is created, and each element is autonomous. Brecht's principle of 'not ... but rather' (*'nicht-sondern'*), which supports difference in performance, defines Bausch's work. Furthermore, her method of 'work in progress' prevents closure, thereby allowing several possibilities. The order is not fixed and any element can follow another. The beginning and end do not demarcate her works. Her main principle is the free association of her motifs, precluding the usual connections with a principle of causality. No emphasis is placed on the importance of any performer, the spectator can no longer identify with the protagonist of the story due to the lack of the normal differentiation of roles in main and supporting performers, thereby further problematizing subject positions.

In its rejection of narrative, dance theatre relies on the transmission of primarily emotive experience.[12] What is important is spontaneity and the fusion of performers and audience, together with the retention of a critical reflective attitude. If Brecht's theatre brought about a 'proper consciousness' through intellectual insight, Bausch's theatre seeks to produce the same with emotive experience. Its opposition is organized not on the basis of rational insight, but on the disruption of the emotions. Where didactic theatre is addressed to the social, Bausch's theatre proceeds from internalized norms and conventions.

In keeping with Brechtian theatre, her performance derives everything from the *gestus*. However, in this instance, the *gestus* is strongly related to the actions of the body: 'It neither supports nor contrasts something spoken; rather, it "speaks" by itself. It is the mode but also the subject of performance', as, for instance, when 'a man has his wife draped around his neck like a scarf to show that she serves only as a decorative accessory' (Servos, 1981, p. 440).

Bausch rejects the theatrical conventions of active stage and passive audience with its 'fourth wall'; she incorporates the audience into her performances whenever she can. In several of her performances she turns on the houselights, indicating to the audience that they share the same world as the performers. As with *Ausdruckstanz*, which rejected expensive stage sets and costumes in favour of stage scenery that focused on the body and emphasized dance, the realism of dance theatre avoids conventional theatrical values; stage design and props are subordinate to the statements intended. This is demonstrated by the performance of the 'stage designer' in *Café Müller*. The costumes — simple dresses, extravagant ball gowns, black suits, high-heeled shoes — are reflections of everyday life and are employed as means of expressing the ways bodies are constricted and confined. Unlike performers in classical ballet, Bausch's dancers do not attempt to make their movements appear effortless. They are physically pushed to the limit and they exhibit their exhaustion and pain quite openly onstage.

Therefore, in contrast to traditional theatrical performance, Bausch's liminal dance theatre takes issue with certain theatrical conventions, such as the notion of completion, the need to exhibit something and the audience's attitude of passive anticipation. No distinction is made between rehearsal and performance; rather, emphasis is placed on the process of adaptation, how the performance develops and so on. By exposing the theatrical process, dance theatre destroys theatrical illusion. Theatre is brought back to life by the continual process of comprehending and exposing the contradictions of urban existence.

Bausch fills her stage with so many images, movements and objects that some critics have been exasperated.[13] Her emphasis on the *mise-en-scène* and the concurrent subordination of language are two aspects which point to the influence of Artaud on her work (Price, 1990, p. 327). Artaud wrote: 'the possibilities for realization in the theatre relate entirely to the *mise en scène* considered as a language in space and in movement' (1958, p. 45). For Artaud, the stage had to be cleansed of psychologisms and social critique. The plastic and the physical were the true domain of the theatre. Certain affinities exist between the works of Artaud and Bausch. Artaud's stage was a theatre of dreams crowded with objects and bodies seen as signs, open to interpretation and without a narrative. The use of montage in *Tanztheater* reminds spectators of some of the bizarre combinations which occur in dreams. Nearly every Bausch work contains dream-like elements. Bausch would appear to agree with Artaud that theatre is 'a kind of organized anarchy' (Artaud, 1958, p. 51). Bausch's theatre in many ways is a dreamscape, a place where the fantastic, the mundane and absurd can and do occur simultaneously, as in *Arien* when the huge hippopotamus rises out of the water. A further example is the manipulation of the oneiric images in *Café Müller* which capture the imagination; a particularly powerful image is that of a woman walking in slow motion over a man. This image has a lasting effect.

For Artaud, the object of theatre is 'not to resolve social and psychological conflicts ... but to express objectively certain secret truths, to bring into the light of day by means of active gestures certain aspects of truth that have been buried under forms in their encounters with Becoming' (1958, p. 70). Artaud's actors were 'animated hieroglyphs' (1958, p. 54), 'bodies that moved about like living ciphers in a type of choreographed cryptography' (Price, 1990, p. 327). Artaud's theatrical writing is a 'writing of the body itself' (Derrida, 1978a, p. 191). Bausch's theatre, too, is literally a writing of the body.

A further similarity between Bausch and Artaud is her refusal to work with a dramatic text. Her *Macbeth* piece, *He Takes Her by the Hand and Leads Her into the Castle, the Others Follow*, mirrors none of the play's dramatic or narrative structure (Price, 1990, p. 328). As Artaud wrote, 'we shall not act a written play, but we shall make attempts at direct staging around themes, facts, or known works' (1958, p. 98). In keeping with the Artaudian theatre, the oneiric sequences in *Café Müller* include actions of 'terror' and 'cruelty'. For instance, a man and woman begin an awkward duet, which culminates in the two alternately slamming each other into the wall. These actions seem to evolve naturally in the course of the performance, almost as though Bausch is suggesting that certain conditions of existence cannot be changed (Price, 1990, p. 330). By presenting in *Café Müller* what appear to be some aspects of inevitability, Bausch appears to agree with Artaud that 'We are not free. And the sky can still fall on our heads. And the theater has been created to teach us this first of all' (1958, p. 79).

However, to make only one interpretation of Bausch's work is to deny the various constituent elements and avoid the true tension, a tension that intentionally leaves unresolved questions of existence. Since Bausch concentrates on the personal and 'the themes are always to do with man–woman relationships' (Servos and Weigelt, 1984, p. 227), it is important in examining her work to determine just what is the nature of those relations. Brechtian theory suggests that the nature of male and female relations is socially constructed and can and must be changed. Artaud, on the other hand, presents these relationships as fixed and unchanging (Price, 1990, p. 331). This latter element in Bausch's work has not gone unnoticed by feminist critics. As Jay Kaplan writes, 'Bausch's feminism is a grim world-view which proclaims biology is destiny. It is male nature to dominate women, and love is a continuation by other means of the battle of the sexes' (Kaplan, 1987, p. 76). This in some way misses the point of Bausch's liminal work. By using Artaudian techniques in her productions, Bausch criticizes the logocentrism of the West. Furthermore, by writing the body in the context of male and female relationships, she rejects the phallogocentrism of our culture (Price, 1990, p. 328). At the same time she emphasizes an intersemiotic signification, for which even the latest critical equipment is inadequate. Therefore, Bausch's work, together with much of the liminal, indicates a need for an analysis that incorporates both linguistic and non-linguistic significatory modes.

Bausch's work is close to Luce Irigaray's concept of the female imaginary, 'which brings into play "scraps" and "uncollected debris", and is not "too narrowly focussed on sameness"' (Irigaray, 1985, pp. 28–30). Her use of the body in performative acts proposes 'gender' not merely as a culturally inscripted artefact but also as irreducible difference, which reveals itself through the imaginary (Price, 1990, p. 328). In dance theatre, both a materialist and an essentialist feminism exist and Bausch, as in other aspects of her performance, presents no resolution; instead, the audience is left to contemplate the opposing points of view. In commenting on feminism, Bausch confesses,

'Feminism' – perhaps because it has become such a fashionable word – and I retreat into my snail-shell. Perhaps also because they very often draw such a funny borderline there that I don't really like. Sometimes it sounds 'like against each other' instead of together. (Hoghe, 1980, pp. 73–4)

Finally, to understand Bausch's dance theatre requires little intellectual preparation. Her theatre, like much liminal performance, appears to work directly upon the emotions. Consequently, individuals who have the most difficulties with it tend to be those who have certain cultural expectations of what constitutes 'dance' and what constitutes 'theatre'. *Tanztheater* can be seen as a shattering of traditional theatrical illusions, a process rather than a product that provides a certain merging of the aesthetic with everyday life, since it resists closure from within a place that is not entirely aesthetic.

'Theatre of images': *Einstein on the Beach*

It is not a question of what *Einstein* means, it is that it is meaningful. (Philip Glass quoted by Obenhaus, 1985)

Einstein on the Beach was revived for the third time in September 1992 at the Festival of the Arts in Melbourne, Australia. Robert Wilson, the 'opera's' director and 'auteur', and his musical collaborator Philip Glass, initially decided on Einstein as a subject since 'Einstein embodied ... [the] mythic gods of our time' (Wyndham, 1992, p. 12).

Starting with a title, Wilson developed the concept and design for *Einstein on the Beach*, an almost five-hour opus that refers to such disparate elements as Nevil Shute's *On the Beach*, a photograph Wilson had come across of Einstein standing at the seashore, Patty Hearst, justice and nuclear war. It has been at different times described as a theatre piece with music, an opera and a dream play. I am referring to it as an opera in keeping with Wilson's own terminology, from the Latin *opus* meaning a work, *opera* being the plural term (Rockwell, 1980, p. 12). Wilson, in describing his hybrid work, says, 'everything in it happens at once, the way it does in operas and the way it does in life' (Arens, 1991, p. 30). Philip Glass wrote the music and Lucinda Childs, one of the original founders of the Judson Church Dance Theatre, created the choreography. First performed in Europe and the United States in 1976, and revived briefly in 1984, it was not performed again until 1992, when it had its premiere in Melbourne, Australia.[14] It is estimated that only approximately 120,000 people had seen the work until its latest revival, which of course has heightened its mystery and made it legendary in contemporary circles.

Encompassing significant incidents in Einstein's life, the highly amplified opera merges vocals, visuals, dance and minimal instrumentation to create a heterogeneous, surreal entertainment of 'spectacle' and 'event'.[15] Comprising thirteen singers, nine dancers, seven instrumentalists, four actors and a production crew of twenty, *Einstein* is a huge musical undertaking, involving state-of-the-art sound and lighting technology as well as sets to rival the biggest touring rock acts.[16] The utilization of such technologies is a central aesthetic feature of much liminal performance.[17]

Wilson's libretto included texts by Christopher Knowles, a gifted but brain damaged youth with whom Wilson had been working for some time (Simmer, 1976, p. 106). Other text from the play includes a speech by Lucinda Childs repeated 43 times during the performance, making the only reference to a 'beach' in the whole work:

> I was in this prematurely air-conditioned super market and there were all these air conditioned aisles
> and there were all these bathing caps that you could buy
> which had these kind of fourth of July plumes on them they were red and yellow and blue
> I wasn't tempted to buy one
> but I was reminded of the fact I had been avoiding the beach.
> (Glass, 1988, pp. 74–5)

Other texts were provided by Samuel Johnson, an elderly man who auditioned for Wilson from off the streets. In France, at the premiere, he surprised both Wilson and Glass by writing and reciting two speeches in French. He later revised the texts for the 1984 performance at the Brooklyn Academy of Music, in which he also performed, though at this time he was in his eighties.

The performances in *Einstein on the Beach* relate to three basic images – a train, a trial and a spaceship – which are seen in various incarnations and from varying perspectives in the course of the opera. The train and the spaceship both relate obliquely to the life of Einstein, who was born in the era of the steam locomotive and died on the brink of the space age which his work helped to bring about. Together the two images trace the trajectory of the physicist's life. The remaining image – a courtroom, with an enormous bed at its centre – did not seem to have any basis in the life or work of Einstein, except that Einstein had mentioned that some of his most important ideas came to him in dreams. The trial in *Einstein* demonstrates Wilson's ability to create images that lack specific meaning, yet are very powerful. What crime had been committed and who was being judged? Wilson commented that he always felt the bed itself was on trial (Shyer, 1989, p. 218). This presupposes the question 'Who is speaking?' In this performance, as with other liminal works, it is clear that the subject's position is a 'vacant' site that may be filled by different individuals (or objects) at varying times (Foucault, 1972, pp. 54–5), thus problematizing notions of fixed identities.

These visual and aural oneiric images are structured mathematically throughout the four acts of the opera, each act preceded and followed by a 'knee play', the 'knee' referring to the joining function that human's anatomical knees perform (Glass, 1988, p. 30). The acts are divided into nine scenes. The scenic and musical development is controlled by permutations of the number three, with each of the dominant visual images recurring every third scene: a train/building (1), a courtroom and a bed (2), a field with a spaceship (3), each appearing three times.

The knee plays contain the most important musical material and feature the violin. Dramatically speaking, the violinist, dressed 'like Einstein', appears as a soloist as well as a character in the opera. His performing position is midway between the orchestra and the stage. He can be seen as Einstein or simply as a witness to the performance (Glass, 1978, p. 64). This particular character demonstrates in literal terms the importance of 'supplementarity', which makes origins dependent on an originary substitution of an absent 'other', showing that an identity is formed but can never be fully established in any rigorous sense.[18]

The images in Einstein are centred on three principal ways of looking at painting and measuring space (Wilson is both an artist and architect): first, portraits in a close-up (the knee plays); second, still life seen at middle distance (the trial and train scenes); third, landscape seen at a distance (the field/ spaceship scenes). The recurrence of the images implies a certain development, a 'happening' in process (Heidegger, 1971b, p. 57), its 'hermeneutic' situation revealing new insights in each stage of that development (Heidegger, 1978, p. 192). For instance, the sequence of 'train' images is presented in a reductive order (each one becoming less 'train-like'). In the first scene, act 1, a young boy looks down from the top of a high platform to watch a full-scale locomotive as it imperceptibly inches its way across the stage, steam pouring from its smokestack. The train reappears in the second scene of act 2, in the guise of either a caboose or the last carriage of a train. Finally, in the first scene of act 4, the visual shape of the previous train scene has been retained, but it has now become a building.

Wilson, instead of explaining the opera and its contents to his collaborators, would provide sketches. Even the published 'text' for the opera is non-verbal; instead, a series of 113 charcoal sketches made by Wilson himself and reproduced in a book which assembles musical scores, spoken texts and choreographic diagrams makes up the performance text. Arranged as a sequence of cinematic stills, these atmospheric drawings chart *Einstein's* progressive arrangement. The pictographic text proceeds from and extends

Wilson's ambition to present a spectacle that cannot be contained in verbal language alone (Owens, 1977, pp. 24–5).

Although they knew the time length for each sequence and what might happen on stage, Glass and Wilson did not discuss the mood or emotional content of a scene. According to Glass, fundamental to their combined approach 'was the assumption that the audience itself completed the work' (Glass, 1988, pp. 34–5). Therefore, active participation is required from the audience. This is because the signs presented by the 'opera' demand more than mere contemplation.

The musical idiom in which *Einstein* was composed had its beginnings in the mid-sixties, when Glass worked with the Indian sitar player Ravi Shankar. He explains, 'I discovered that a piece of music could be organized around the idea of rhythm rather than harmony and melody as I had been taught' (Shyer, 1989, p. 120). Glass 'developed a vocabulary of techniques (additive processes, cyclic structure and combinations of the two to apply to problems of rhythmic structure)' (Glass, 1978, p. 67). His main approach throughout *Einstein on the Beach* was to link harmonic directly to rhythmic structure, using the latter as a base. The usual tradition of Western music, which prioritizes harmony and melody above rhythm, was reversed. In *Einstein*, the rhythmic structure is prioritized above harmony and melody. The result is the reintegration of all three into an idiom 'accessible to a general public, though admittedly somewhat unusual at first hearing'. The vocal texts used throughout the opera are based on numbers and solfège ('do, re, mi ...') syllables. When numbers are used, they represent the rhythmic structure of the music. When solfège is used, the pitch structure of the music is presented; 'in either case the text is not secondary or supplementary, but is a description of the music itself' (Glass, 1978, pp. 67–8). As well as seeming appropriate for the subject of Einstein, a vocal text based on numbers could be easily understood by an international audience. By such means, this work can be seen to challenge traditional musical and theatrical practices.

The second revival of *Einstein on the Beach* retained the revised texts from 1984, the only difference being the performers.[19] Knee play 1 began unobtrusively. It was in progress as the audience entered the auditorium and ran for approximately thirty minutes. Two women stenographers, one black dressed in white and one white dressed in black, sit at desks at the right front of the stage, counting and reciting, their fingers performing a repetitive slow dance on the desktops. They are dressed in 'Einstein-like' attire.

It is no accident that one is black and the other white, that their trousers reverse the colour scheme of their skin and that they are both positioned in front of a brightly lit white area bordered by a black space. While one engages in distinct hand gestures, the other hardly moves, and when one of them recites a sequence of numbers, the other recites text repetitively. Philip Glass, in commenting on repetitiveness within the work, claims that 'the difficulty isn't that it keeps repeating, but that it almost never repeats' (Obenhaus, 1985). The difference within repetition, which Glass implies, is clearly demonstrated in the above performance. 'Iterability' is a useful tool for helping to explain this difference since it marks the relation between repetition and alteration. It supposes a 'minimal remainder'; as 'it alters something new takes its place' (Derrida, 1977, p. 175).

Fifteen minutes into the scene, the chorus slowly enters the orchestra pit. As the theatre lights gradually dim and spotlights come up on the chorus, they begin to count. The women on stage continue their recitation until a blackout ends knee play 1. In act 1, scene 1, a small boy stands on top of a high platform or tower. During the course of the scene, he occasionally tosses paper aeroplanes on to the stage below. A solo dance performed by a woman follows: an accumulation of skips, steps, turns on three diagonals, a restless, almost violent pacing and retreating along the diagonal lines. She appears to grip a pipe in her left hand (Einstein was often photographed with a pipe). At the front right corner of the stage, a man scribbles equations on to an imaginary blackboard. A full-scale, though obviously two-dimensional, locomotive, complete with pipe-smoking driver, edges its way across the stage, steam pouring from its smokestack. Two women slowly move across the stage, one reading a newspaper while the other makes birdlike motions. Three other dancers move across the stage holding strings that form a carpenter's triangle.[20] Three times during this train scene, a beam of light descends through the scene, cutting it in half. In this scene, the spectator is presented with a chaotic interplay and superimposition of different energies and speeds of movement, together with associations from Einstein's life, creating a scene of disruption and dispersion:[21] from Einsteins's childhood in the age of steam to the technological realization of mechanically powered flight, alluded to by the looping flight of the paper plane.

In act 1, scene 2, three illuminated rectangular horizontal beams of lights form the major visual theme of the trial, augmented by a huge clock without hands[22] and an enormous bed. The members of the chorus take standing positions in the jury box, their fingers moving together in unison to form intricate patterns under individual spotlights. An elderly black man and a young boy, both wearing wigs, take their places on the judge's bench between two globes of light. The defendant slowly mounts a stool. She is escorted by the prosecutor and the witness. The trial proceeds at a leisurely pace, a young lawyer carries an illuminated briefcase and the chorus takes a coffee break. A large black disc eclipses the clock, leaving two bright lights at either side of the blackened clock.[23] The trial concludes with Samuel Johnson's speech.

In knee play 2, the principal women actors, again in a square pool of light at the front of the stage, sit on chairs and recite. Behind them images of Einstein appear on a screen, while in front Einstein plays his violin. In act 2, scene 1, a hovering spaceship is seen in the far distance above a group of dancers. Lucinda Childs's choreography produces a mathematically precise piece, with an emphasis on clean lines and an exact match of movement to music.[24]

Dance was conceived by Wilson as the most 'separate' element in this 'theatre of images'; its relation to the stage space is revealing. All five of the knee plays and the opera's three major images are essentially tableaux.[25] The stage is divided into a grid. Within this grid, patterns of 'repetition' and 'difference' are developed (Derrida, 1981a, p. 265). The architecture and the design of these tableaux appear two-dimensional, or 'it is more accurate to say that the space they create is very shallow' (Sayre, 1989, p. 131). However, dance is different: it appears to be more three-dimensional, giving the allusion of occurring in a vast open space.

In act 2, scene 2, the train image reappears, but from a completely different perspective. The scene is a midnight-blue space, and the moon appears in various phases, from new and crescent to full and round. A gaslit, late nineteenth-century train rests on a flat and barren plain. An elegantly clad Victorian couple emerge from the bright compartment, stand on the platform and mimic a love duet. At the same time the chorus chants numbers and solfège syllables from the orchestra pit. A lunar eclipse occurs, paralleling the eclipse of the clock in the first trial scene. As the moon is obscured, two stars become visible on either side of the black disc (a visual repetition of the two lights at the side of the trial clock). Towards the end of the scene the couple return to the train compartment, the woman takes a gun from her handbag and aims it at her lover. He raises his arms. After a brief blackout, the train is seen again from a great distance.

Knee play 3 follows: as the chorus chant numbers and solfège syllables from the orchestra pit, the two principal female actors stand in their square at the front of the stage at a control board of flashing lights. The chorus makes steering motions, and its members, producing toothbrushes, begin brushing their teeth.[26]

The second trial, in act 3, scene 1, is now both trial and prison combined. The chorus and the principal actors take their place as before, the defendant again positioned on the high stool. She has now shed her 'Einstein look' and is wearing a white dress with white stockings and white shoes. The stage divides, a towering screen of bars cutting off the right side. Two prisoners, one male and one female, sit on two benches which have appeared behind the bars. They begin an angular seated dance, moving or sitting, chin in hand, presenting postures of dejection. The defendant slowly moves from her stool to the bed, where she lies writhing about, reciting the 'supermarket' speech. As the speech continues, her movements become jerkier and increasingly disjointed. Meanwhile, stagehands deposit props along the stage floor. She moves slowly along the front of the stage, collecting the props and changing her clothing. When she turns back to the audience, she is Tanya, alias Patty Hearst; in black pants and a black jacket, machine-gun held in her hand, pointed at the audience, still reciting her speech.

For the second dance sequence, in act 3, scene 2, the space is an open field. The spaceship is much nearer this time, and is moving dramatically across the scene as the dance continues. In knee play 4, the two principal female actors, again wearing their Einstein attire, lie writhing on the tops of narrow, glass-covered chrome tables.[27]

In act 4, scene 1, the visual shape of the night train scene remains, but the train has become a building. A crowd gathers and stares at an 'Einstein-like' figure who is visible at a window, scribbling equations. Eventually the crowd casually strolls away. Act 4, scene 2 presents the horizontal illuminated lines of the previous trial scenes, now metamorphosed into one beam of light, which merges with the bed. During the organ cadenza, the beam rises to a vertical position very slowly. A soprano begins to sing and the beam slowly disappears into the heights of the stage backdrop.

For act 4, scene 3, flickering lights outline the panels of a spaceship at the back of the stage. This is composed of scaffolding, compartmentalized by its girders into a three-tiered board of approximately fifteen squares. In front of the lit panels are cast members, musicians and even stage hands. The music bursts out in full strength, different combinations of lights go on and off. Up from the stage floor comes a glass booth, a young boy inside. There is a clock on the booth. The booth moves slowly up and down throughout the scene. At the same time another glass booth, bigger than the first, moves sideways with a woman inside, moving from left to right and back again. A black clad figure darts out, making semaphore signals with a pair of flashlights. As the scene continues, a sense of chaos increases. Banks of control lights in the performer's cubicles flash wildly, together with throbbing synthetic pulses of sound. Finally, smoke pours from two plastic 'bubbles' which have appeared on the floor near the front of the stage. The bubbles burst open and two astronauts climb out and slowly collapse. A curtain descends, cutting off the scene. It bears Einstein's famous equation: $E = Mc^2$.

In the final scene, knee play 5, two solitary figures sit on a park bench, representing two lovers in a post-Armageddon 'no-man's land'. They are the two original female performers, reciting text and displaying hand gestures in the same silent ballet which began the opera. A bus, headlights glaring, edges from the right side of the stage. As verbal phrases overlap and the chorus chants numbers, the bus driver delivers a speech. The text, originally from Samuel Johnson, contains a variety of poetic images, such as 'the moon and stars' and 'lovers in the moonlight'. The words and music cease. The bus moves in the direction of the lovers. The curtain falls.

Thematically, in this opera, Wilson seems concerned with a loss of innocence associated with technological advancement, leading to the alienation of individuals and the imminence of an apocalypse. In the penultimate scene, an atomic explosion is simulated in a spectacular vision of the future. However, ultimately, any significance in Wilson's work is ambiguous and inconclusive. Wilson's principal aim is to create a mode of heightened perception in his audience. His three major areas of concern are the manipulation of time, the construction of visionary images and the fracturing of verbal language. According to Wilson:

> My purpose in this method of working is to emphasize the importance of each separate element. ... In many of my pieces, what you see and what you hear do not go together. ... What I am trying to do is give individual lives to both sound and picture. (Arens, 1991, p. 24)

Wilson's theatre can be viewed as a type of collage and not as an integrated whole. It disconnects text from image and music, producing 'defamiliarization' effects and disrupting traditional narrative. Imagination is the crux of Wilson's perceptual art. Wilson's audience is free to combine or to develop separate meanings from his visual and aural resources. The spectators' freedom includes their emancipation from the specific textual interpretation of directors and actors, what Wilson calls the 'fascist directing and acting' of Western theatre today.[28] In liminal performance, in contrast to traditional performance, there is a loss of authority, together with the decline of the genius of the artistic producer, though not their disappearance.[29]

In creating a heterogeneous form of liminal theatre which simultaneously and multidimensionally provides neutral choices for the audience to make, Wilson points to an intuitive, non-verbal, non-rational mode of interpretation. Hallucinations and daydreams are acceptable and are even suggested by his work, as are many forms of non-linear, non-narrative mental activity. The challenge is for the audience to put the images together. This inverted theatrical process make the actor's job in this kind of production doubly difficult. The actor must present not one but all the possibilities of the moment. Wilson believes that in conventional acting the spectator's freedom to imagine is lost. He advises actors to 'break down every emotion, until you fully understand it, fully control it; only then are you free' (Dyer, 1985, p. A4). In much of this performance, no emphasis is placed on the importance of any performer; therefore the audience can no longer identify with any protagonist. Showing the formation process, not just of subjectivity but also of narrativity and visual representation, is fundamental to the liminal.

In Wilson's productions, acting technique is essentially reduced to the level of metronomic repetition, a mechanical dance sequence of synchronized movements. This had left Wilson vulnerable to accusations of using dictatorial directing methods (Holmberg, 1988, p. 455). However, he explains:

> The more mechanical we are, the more we do it, the more we understand about it. Many people think that too, it loses life but I don't think so. You're freer and in this work it is very formal, the gestures are counted, repeated and rehearsed. (Obenhaus, 1985)

In *Einstein*, Wilson's non-linguistic stance is evident in his refusal and even inability to discuss the work in anything but pictorial terms and in his use of the fragmented text of Christopher Knowles. Although Derrida has pointed out that there is no getting beyond language and culture, since what we think of these discourses is 'inscribed' by the cultural traces which create and maintain language (1982a, p. 329), it is a mistake to believe that by language Derrida is referring to a purely linguistic significatory practice.[30] It is evident that for this particular liminal performance, with its eclecticism and mixing of codes together with its semiotics of gesture – kinetic, visual, aural and gravitational, much of which produces disconcerting sensations[31] – an analysis based primarily on a linguistic model, such as Lyotard's (1988, p. xii), is inadequate. An intersemiotic analysis is required that can go beyond current critical theorization. It is only by such an analysis that non-linguistic modes of signification can also be provided for. In this way, the sublime, which exceeds the (linguistic) sign and is 'an outrage to the imagination', can be presented through such liminal performances as *Einstein on the Beach*.

'Synthetic fragments': Müller's *Hamletmachine*

I am neither a dope- nor hope-dealer. (Müller, 1984, p. 140)

Hamlet/Machine (1990) was first performed at the Deutsches Theater in Berlin and repeated the following year, again at the Deutsches Theater (a nocturnal performance which I attended in June of that year). *Hamlet/Machine* was a marathon eight-hour performance composed from both Shakespeare's *Hamlet* and Heiner Müller's own Hamlet deconstruction, the fragmentary *Hamletmachine* (1977).

Using *Hamletmachine* to reflect on Shakespeare's play as a testament to a juncture, the end of feudalism and the commencement of the Renaissance, with its concomitant age of reason, the production marked the demise of the Democratic Republic of Germany. Critics referred to it as a 'state funeral' because of both its content and its context, the 1990 production beginning work scarcely weeks before the fall of the Berlin Wall in November 1989 (Brenner, 1991, p. 160).

Müller's earlier plays explored the problems of reconstructing Germany on the socialist model. Residual Nazi consciousness among citizens, the gap between party rhetoric and daily reality and the personal sacrifice needed to fulfil eventual utopian goals were the basis of plays like *The Scab* (1956), *Tractor* (1955–61), *Correction* (1957–8) and *The Farmers* (1964), which exhibited a strong Brechtian influence, written in the 'epic' mode Brecht had established. Müller emulated ideas that Brecht had discussed in his later life, which included a new dramaturgy termed a 'dialectic theatre', replacing the earlier 'epic theatre'. In some of Müller's plays, such as *Philoctetes* (1966), he reworked classical materials in order to achieve an aesthetic distance which he refers to as 'alienating the whole' (Calandra, 1983, p. 119).

Although definite Brechtian traces exist in Müller's work, certain differences are apparent, even in his early works. In *Mauser* (1970), a parallel of Brecht's *The Measures Taken*, Müller exhibited a new disseminated style of what he referred to as 'synthetic fragments' (Müller, 1984, p. 17). Seemingly disparate scenes or part scenes are combined without any traditional notion of a coherent linear plot, to form an assemblage of intertextual fragments.[32] At the same time, the fractal nature of culture is exposed, pointing to the gaps, disjunctions and inconsistencies that make up conflicts without offering any resolution or closure (this is especially apparent in the *Hamletmachine*), unlike Brecht's 'A-B-C dramaturgy', which underlies and reifies an aesthetic built on closure and final solutions.[33] Where Brecht manipulates an audience into accepting his answer as the only correct solution, Müller refuses to give answers. He offers the problem, poses the question, presents the conflicting attitudes and opinions: 'I believe in conflict. I don't believe in anything else . . . I'm not interested in answers and solutions. I don't have any to offer' (1984, pp. 17–18). Thereby, he challenges the spectator to take sides or to withhold involvement. Müller does not pretend to know more than his characters; in this way he delegitimates the authority of himself, the author.[34] According to Müller, 'Writing drama you always have masks and roles and you can talk through them' (1984, p. 138).

In the early seventies, Müller was dramaturge and playwright-in-residence at the Berlin Ensemble. However, he has since expressed distinct reservations about the Brechtian 'father-figure', even using the term 'parricide' to define his relationship to Brecht, and stating that 'it's treason to use Brecht without criticizing him' (1984, pp. 16–18). In defending the fragmentary character of his later plays, a feature of much liminal performance, he points to the crux of his disagreement with Brecht's dramaturgy when he writes: 'I don't believe that a story which has "hands and feet", the fable in its classical definition, can grasp today's reality anymore' (Weber, 1980, p. 139).

While acknowledging Brecht's contribution, Müller claims that Brecht's plays have lost all their virulence in today's society. Contemporary theatre needs new instruments and Müller's use of fragmentation in his dramaturgy is one attempt to achieve this. Therefore, Müller's liminal theatre is a theatre of signification, 'dissemination' and 'dispersion' rather than of grounding (Derrida, 1981a, p. 25). Müller claims that the increased momentum of history today allows us

> Hardly any time to act and to bring about change. This also means that we no longer have time for a discursive dramaturgy. . . . When I write I always feel the need to load people with so much that they don't know what to take on first. . . . It just doesn't work any longer when you give them one piece of information and then tell then that the next one is coming. . . . Today, I think, you can only work with inundation. (Fehervary, 1976, p. 96)

The *Hamletmachine* is an evolving piece in the development of Müller's thinking and writing. Although quotes from his previous works have been included, he is exploring a new issue, quite different from his previous plays. According to Müller, 'The *Hamletmachine* isn't anymore simply a description of people missing the occasions and chances of history. . . . It is . . . about history as a story of chances lost' (Weber, 1980, p. 138).

Müller is aware of the fact that he has been influenced by the contemporary 'theatre of images' ('seduced' by the 'hyperreal spectacle'; Baudrillard, 1979, p. 32), as demonstrated in the work of Wilson and Foreman in the United States, and Mnouchkine in Paris. Robert Wilson collaborated with Müller on a production of the *Hamletmachine* in 1987, at the Almeida Theatre, London. This particular production, however, probably to the disappointment of some, had the actors intone the description of the *mise-en-scène*, as though it were part of the dialogue, rather than realizing it visually. Wilson's approach was entirely in accord with Müller, who referred to the performance as the 'best production ever' of one of his plays (Shyer, 1989, p. 131). Other influences, especially in his later works, have been Grotowski and Artaud.[35]

However, although Müller emphasizes the prominence of the visual aspect in the contemporary theatre, and devaluation of the text, he believes they are symptoms of a crisis, 'the Playwright's position versus the theatre and the audience, i.e. society has changed'. He continues with the observation that the playwright has moved away from the interests of the audience, society and even the director, therefore leaving the theatre with the problem of finding its function in today's society (Weber, 1980, p. 139), and producing a 'vacant' subject site that can be filled with different subjects at varying times. This focus on *énonciation*, which is central to liminal art in general (Foucault, 1972, p. 50), points to a self-conscious awareness of both the production and reception of art. Moreover, Müller believes that the abolition of an 'ordered' dramatic structure is conditioned by our contemporary history and is replaced by a system of differences. The *Hamletmachine* has no continuity in the sense of a conventional progression. Müller refers to the first scene of the play as the 'shrunk head' of Hamlet, and also points to the importance of Michel Foucault's work for him while he was writing the play: 'The final scene is defined by this feeling: that it is too late ... Ophelia/Electra, is finally silenced ... by the psychiatrists or whatever we assume these men in their white smocks are' (Weber, 1980, p. 140).

Hamletmachine was completed in 1977 and published in *Theater Heute* (No. 12, Seelze, 1977). References to the play in this work are from Müller's *Hamletmachine and Other Texts for the Stage* (1984). However, its inception was in the early fifties, originating from Müller's first reading of the play in its original language. Müller claims that 'Hamlet is really more a German than a British character' (Shyer, 1989, p. 126).[36] According to Müller, this is indicated by the propensity of German texts written on *Hamlet* in German. Furthermore, according to Müller, *Hamlet* reflects the situation of the intellectual in German history, a situation which seemed to change after 1945. He writes:

> In 1956 ... it became evident that Hamlet was becoming a topical character again. Quite as Brecht once defined him: The man between the ages who knows that the old age is obsolete, yet the new age has barbarian features he simply cannot stomach. (Weber, 1980, p. 137)

The final work contains many 'traces' and quotes from Müller's early notes on *Hamlet*, together with texts from his other plays.[37] The original concept for the piece was quite different from the *Hamletmachine* that was eventually produced. Originally, Müller intended the play to have 200 pages of text. It was meant to be a variant on the *Hamlet* theme, based on the situation in a socialist country after the abolition of Stalinism in 1956. However, 'the 200 pages started to shrink, eventually to eight pages'. Müller explains that, since translating the work, he developed a very free attitude to the 'material' and therefore did not want to use too much of it. For instance, in the scene in the graveyard where Horatio appears to Hamlet as an angel, Müller decided there was not enough historical substance for such a dialogue and instead produced separate monologues for Ophelia and Hamlet (see Weber, 1980, p. 138).

Müller's play *Hamletmachine*, given its fragmentary nature, can be summarised only in a similar way. In scene 1, during the state funeral of his father, Hamlet feeds the corpse to the hungry crowd, his father's ghost appears and Hamlet rapes his mother.[38] In the next scene, Ophelia destroys the home which has been her prison and runs out into the street covered in blood. In the third scene, Hamlet tells Ophelia, who is accompanied by Claudius, that he wishes to be a woman. He dances with the angel Horatio dressed in the clothes he has taken from Ophelia. Above them on a swing sits the figure of a madonna with a cancerous breast. In scene 4, the Hamlet player sheds his role and heads home, retreating into his own 'shit' and 'blood' (p. 57). He crawls into a suit of armour, and taking up an axe, he splits the heads of Marx, Lenin and Mao. In the final scene Ophelia sits wrapped in white gauze in a wheelchair, while 'fish, debris, dead bodies and limbs drift by'. She is left on stage 'motionless in her white wrappings' (p. 58).

The text is divided into five scenes and dominated principally by two characters: Hamlet (scenes 1 and 4) and Ophelia (scenes 2 and 5). Fundamental differences are immediately apparent between the Hamlet and the Ophelia scenes, displaying a certain 'deconstruction' of the text. The longer scenes, which are devoted to Hamlet, display a variety of literary forms, from multi-narratives in past and present tenses to lyric in free verse, containing various intertextual quotations from Shakespeare but also including text from Müller's previous works and from T. S. Eliot.

This intertexuality, a central feature of much liminal performance, continually disrupts the continuity of the text. Lyotard's subscription to the verbal in his analysis of the differend goes some way to providing a theorization of the sublime (1988, p. 166), which is demonstrated in the disruption of the play's narrative. However, when applied to Müller's work, Lyotard's theorization again proves unsatisfactory, since any theorization must ultimately allow for an intersemiotic significatory practice.

In contrast to the Hamlet scenes, the Ophelia scenes are much shorter and striking, consisting of a central, uninterrupted speech by a single voice. The interim scene, 'Scherzo', is more obscure. The term denotes the quick middle movement of a sonata, and is perhaps a 'joke' by Müller on the seriousness of bourgeois drama, which demands that the dramatic figures confront each other in a heavy, philosophically significant dialogue; instead, we are provided with monologues from Ophelia and Hamlet.

Scene 1, 'Family Scrapbook', opens with Hamlet at his father's funeral, reciting details in the past tense of the murder of his father by his uncle, his mother's lover:

I was Hamlet. I stood at the shore and talked with the surf BLABLA, the ruins of Europe in back of me. The bells tolled the state-funeral, murderer and widow a couple, the councillors goose-stepping behind the high ranking carcass' coffin, bawling with badly paid grief. (p. 53)

This first scene essentially presents a dramatic development of Hamlet's progression from detached observer to active participant, beginning with the state funeral of his father as above and ending with the murder of Polonius and the rape of his mother. The funeral is followed by a collage of quotations, delivered in the present tense and calling for definitive action from the hero:

I'M GOOD HAMLET GI'ME A CAUSE FOR GRIEF ...

RICHARD THE THIRD I THE PRINCE-KILLING-KING ... (p. 53)

Therefore, the action that Hamlet must accomplish becomes clear: he is to become the king-killing-prince, in contrast to Richard the Third, the prince-killing-king. The ghost of his father appears: 'Here comes the ghost who made me, the ax still in his skull' (p. 53). Hamlet, disinclined to fulfil his father's demand for revenge, desires a world without mothers, thereby ending the endless repetition of murder passed from father to son: 'Women should be sewed up' (p. 53). Hamlet questions the necessity of committing murder to avenge murder when he asks:

SHALL I
AS IS THE CUSTOM STICK A PIECE OF IRON INTO
THE NEAREST FLESH OR THE SECOND BEST ...
(p. 54)

Finally, Hamlet decides to act. He murders Polonius: 'Exit Polonius' (p. 54). Rapes his mother: 'A MOTHER'S WOMB IS NOT A ONE-WAY STREET' (p. 54). Addressing Ophelia: 'Then let me eat your heart, Ophelia, which weeps my tears' (p. 54).

The development from a passive, aloof Hamlet to an active, involved Hamlet is reflected in the discourse of the text. This is a device which again problematizes subject positions as the 'passive' subject becomes the 'active subject', illustrating that subject positions are always 'vacant' and up for grabs (Foucault, 1972, pp. 54–5). In the role of distant observer, Hamlet speaks in the past tense. However, any reference to action is spoken in the present tense. Therefore, dramatic action is expressed as happening in a dramatic present: 'Now, I tie your hands ... Now, I take you, my mother' (p. 54).

While Hamlet addresses the ghost of his father in what seems to be a dialogue, only a monologue is heard. The speech of the hero expresses reluctance to act in accordance with his role as his father's son, in other words to be a link or a 'mark' (Derrida, 1981a, p. 265) in the patriarchal chain. However, he eventually succumbs and begins to accept his designated role, though still trying to disclaim it: 'HoratioPolonius, I know you're an actor. I am too, I'm playing Hamlet' (p. 54). For Müller, the character of Hamlet, who dispenses with his knowledge and kills according to his prescribed role, represents the type of failed intellectual in modern Western political thought. The bloody deed required by tradition reaffirms the continuation of the established order, the institutions of oppression. In raping his mother he becomes his father, preserving the continuation of his family and his society. Hamlet finally accepts the violent role, which makes him the traditional hero who, in destroying others and himself, reaffirms the order of the world. Müller depicts Hamlet not as a hero but as a traitor figure: 'SOMETHING IS ROTTEN IN THIS AGE OF HOPE' (p. 53). For Müller the hope has failed, the establishment has not been toppled.

The second scene, 'The Europe of Women', is set in an enormous room. Ophelia is present, her heart is a clock. The scene again makes reference to previous texts of Müller's: the vision of a dying worker in *Germania Death in Berlin* (1976) and a short prose piece Müller wrote on the suicide of his first wife, Inge, in 1966. However, Ophelia's speech, in contrast to Hamlet's, maintains its unity as a speech from a single voice: 'I am Ophelia. The one the river didn't keep. ... I wrench the clock that was my heart out of my breast. I walk into the street clothed in my blood' (pp. 54–5).

While Hamlet represents the dominant, ruling male tradition, Ophelia represents all the aspects of life which are systematically repressed; in fact, she represents a threat to the security of that male order. She is a captive of the Enlightenment state, her dramatic role being defined by her refusal to participate in this order by rejecting her role as lover or lust object, destroying her dramatic setting, which defines her being and her final absolute silence and immobility. While the continuous motion of history is acted out and represented by Hamlet, Ophelia presents a discontinuous and fractal history. With her renunciation of womanhood, she is a revolutionary, in contrast to Hamlet, an intellectual turned counter-revolutionary. Müller writes:

Ophelia has to do with Ulrike Meinhoff and the problem of terrorism in Europe. ... The Ophelia-character is a criticism of Hamlet, consequently a self-critique; it contains autobiographical material dealing with the man–woman relationship of today. (1984, pp. 50–1)

Müller has even stated that 'the main character here could rather be Ophelia than Hamlet. I wouldn't consider this a disadvantage' (1984a, p. 51).

The third scene, 'Scherzo', is the only scene where Hamlet and Ophelia actually meet. It is also different to the other scenes, resembling more a pantomime than a serious dramatic piece. In the other scenes, Ophelia and Hamlet are seriously concerned with preserving their own identities – 'I was Hamlet', 'I am Ophelia' – but in this scene there is a mixture and diffusion of personalities, almost a labyrinth develops. Claudius is also Hamlet's father; Ophelia is also Hamlet's mother; Hamlet wants to become a woman and takes Ophelia's clothes; Ophelia flirts with Claudius/Hamlet's father and joins him in the coffin; the angel Horatio (his face at the back of his head) takes Ophelia's place as Hamlet's partner in a dance; a cancerous madonna sits above on a swing and observes the scene below.[39] The traces of each personality produce not sameness but difference. 'Iterability' marks the relation between repetition and alteration and therefore acts as a critique of pure identity (Derrida, 1977, p. 190).

In this scene, the 'Angel of Despair' makes his appearance as the angel Horatio, with his face turned towards the past, witnessing the catastrophic destruction, but driven unwillingly and inescapably into the future, representing past oppression unredeemed by revolution. The 'Angel' concretizes the 'Angelus Novus' image of history described by Walter Benjamin. Benjamin's angel has his face turned to the past, which he is fixedly contemplating and where he 'would like to stay, awaken the dead, and make whole what has been smashed' (Benjamin, 1969b, p. 257). Müller, in contrast, would have his 'Hapless Angel' looking into the future, but the future into which he wants to fly blinds him, while the past piles its wreckage upon him and brings him to a standstill.[40]

Benjamin's angel tends towards an eschatological image of history. A storm from paradise 'propels him into the future to which his back is turned, while the pile of debris before him grows skyward. This storm is what we call progress' (Benjamin, 1969b, p. 258). Müller, in exchanging the perspectives of past and future and at the same time arresting the dialectical movement of (the 'Angel of') 'History', stresses the point of *subjective* insertions in the historical process, combining his critique of the modernist conception of history with his dramatic manipulation of fragments, thereby introducing traces of the 'other' into the discourse of history.[41] Müller's 'Angel of Despair' 'combines hope with blood shed, lust with terror'.[42]

Scene 4, 'Pest in Buda/Battle for Greenland', defines its location with respect to specific historical events and places. If scene 2 was the 'Europe of Women', scene 4 is the 'Europe of Men'. However, in this scene the places are specified – Budapest, Greenland and so on – in contrast to the historical and politically unspecified location of the Ophelian scene. The Russian Revolution is evoked by the reference to Doctor Zhivago (p. 55); Stalin's death in 1953 and de-Stalinization in 1956 is alluded to by the toppling of the monument into dust ('razed by those who succeeded him in power three years after', p. 56); and the October 1956 uprising in Hungary is referred to by the scene title of 'Pest in Buda' and also by the line 'the stove is smoking in quarrelsome October' (p. 55). As in the earlier Hamlet scene, a multitude of texts are quoted: 'A kingdom for a murderer' (p. 57) is a quote and distortion of Shakespeare's Richard the Third, 'My kingdom for a horse'. Other quotes and misquotes are again taken from Müller's previous texts.

Hamlet in the first part of the scene represents the individual caught between two historical epochs – 'Doctor Zhivago weeps for his wolves' (a symbol of the Cossacks and pre-revolutionary Russia) – or Müller quoting Brecht: 'The man between the ages'. Set in the destroyed room of the Ophelian scene 2, scene 4 transpires against the background of Ophelia's rebellion. 'An empty armour, an ax stuck in the helmet' completes the set and symbolizes the traditional role prescribed for Hamlet. The Hamlet player begins by refusing to play his role (denying his prescribed subject position), rejecting the established political order: 'I'm not Hamlet. I don't take part any more. ... My drama doesn't happen any more' (p. 56).

He is beset by nausea at the privilege of the intellectual who ignores societal injustices under the auspices of 'reason'. Nausea 'Is a privilege' (p. 57). This image is particularly relevant, especially as an analogy to Ophelia's emancipatory gestures in scene 2. In the context of Müller's liminal aesthetics, it points to the privileged author's contradictory endeavour to secure the deprivation of the talented elite, problematizing that activity and authority. In addition, it is an expression of Müller's own self-denial. However, paradoxically, this symbolic rejection of privilege is a possibility itself open only to the privileged.

At the end of scene 4, Hamlet betrays his own revolutionary insight into the oppressive nature of his role and privilege, thereby betraying his own emancipatory resolution: 'AND SHORTLY ERE THE THIRD COCK'S CROW' (p. 58). Hamlet, like Peter betraying Christ, shortly before the third crowing of the cock, becomes the fool who tears away the costume of the 'philosopher' and becomes the fat 'bloodhound' who crawls into his father's armour. He takes up his axe and splits open the heads of Marx, Lenin and Mao, thereby destroying the 'other' as alternatives to the established order of oppression. While Ophelia's actions signify her emancipation, Hamlet's actions indicate his betrayal of humanity.

In the final scene, Ophelia sits in a wheelchair by the 'deep sea', and debris drifts by. Two men in white smocks wrap gauze around her and the wheelchair. If scene 2 depicts Ophelia's emancipatory awakening, symbolizing an awakening of the oppressed from a long period of subordination and exploitation, in scene 5 Ophelia's revolution is realized, the victims have finally turned against their oppressors. The radicalized Ophelia now repudiates all birth and growth and womanhood in general: 'This is Electra speaking. In the heart of darkness. ... In the name of the victims. I eject all the sperm I have received. I turn the milk of my breasts into lethal poison. I take back the world I gave birth' (p. 58).

The character of Ophelia, unlike Hamlet, specifically rejects the role required of her, as the lovelorn Shakespearean character who commits suicide. In this play, Hamlet is representative of the disintegration of the bourgeois intellectual hero, whereas Ophelia signifies an emergence of a new type. Hamlet belongs to a discourse based upon rationality, which unfolds as an inescapable teleology. Ophelia, on the other hand, represents the suppressed darker forces associated with intuition, chthonic myth and an almost Artaudian theatre that appeals directly to the senses. One is the essentially Hegelian model of continuity and inescapable progress, the other is a fractured timeless dreamscape. With the failure of Hamlet, together with the revolt of Ophelia, Müller's *Hamletmachine* would appear to signify a deterioration in the predominant, rationalist Western way of thinking.

Müller's liminal theatre is a scene of aesthetic intervention. However, it does not share the objectives of the Artaudian theatre, which is to present certain secret truths, or the Brechtian theatre in its didactic intention. Rather, the direct, intertextual nature of Müller's theatre, like much of the liminal, has an *indirect* effect on the political and the social. With its 'perceptive strategies', it provides both an experimental extension and a questioning of accepted ideas and belief systems.

'Social sculptures': Viennese Actionism

Viennese Actionism represents a new hybrid form of art, referred to by Joseph Beuys as 'social sculpture' (Oberhuber, 1989, p. 18), its strongly ritualistic character seemingly growing out of the religious ferment of postwar art in Vienna. The main exponents of this movement, which covered more than a decade from the sixties to the early seventies, were Otto Mühl, Hermann Nitsch, Rudolf Schwarzkogler and Günter Brus. Dionysian elements are central to this liminal theatre, with its expression of immediacy, disruption and excess (Nietzsche, 1956, p. 97), performing always to the edge of the possible. One of the central aims of Actionism was to deconstruct the representational language of art. During this process the Actionists came to extreme results, their 'will to art' being developed by their 'powers of invention and dissimulation' and 'the art of experiment' (Nietzsche, 1973, p. 54). Their desperate type of protest, which led to orgies of hatred, mutilation and even suicide, seems to have resulted from the specific Austrian situation, where because of the restrictions placed on society by a slow, outdated and cumbersome government, effective protest could find its place only through the deeds of creative individuals.

Viennese Actionism goes beyond a structural theory of cognition, in favour of a 'psycho-archaeological existentialism' (Klocker, 1989a, p. 42). At the centre of its psychoanalytical structure are: a longing for the primordial nature of the creative act (the pursuit of the chthonic);[43] a reconciliation of mind with matter; a utopia, brought about by blending pure, sensuous experience with total acceptance of existence. It is concerned not only with destroying structures and languages, but also with the expressive cathartic act that goes beyond language. There is a very real attempt to synthesize mind and matter as *mysterium*; whether in the *Gesamtkunstwerk* of Nitsch's Mystery Theatre, in the individualistic 'synaesthetic-alchemistical' laboratory of Schwarzkogler, in the 'analytical-shamanistic' ritual of Brus or in Mühl's 'psycho-dynamic' and taboo-breaking liberation actions (Klocker, 1989a, p. 44). It is in this way that Actionism is closely connected in its pre-mimetic rites to primordial religions, the longing for death and resurrection in Catholicism and the life affirmation of the Dionysian rituals (Nietzsche, 1979, p. 79). Similarly, it is related to the artistic movements of romanticism and expressionism, especially to the destructive aesthetic existentialism of Artaud and Schwitters. However, certain differences do exist, such as the varied use of 'abreaction', induced by the demonstrative, gestural act of overcoming illusion.[44]

Two directions developed from the early stages of Actionism. The first was a tendency towards the behavioural-analytical activity of pure 'action' demonstrated by Brus and Mühl, which concentrates on the role and function of artist and art. The second direction, taken by Nitsch and Schwarzkogler, was the elevation of art to a mystic-religious and romantic *Gesamtkunstwerk*, which incorporates its anti-representative destructive potential (Schwarzkogler's penile self-mutilations and Nitsch's lamb evisceration and blood pouring) into a strictly ritualized dramaturgical event or happening, to be experienced in a synaesthetic manner (Klocker, 1989b, p. 90).

A striving for freedom, 'the will to be free' (Schwarzkogler quoted by Oberhuber, 1989, p. 18), was a main tenet of this movement. Freedom was to be reached by an acting out of the drives from one's own inner being. According to Otto Mühl, 'the free admittance of the true creative drives is the ethical intention of my apparatus. ... I would have all people exterminated except for the ones necessary for entertainment' (Oberhuber, 1989, p. 18).

Initially, freedom for the Actionists meant the need to follow suppressed drives and desires. As Hermann Nitsch writes, 'when I still believed in the meaning, the stability and moral order of a human society, I thought I could offer with my work a kind of outlet, through which all the suppressed and inhibited could be abreacted and eliminated.' However, he continues, 'The structure of form has become a deeper metaphysical reality than morality' (Oberhuber, 1989, p. 19). Nitsch's later works deal with the spiritual foundation of existence, seeking the distinction between the 'temporal and the eternal' and 'the strength to renounce the gratifying experience of the fruits of one's works'. Nevertheless, a historical consciousness does pervade the whole movement. Most of the actions were well documented by photos, film, descriptions in private correspondence and conceptual argument:[45]

> An apartment – a naked male body lies on a freshly made bed – with legs straddled and hanging over the edge of the bed – the brain of a freshly butchered cow lies on testicles – brain and penis are poured with a slimy transparent fluid from above – the fresh sheet becomes befouled – black and white. (Hermann Nitsch, *Penis Rising*, Action photograph, 1964)

> Part of a picture – the pubic area of a naked male body behind a white covered table – a black square rubber mat on the table – the penis wrapped in fat and a white gauzed bandage lies on the black field – right over the pubic hair surgical gauze is stuck to the stomach with a strip of bandage – surgical instruments, a syringe and two scissors lie in such a way on the black square that points to the penis – dark plastic crab touches with the tip of its claws the penis wrapped in fat and a gauze bandage – several razor blades lie scattered over the black square mat – black and white. (Rudolf Schwarzkogler, *2nd Action*, Action photograph, 1965)

The central aesthetic concern of Actionism is the transformation of the fragmentary nature of a 'normatively understood reality' into a 'new subversive significance' (Klocker, 1989b, p. 90), producing a new 'shift-shape' style of intersemiotic signification. It requires the presence of a creative agent and a relationship to the psychoanalytical. It is a momentary art and as such can only be fully realized in the 'immediate' action-like course of the performance itself. However, beyond the spontaneity and theatricality, a constant tendency towards an aesthetic manifesto and its pictorial image led to Actionist works becoming fully valid images in themselves.

From the beginning of the movement, the Actionists were aware of the significance of photographs and films for their future artistic statements. Parallel to the actions they performed, they worked with multimedia, in either a creative-artistic or a documentary-voyeuristic way. For instance, Rudolf

Schwarzkogler's creative-artistic action photographs are exemplary of a 'staged photography'. For him, the possibility of his own experience of the act of painting extended to the event, and photography was the ideal possibility of information. It freed the artist from leaving an autonomous work behind; at the same time questioning the work's identity and legitimation.[46] Therefore, Schwarzkogler tended not to realize his actions as a public dramatic event for the audience. Only the action collage designed for his own sensuous experience was to be fixed in the reproduced image. Schwarzkogler's later art developed into the radical notion of an alchemistical art. The synaesthetic conditions and ritually controlled physiological influence over the environment were to bring about a healing process of the body.

Despite the glaring disparity between the detached illusional essence of film and the demand of 'action' to work with a direct 'reality', Nitsch, Brus and Mühl were inclined to document their performances with the film camera. For them, this was the only way of bringing their actions (many of which were privately realized) to the public. According to Nitsch, 'My actions can be documented only to a very qualified extent. Decisive is and remains the execution. The direct sensuous experience of the real occurrences will remain most essential and is what was intended' (Klocker, 1989b, p. 98). In a number of joint projects Brus and Mühl combined to form works called 'total actions'. Painterly references were discarded and the actions became increasingly of a theatrical-literary character, requiring the audience's interactive participation, and thus destabilizing and delegitimating authorial authority.

The 'total actions' began a process in which it was no longer a matter of overcoming possibilities in art but of attacking the essence of representation itself, 'of calling into question the art system ... and the stereotype of culture and of going to the limit, of "peeling art from the body" so to speak' (Klocker, 1989b, p. 95), or of a 'writing of the body itself' (Derrida, 1978a, p. 191). The works also known as 'Direct Art' required the direct and immediate spontaneity of the 'event' itself, in which the bared body appeared before the public and therefore in a social context: for instance, Otto Mühl's *Leda and the Swan* (1964), where a mixture of egg yolk, paint, nails and feathers is poured over a naked female torso, or Günter Brus's *Action Breaking Test* (1970), where a naked, mutilated male body lies surrounded by razor blades.

If the earlier works of this type of action were still theatrical and therefore representational, they provided a transitional step for the radical nature of Brus's later purely gestural practice of 'faeces and body analyses' and Mühl's 'psychodramatical' actions.[47]

The attack of 'Direct Art' against cultural stereotypes became an attack against the art system itself. In the late sixties Brus began his corporeal 'analysis', a process not completed until the seventies. Together with the 'psychodramatical actions' of Mühl, many of his actions were conceived only for film owing to their extreme, radical nature, which prevented them from being performed live for fear of arrest. The style of this film was intended to be purely voyeuristic and documentary.

As well as being a series of 'direct' synaesthetic events, the history of Actionism is a history of its reception through a changing aesthetic in its photographic and filmic style. In striving for an extreme that was necessary for their creative act, they consciously limited themselves to those media which make a later reception of content possible. In this sense no art fully escapes the picture, because the picture constitutes its essence. This fact was taken into account by the Actionists in their continual pictorial reproduction through photographs and film. It is in the tension between 'representativeness of the image and immanence of the action', between 'distance and participation' and between 'hierarchy and anarchy' (Klocker, 1989b, p. 101) that Actionism is deconstructive. The Actionists' apparent complicity with dominant means of representation would seem to be at odds with their realized actions.[48] Deconstruction, and such motifs as death and eroticism, self-effacement, sensuality and the interdisciplinary (*Gesamtkunstwerk*), are central to Actionism.

From the moment of its inception, Viennese Actionism has developed in a particularly intricate and complex way. At its centre is an almost chthonic longing for the unity of spirit and the material. An attempt is made to retrieve or 'disclose' such an identity by direct corporeal insertion in the creative act by way of a 'happening'. Each turn of interpretive spiral or 'hermeneutic helix' reveals new insights (Ruthrof, 1992, p. 141). In this sense, identity is supplemented by the body itself, which compensates for this perceived lack. The entrance of the body into the performance is necessarily in this context as victim. The human body, as direct working material which goes beyond the representational role-playing of theatre (though no body, not even a naked one, can abandon representation altogether), becomes 'the dramaturgy of the organic'. Therefore, following Artaud, 'like one condemned to burn at the stake from where he makes signs', Viennese Actionism presents its 'aesthetic strategy of survival' as a reaction to an increasing alienation and loss of identity in contemporary society (Klocker, 1989b, p. 112).

Notes

1. According to Derrida, although all texts participate in a genre, 'such participation never amounts to belonging' (1980, p. 212).
2. Derrida explains how closure is prevented by 'différance', 'trace' and 'mark' (1981a, p. 25).
3. Deborah Jowitt of the *Village Voice* writes: 'I can't image American choreographers wishing to imitate "Tanztheater", no matter how much they are impressed by the work. It may be instructive to see that extremes of emotions can be dealt with onstage in innovative ways, but I think that American dancers still have faith in the expressive powers of dancing and form, and believe that trust, affection and uncomplicated love, as part of our emotional life, are worth showing onstage' (1986, p. 81). Anna Kisselgoff of the *New York Times* writes: 'It should be pointed out that German choreographers ... are ... strict about using formal structures. But these are underpinnings. They are used as means to an end, to express feelings, and this expression is usually pictorial. ... Miss Bausch ... asks the viewer to bring his or her reactions to her works, knowing that a specific image might evoke contrasting reactions. Hence the reason why we cannot agree on the "point" of the German pieces' (1986, pp. 81–2).
4. According to Bausch, 'When somebody stands there alone singing, isn't that somehow lonely? Someone standing quite alone and then this singing' (Servos and Weigelt, 1984, p. 131).
5. This corresponds to certain Nietzschean features described by Blanchot as *parole de fragment* and *écriture fragmentaire* (Hartman, 1970, pp. 97–103).
6. 'Inscription', according to Derrida, is a strategy of deconstruction with the aim of 'overturning and displacing the conceptual order' (1982a, p. 329).
7. According to Nietzsche, Dionysian art 'annihilates' illusion (1956, p. 97).
8. See Derrida for a detailed discussion on metaphor and metaphoricity (1982b, pp. 219–20).
9. In 'Parergon' (1987a, pp. 59–60), Derrida questions art in terms of its borders and the effects on it of forces coming from 'outside'. Derrida considers the notion of a fixed border to be a sign of critical dogmatism. He problematizes the notion of frames ('*parerga*'), since their exteriority defines them less than does the necessity that links them to the internal structure of the work ('*ergon*').
10. Foucault writes: 'The body is the inscribed surface of events (traced by language and dissolved by ideas), the locus of a dissociated self (adopting the illusion of substantial unity), and a volume in disintegration. Genealogy, as an analysis of descent, is thus situated within the articulation of the body and history. Its task is to expose a body totally

imprinted by history and the process of history's destruction of the body' (1977, p. 148).

11. According to Lyotard, '"our" destination ... in regard to Ideas, [is] to exceed everything that can be presented' (1988, p. 166).

12. See Nietzsche for a discussion of the Dionysian, which is 'the tremendous awe which seizes man when he suddenly begins to doubt the cognitive modes of experience' (1956, pp. 219–20).

13. Marcia Siegel writes of a 'gigantic and irrelevant *mise en scène* which completely takes over the production ... no plots, progressions, developments or denouements ... fascination with costumes ... accumulation of objects ... the eclectic and nonlinear choice of music, verbal text, visual reference ... are action based and essentially formless' (1986, p. 108).

14. According to Glass, 'the work was certainly considered strange and avant-garde in 1976 but when it was presented in 1984 it didn't seem so odd. It is probably more radical than ever because most of today's music theatre is incredibly conservative by comparison. *Einstein* looks as though it came from the moon' (Hallett, 1992, p. 5).

15. Baudrillard argues that an outcome to an 'event' is sought from its 'maximum disequilibrium'. It is therefore a fatal strategy, 'a form of catastrophe' (1990, p. 191).

16. Glass claims that 'In the past sixteen years technology has become more evolved and technical standards are higher. It was conceived as a high-tech piece and technology has caught up with our original vision. It is now much cleaner and sharper' (Hallett, 1992, p. 5).

17. The 'sublime' is seen by Lyotard as a response to art deprived of rules and limits, and is therefore analogous to the liminal. This new 'sublime' as 'a contradictory feeling ... of both pleasure and displeasure' allows us to challenge new 'complex' techno sciences by concerning itself with such things as the unrepresentability of technology and the ineffability of the multinational corporation (Lyotard, 1986c, p. 10).

18. The 'supplement occupies the middle point between total absence and total presence' (Derrida, 1976, p. 157).

19. I attended the 1992 premiere in Melbourne.

20. Frequent reference is made during the opera to certain geometrical angles and shapes, particularly triangles, apparently representing the fixity of a Euclidean conception of the universe. These forms contrast with Einstein's revolutionary vision of a space–time continuum, evoked in the music and the plastic images of the work.

21. See Nietzsche's discussion of the Dionysian aesthetic (1956, p. 22).

22. Given the temporal concern at the centre of Einstein's research, Wilson

makes frequent use in performance of a variety of instruments for the measurement of time (see Stefan Brecht, 1978, p. 330).

23. This alludes to the solar eclipse of 1919, in which the appearance of two stars on either side of the sun demonstrated to Einstein the curvature of space, supporting his theory of relativity.

24. In the 1976 production of the opera, Andrew De Groat's choreography emphasized more a dervish-like spinning movement.

25. As Craig Owens notes: 'Wilson's theatre is pictorial; it proceeds from visual images' (1980a, p. 115).

26. This refers to a famous photograph of Einstein sticking his tongue out at a photographer.

27. According to Wilson, 'you see two characters lying on plexiglass tables: they are supposed to be floating in water. In 1900, there was 25 ft. diameter barrel of water that had mercury in it. They shot two beams of light through this to measure the speed of light' (Stefan Brecht, 1978, p. 167).

28. Wilson argues, 'I don't want the audience to wander around in my mind, or in the minds of the actors. I want them to wander around in their own minds' (Dyer, 1985, p. A4).

29. Foucault asks, '*Who is speaking*? Who has the right to use this sort of language (*langage*)?' (1972, p. 50). In liminal performance, 'speaking positions' such as the director's are similarly brought into question. In this way, authority is both destabilized and delegitimized, giving the liminal a further political and social dimension.

30. Derrida writes, 'the general text is not limited … to writings on the page' (1981b, pp. 59–60).

31. Sensations which correspond to the 'negative pleasure' experienced by the Kantian sublime (Kant, 1978a, p. 91).

32. Müller exhibits a certain Nietzschean style as *écriture fragmentaire* (see Hartman, 1970, pp. 97–103). This 'fragmentation' blurs and destabilizes genres.

33. See Derrida for a discussion on 'closure' (1982a, pp. 130–1).

34. By the foregrounding of subject positions in the text, authorial authority is destabilized (see Foucault, 1972, p. 52).

35. According to Müller, 'Artaud tried to use his psychosis – or neurosis – as the point of departure in his theatre work. That, of course, was disturbance of "business as usual" in the theatre. This, it seems to me, is the function of today's playwright and theatre-person: to disturb the peace, the corruption, the habits, the comforts, etc. Today the negative attitude is the positive one' (Weber, 1980, p. 140).

36. Müller is alluding to the fact that Frederick the Great was descended on

both sides genealogically from James the First of England, the supposed model for Hamlet. According to Müller, 'James knew his mother [Mary, Queen of Scots] married the murderer [Bothwell] of his father [Darnley] – Frederick could be Hamlet', the tormented blundering protagonist haunted by the 'nightmare of history' (Shyer, 1989, p. 126).

37. For Derrida, 'trace' is a metaphysical (quasi-)concept which names an originary tracing and effacement (1976, p. 62).

38. See Arlene Akiko Teraoka, 'Scenes 2–4: The Dramatic Hero and the Undramatic Victim' (1985, pp. 89–97).

39. At the production I attended in Berlin, this scene was certainly treated by the audience as a pantomime providing light relief in comparison to the other scenes in the play.

40. Fehervary points to Müller's 'image of history' as being exemplified by 'The Hapless Angel' described in his 1958 libretto *Glücksgott*, where he writes, 'behind him the past washes ashore, piles debris on his wings and shoulders with the noise of buried drums, while before him the future dams up. . . . Then the moment closes down over him: standing buried by debris quickly, the hapless angel comes to rest, waiting for history in the petrification of flight glance breath. Until the renewed roar of mighty beating wings propagates itself in undulations through the stone and announces his flight' (1976, p. 93).

41. Müller writes of 'a new magic healing of the rift between humankind and nature', insisting on a place for the 'other', yet insisting that 'hope guarantees nothing. . . . A better world will not be achieved without blood shed; the duel between industry and the future will not be fought with the songs which allow one to feel at ease' (1979, p. 56).

42. See Sabine Wilke (1991, pp. 282–3) for a more detailed discussion of Müller's deconstruction of the 'Angel of History'.

43. This echoes the Heideggerian quest for the 'primordial' way of knowing (see Heidegger, 1978, pp. 172, 186). It also bears 'traces' of Artaud's 'theatre of cruelty' (1958, p. 70).

44. 'Abreaction' (a psychoanalytical term) is the release and expression of emotional tension associated with repressed ideas by bringing those ideas into consciousness.

45. The following documented readings are presented by Hubert Klocker (1989b, p. 89).

46. By problematizing its genre, the work of art's identity is destabilized and delegitimated; 'origin' in this instance is shown to be merely an intentional (mis)representation (see Derrida, 1980, p. 212).

47. These performances, in keeping with liminal performance in general, not only foreground the body but also form wide, disconcerting metaphors,

since they refute closure and play with meaning (see Derrida, 1981a, p. 258).

48. Derrida argues that it is not possible to escape complicity 'without also giving up the critique we are directing against this complicity' (1978c, p. 281). Similarly, Craig Owens, writing on postmodern art, points to a problematizing of the 'activity of reference', which involves an 'impossible complicity' (1980b, pp. 79–80).

5

Liminal film

Liminal film is heterogeneous, experimental and marginal. Its employment of the most recent developments in media technology is a quintessential feature that has led to an increased creative potential. Other aesthetic traits are self-consciousness and reflexiveness, montage and collage, extreme stylization, eclecticism, pastiche, playfulness and the mixing of filmic codes. Liminal film is usually screened in localized arthouses rather than in mainstream theatres and attracts a smaller audience, thereby creating alternative 'institutional sites' of performance. Such liminal films as *Prospero's Books, Edward II, Der Himmel über Berlin/Wings of Desire* and *Europa/Zentropa* are typically parodic, metacinematic and, questioning, and, like all liminal performance, are experimental extensions of our social and political milieu.

'Painterly' aesthetics: *Prospero's Books*

Peter Greenaway's most ambitious work, *Prospero's Books*, is an adaptation of Shakespeare's *The Tempest*, at once fanciful and exact. It is operatic in its use of music, song, dance and the choreography of scores of extras. Against opulent settings of Renaissance architecture, naked bodies form heterogeneous tableaux based on classical mythology or European art. The spectacle is further enhanced by the density of the images, producing a 'pure event' of 'ecstasy' and 'obscenity' (Baudrillard, 1988, p. 192).

Greenaway uses both conventional film techniques and the resources of 'high definition television' to layer image upon image, superimposing or opening out a second or third frame within his frame. At the same time, the text is highly literary and self-referential in its constant reminders that *The Tempest* is the text. Greenaway conceives the play as Prospero's invention, and we see the pen of the magician-playwright as it moves across the parchment, leaving in its wake 'traces' of 'difference' (Derrida, 1982a, pp. 130–1) in the baroque, calligraphic lines. The film was shot in the Netherlands with a multinational cast headed by Sir John Gielgud, and edited on videotape in Japan in one of the world's most advanced high-tech post-production suites. It was released in 1991.

Greenaway has a 'formal, rigorous, near-algebraic' approach to narrative: 'there's a way in which the scripts themselves are almost constructed on a grid' (Rodman, 1991, p. 36), which is, in his films, almost always disguised by a luscious painterly richness. However, in *Prospero's Books* he goes completely over the top, as layer upon dazzling, stunning layer of text and image float across the screen like a Cecil B. De Mille production gone completely deranged. The visual imagery of the film is excitingly profuse. Actors compete for screen space with Muybridge-like animatics, all manner of corporeal parts and superimposed calligraphy. Greenaway's trademark of long lateral shots presents at one moment a tableau from the Dutch masters, Hals or Vermeer; the next, a young boy urinating with exhilarated abandon into a swimming pool where Prospero/Gielgud is bathing; then a near-naked woman with a skipping rope; all competing with cadenced drops of water and orbs of fire, pulsating rhythmically. Consummating the scene is the delicate presentation of pen scraping against parchment.

Greenaway's films, in flaunting their esotericism and relishing their overt staginess, divide audiences. There are those who attempt to follow the plot and there are others who think a Greenaway film is about as exciting as taking a trip through a museum without a catalogue. However, what is not in doubt is the fact that Greenaway has made, from early shorts such as *H for House* (1976) through to *The Cook, The Thief, His Wife and Her Lover* (1989), a string of films that have been among the most challenging bodies of work in cinema today. Not surprisingly, his films have been successful mainly in arthouse cinemas rather than in the commercial mainstream; and more so in European than in American markets (though they would appear to have some popularity in the art house cinemas of New York). These 'other' marginalized performative sites suggest the alternative 'institutional sites' (Foucault, 1972, p. 51) of much of the liminal.

Prospero's Books is a hybridized version of *The Tempest* and provides 'traces' of that chain of signification. Shakespeare's play centres on Prospero, Duke of Milan, who has been deposed by his brother, Antonio, and now lives on an island with his daughter, Miranda. Opening with a storm in which the corrupt brother and his courtiers are shipwrecked on the island through Prospero's magic, *The Tempest* shows Prospero's manipulation and staging of the action in which he intends to take his revenge on his usurping brother.

Initially approached by Gielgud, who had wanted to put the enigmatic drama on screen for some time, Greenaway rapidly transformed the play into his own idiosyncratic vision. While remaining faithful to the Shakespearean text, Greenaway put the words of all the characters into Gielgud's mouth for two-thirds of the film. The results are fascinating, even more so than any of his previous films.

Prospero's Books is essentially a set of perpetual interpretations. The first is Greenaway's interpretation of *The Tempest*, in which one line of Prospero's — 'knowing I loved my books, he [Gonzalo] furnished me from mine own library with volumes that I prize above my dukedom' — is made to serve as the metaphor for the whole enterprise. Greenaway then assumes that this library contained some 24 books. The books provide Greenaway with his 'grid'.

The second interpretation is the technological one, that of film to tape to film. Shot on 35 millimetre film, *Prospero's Books* was then transferred to 1125-line high definition widescreen video. Superimpositions, special effects and opticals were added in the video domain and then transferred back to film, to be joined with the original celluloid.[1]

Underlying all this is the translation whereby Prospero becomes Shakespeare and Gielgud becomes Prospero, with Greenaway taking the role of 'master artist' or 'auteur'. Greenaway explains:

> *The Tempest* is extremely self-referential. . . . I very much like the idea that when somebody sits in the cinema and watches a film of mine, it's not a slice of life, it's *not* a window on the world. It's a constant concern of mine to bring the audience back to this realization. (Rodman, 1991, p. 80)

For Greenaway, *The Tempest* is an ideal medium for this 'hyperrealization' (Baudrillard, 1983a, p. 147) or 'happening' (Heidegger, 1971b, p. 57). Underpinning these interpretations is the Nietzschean 'perspectival attitude', which displaces the truth — falsity opposition (Nietzsche, 1924a, p. 16), together with the Heideggerian *Auslegung*, a term which means explanation as well as interpretation (Heidegger, 1978, p. 188). By a correct entry into the 'hermeneutic helix' of the work (Ruthrof, 1992, p. 141), fresh insights are 'disclosed' with each turn of the spiral (Heidegger, 1978, pp. 192–3).

First, there is a way in which Prospero himself is a portrait of Shakespeare taking leave of the audience, the theatre and the world of illusion. *The Tempest* was allegedly Shakespeare's final play.[2] Since there is a way in which Prospero is both Gielgud and Shakespeare, Prospero himself invents the dialogue for all the other characters. Throughout the film Gielgud/Shakespeare/Prospero is seen writing the dialogue; ultimately Gielgud's voice is everyone. Greenaway remarks that, since this is a Jacobean play, it might have been a classic revenge drama. However, it does not end in revenge, it only goes to a certain point and then there is forgiveness by the wronged Prospero of those who sought to persecute him. However, if Prospero has renounced his artifice, it is apparent that Greenaway is not about to do the same thing. According to Greenaway, the reason the film was called *Prospero's Books* rather than *The Tempest* was to indicate that the film is not just an attempt to reproduce a familiar text; thus, through its 'traces', it self-consciously inscribes differences and destabilizes any fixed 'identity' (Derrida, 1976, p. 62).

Greenaway's main interest was to pursue the 24 books that Gonzalo, Prospero's loyal courtier, put into the bottom of the vessel in which Prospero and Miranda were sent out into exile. That idea would appear to hold the material together. As Greenaway remarks, '*Prospero's Books* is a film about "You are what you read". We are all products of our education and our cultural background, which very largely is perceived through text' (Rodgers, 1991/2, p. 15). The film opens with Gielgud sitting at his desk experimenting with the first word of the play, which is 'Bosun'. This is an interesting word, because it is one that was never written but used only by illiterate seamen, and when the word was eventually written it became 'boatswain'. This emphasis on disorder in the use of oral and written language is intentional by Greenaway. The word is written up on the screen many times, accompanied by droplets of water. The evocation of that word in conjunction with the first book of the film, which is the 'Book of Water' (supposedly put together by Leonardo da Vinci), determines the film and marks its differences (Barker, 1991, pp. 27–8). Therefore, from the beginning the audience is aware that it is at the origin of the play and there is going to be no simple illusion. The film throughout draws attention to its own artifice. At the end of the film the books are all destroyed except for two, one of which is *The Tempest* and the other a collection of Shakespeare's plays. Of course, if these books were destroyed there would be no means with which to make the film – a typical liminal self-referential gesture from Greenaway. The books are rescued by Caliban, the image of the negative aspect of the island, which is quite an ironic gesture. Hence, the books, which never existed, are created in the first minute and destroyed in the last minute of a two-hour film. They exist only for the duration of the film.

Greenaway produces fantastic volumes that encompass the vast knowledge Prospero needs to create his island utopia. The 24 books, which punctuate the narrative and create the structure of the film, include books of architecture with buildings that spring out fully formed, and anatomy texts with organs that throb and bleed and even illustrate graphically the processes of reproduction and birth. Greenaway designed the pages of the books, which were drawn up and transferred on to video tape. They were then manipulated using techniques that can produce almost limitless combinations of words, moving images and colours. For instance, 'A Harsh Book of Geometry', a handbook of the newly emerging science which allows for the mathematical formulation of physical space, is composed of complex three-dimensional geometric diagrams rising up out of the pages like models in a pop-up book. Angles are measured by needle-thin metal pendulums that swing freely.

This employment of the most recent means of technology is a main feature of much liminal performance, pointing to the 'cool seduction' of the audience by the proliferation of media objects (Baudrillard, 1979). However, this is not, as Baudrillard argues, inducing 'entropic inertia' but rather as part of an innovative project that creates new aesthetic styles.

The final, almost ominous, release of the Ariels shows them running through fire and water, through the main elements.[3] The smaller Ariel appears to be running towards the audience but instead takes flight, thereby escaping the audience's grasp. All that remains is the equivalent of a safety curtain that separates the audience and the world, pointing to the illusion of accepted 'realities'. This whole universe gradually disappears, leaving a few scribbles and some animated graffiti. A huge splash is heard and the film is back right at the beginning with those drops of water. Greenaway's film would seem to indicate that the final release of the spirit is when knowledge is thrown away, pointing to the need for immediacy, rather than for any intellectual mediation (Nietzsche, 1956, p. 24). In addition to the labyrinthine complexity of its narrative, *Prospero's Books* is visually the most dense of Greenaway's films. This is largely due to the use of high definition television processes for the big screen. High definition television uses twice as many lines as conventional television to achieve better resolution, higher contrast and a wider range of colours. The resulting image, which also has a wide, cinema-like screen ratio, can be manipulated using all the sophisticated techniques of video editing: slow motion, superimposition, and animation. *Prospero's Books* was edited using a combination of conventional film techniques and television post-production. Three versions of the film were edited by Greenaway and ultimately mixed together into a two-hour narrative. Much of the post-production work was undertaken in Tokyo. NHK, the Japanese television company, provided state of the art high definition television editing equipment. In order to test the potential of the technology, NHK contributed US$4 million worth of editing time free of charge (representing more than the entire production budget of US$3 million).

These high definition techniques allow Greenaway to unite lavish cinematography with complex image manipulation. Greenaway admits that the reason he became interested in the cinema was because of the extraordinary opportunities it provided to play about with images, to play with words and to play with their interaction. He began his career as a painter, and still believes painting is the supreme visual means of communication. For

Greenaway, nothing in cinema is comparable with the twentieth-century inventions in painting, and he believes that 'the cinema ... seems to be an opportunity to expand on those things which my rather small painterly talent would never allow me to' (Rodman, 1991, p. 37); expanding 'on those things' includes the use of Hi-Vision equipment.[4]

In the 'paintbox' room of the television studio in Tokyo, images were entered into the computer via a high definition video camera. The images, plundered from a variety of books featuring the works of da Vinci and Muybridge among others, were treated: that is, colourized, resized, rotated and enhanced. The paintbox images were then taken to the edit suite, and various layers were tested, tailored, adjusted and combined under Greenaway's direction and editing.

However, sometimes new technology causes more problems than it solves as Chris Wyatt, Greenaway's 'dubbing editor', pointed out during a film forum in Melbourne, Australia, at which he was the main speaker.[5] Wyatt explains that the original scheme was to: shoot on film; edit a kind of 'foundation' to achieve the film's length; transfer the material to high definition; as with online video edit, conform the edit on tape but at the same time play with the multilayering, boxes and paintbox; transfer back to film; complete; dub; print; and, finally, go to the Cannes film festival. This is a simple scenario and, apparently, the first part did go well. During the film edit, a single strand cutting copy was made with the 'box' inserts cut into the very long background shot. The next stage was not so straightforward. This was when the film crew, including Greenaway, went to Japan to execute the high definition stage and to start generating the paintbox material. According to Wyatt, it was quite clear that the enormous task of completing an entire feature film on this format in the time that was available was too great and too ambitious. The first problem was converting the film edits to tape edits. This was mainly because of the different frame speeds – the film at 24 frames per second (f.p.s.) and the NTSC at 30 f.p.s., and after numerous systems the crew made it up as they went along. Together with the technological difficulties, there were also communicational and cultural problems in working in Japan.[6]

Still, with all its drawbacks, new technology is obviously here to stay and Peter Greenaway, without a doubt, will continue to take full advantage of it in his future projects. The overall effect of *Prospero's Books* is stunning, with its self-conscious manipulation of the text and imagery. Linda Hutcheon could be referring to Greenaway's work when she writes, 'it simultaneously destabilzes and inscribes the dominant ideology through its overly self-conscious "interpellation" of the spectator as subject in and of ideology' (Hutcheon, 1990, p. 125).[7] Showing the formation process, not just of subjectivity but also of narrativity and visual representation, has become fundamental to contemporary metacinema. This liminal self-reflexivity calls attention to the acts of production and reception of the film itself. Furthermore, the lack of closure calls for active identification and therefore participation by the audience. However, this identification is not intended to produce mere passive contemplation or an empathy for the characters. In *Prospero's Books* the audience is placed in the same position as Prospero, as the conventions of movie-making are both used and abused, bared as conventions in a self-conscious way, thereby problematizing subject positions and challenging 'who is speaking' and who is allowed to speak. This focus on *énonciation* (Foucault, 1972, p. 55) is typical of the liminal in general, with its overt awareness of both the production and reception of art within a social, ideological and aesthetic context. It would seem, then, that this could be seen as a typical liminal film; parodic, metacinematic and questioning. Its constantly contradictory discourse foregrounds the issues of the ideological construction of subjectivity and of the way that history can be known. It challenges the spectator's expectations; its contradictions, though not really resolved, are stylized in the extreme.

Greenaway's constant use of double-encoding in his films, inscribing and subverting prevailing conventions, denotes a Derridean double displacement of the Heideggerian Being which is also inscribed in a system of differences (1982b, p. 254), and is probably what causes critics either to reject his work or enthusiastically to applaud it. Whatever, *Prospero's Books* is a self-consciously filmic film that, paradoxically, wants to challenge the outer borders of film, and question ideology's role in subject formation and how we can ever know the past in the present, except through its 'traces': that is, its texts or, in this case, Prospero's books.

Liminal politics: the 'queer' aesthetics of *Edward II*

It is difficult enough to be queer, but to be a queer in the cinema is almost impossible. ... Marlowe outs the past – why don't we out the present. Fuck poetry. The best lines in Marlowe sound like pop songs. ... *This ... is dedicated to the repeal of all anti-gay laws, particularly Section 28.* (Jarman, 1991a, Preface)

Cineaste: 'You like to use classical material, don't you?'
Jarman: 'Well, it's a way of getting things through isn't it? I don't think if I had written this I would have gotten any funding. I couldn't believe they'd actually let me do this. Take the murder scene: Edward is killed by a red hot poker shoved up his ass. How is this going to look on the screen? But the BBC put half a million into it.' (Grundman, 1991, p. 26)

In *Edward II* (1991), Derek Jarman attempts to shape the present by means of the past. He reworks Christopher Marlowe's 400-year-old play into an 'improved' version (Jarman, 1991a, p. 3), in order to emphasize the obsessional gay love story of the Plantagenet king Edward the Second (1307 to 1327), whose onstage execution, buggered with a red hot poker, gave the Elizabethan audience its titillation. In doing so, Jarman demonstrates that in any rigorous analysis all 'origin' is merely difference. Marlowe's text itself is only another signifier in an endless chain of signification and 'dissemination' (Derrida, 1981a, p. 25).

Jarman creates a world where Edward's obsessive and tragic love for the ambitious Gaveston is presented as a modern gay love affair set in contemporary England, while at the same time retaining a medieval simplicity in his *mise-en-scène* (indeed, only one set is used for the whole production), thereby presenting an example of an alternative 'institutional site' of performance (Foucault, 1972, p. 51), one of the primary features of much liminal performance. Much has been made of the painterly nature of Jarman's films, and they are often contrasted with the films of Peter Greenaway. However, unlike Greenaway, Jarman tends to use extremely minimalist sets; nowhere is this contrast more striking than in the comparison between Jarman's *Edward II* and Greenaway's *Prospero's Books*. Greenaway's film was released at the same time as *Edward II* in 1991. Although *Edward II* is no less studio-bound than Greenaway's lavish production of *The Tempest*, it is shot largely in close-up, with a mainly static camera. The faces are dispassionately eloquent and the design is elegantly impoverished: dirt floors, looming concrete walls, rooms furnished with a few strategic props (a mud-walled dungeon stands in for the cavernous interior of Edward's castle and for exterior locations, with forbidding metal work added for the prison). As J. Hoberman remarks, 'since everyone is also a raving fashion plate, it gives the impression of being filmed in a Soho emporium like *Comme des Garçons*' (Hoberman, 1992, p. 57). By flaunting the relative poverty of the film's resources (much of the backing was from the BBC), as well as his ability to transcend them, Jarman declares his allegiance to the aesthetics and ethics of low-budget film making, and affirms his stance as an economically and ideologically marginal director.

In Jarman's hybridized *Edward II*, the contemporary is determined by the emotional and dramatic demands of the play. Sixties gangster fashions (the Krays) are juxtaposed with thirties *Vogue* fashion, the balaclava hoods of modern day terrorists and the military (who bear a strong resemblance to British SAS paratroopers in Northern Ireland). Edward's rebellious noblemen are transformed into pillars of the modern British establishment: bishops, generals and businessmen. Edward's wife Isabella[8] colludes sexually and politically with Hugh Mortimer, who, envious of Gaveston's prestige and believing that Edward is neglecting his regal responsibilities, violently opposes him in a bloody civil war. The themes of love and death, the role of institutional violence in society, especially by the military, and an overwrought sexuality are all reworked in *Edward II*. Jarman's ambivalence to the military is noted in his remark, 'if we must have troops, let's have them in bed' (O'Pray, 1991, p. 8). The violence is brutal and ambiguous, as demonstrated by Isabella murdering Edward's brother Kent by biting out his throat, and the murder by Edward of Gaveston's assassin, both being at the same time horrific and intensely erotic. The aesthetic features of the performance provide the audience with feelings of discomfort and disquiet or, in other words, a certain 'negative pleasure' (Kant, 1978a, p. 91).

In *Edward II* Jarman's two passions, his Englishness and his homosexuality, are analysed. Central is the constitutive relation that founds the modern English state on a repressive security apparatus and a repressed homosexuality. Therefore, in Foucauldian terms, this could be seen as the 'surface of emergence' of Jarman's 'objects of discourse' (Foucault, 1972, p. 41). The words 'come death' are spoken at the end of the film, but it appears that it is no longer Marlowe or Edward who addresses us but Jarman himself (MacCabe, 1991, p. 12). Jarman was diagnosed as HIV positive a few years ago and in some ways this film can be seen as his death-work.[9] The film, although primarily directed by Jarman, was also ghost-directed by Ken Butler; this was due to Jarman's periods of ill-health suffered as a consequence of his condition.[10]

The repression of homosexuality by the state is not new, as amply demonstrated by that 'great reckoning in a small room', as Shakespeare described the death of Christopher Marlowe. Ingrim Frizer stabbed Marlowe to death, days before he was to appear before the Privy Council to answer charges of blasphemy. Four hundred years on, mystery still surrounds his death, though it is not unreasonable to assume that it was owing to him having access to too many political and sexual secrets. In an age when sodomy was a capital offence, more than one Privy Council member may have feared for his life, afraid that Marlowe's testimony would reveal not only his spying activities (he was a member of one of the foundations of the Elizabethan state, Francis Walsingham's state-organized secret service, which in contemporary times would be close to the MI5), but also the sexual activities of some of the Council's members.

Marlowe ruthlessly edited his sources, running together two barons' revolts separated by eleven years and transforming Edward's favourites from members of the nobility into members of a new Renaissance class of which he was a prominent member. Jarman is just as ruthless at destabilizing identity (MacCabe, 1991, p. 12). Derrida's critical tool of 'iterability' is valuable in this instance, since it marks the relation between repetition and alteration and acts as a critique of pure identity (Derrida, 1977, p. 190).

All questions of national politics are reduced to one, the determination of the barons to deny the king the love he needs. Jarman follows Bertolt Brecht, who adapted Marlowe's chronicle in 1924, by making sex central and concentrating on four characters, instead of the multitude of characters in Marlowe's play. The central characters consist of Edward, the king, Isabella, his queen, Gaveston, his love object, and Mortimer, his rival and his wife's lover. Brecht's *Edward II* contributed much to his subsequent theories of 'epic theatre', with Elizabethan stage conventions and the medieval English setting providing ideas for a 'defamiliarized' performance. Jarman presents some *Verfremdung* effects of his own, not the least of which is a dreamscape of Annie Lennox singing 'Every time we say Goodbye', as Edward and Gaveston dance together bathed in a spotlight, dressed in 'Marks and Spencer' pyjamas.[11]

In Jarman's version of *Edward II*, the barons led by Mortimer and Isabella are intent on one thing only, the destruction of Gaveston. This inevitably leads to the assumption of power and the concurrent murder of Edward. The connections between power and sexuality that run through Marlowe's life and work are drawn by Jarman with all the deftness of a painter's hand. The simplicity of the story allows the film to present homosexuality as the key term to the understanding of the structure of English society, pointing to its 'discursive formation' as a deviant 'object of discourse' (Foucault, 1972, p. 38).

Jarman depicts both of Edward's lovers, Gaveston and later Spencer, as working class, in contrast to the aristocratic class from which they both originated. Gaveston is a sneering youth with a two-day beard, full of unrestrained class resentment.[12] One of the scenes has him prancing naked on the throne, taunting the outraged Mortimer, who appears as a British officer with a trim moustache, dressed in battle greens and representing the military posture of a colonizer or occupier. Mortimer is an alternative, heterosexual, erotic ideal, a sort of sexy fascist, featuring sado-masochistic traits. In one scene, Mortimer wears a studded collar and chain and is whipped and beaten by three stilettoed, scantily leather-clad females, singing:

Maids of England, sore may you mourn
For your lemons you have lost, at Bannocks borne
With a heave and ho.
What weeneth the King of England
So soon to have won Scotland,
With a rombelow.[13]

Isabella introduces another erotic ideal. Edward's spurned queen evolves into an implacable monster, especially as her evil seems a direct corollary to her sexual gratification. This is manifested in her murder of Kent, where she literally tears out his life by biting his throat, reminiscent of the *vagina dentata*, and eventually culminates in her seduction of Lightborn with the intention of persuading him to murder Edward in a particularly horrendous manner.

Isabella first appears in a demure pale satin slip with marabou trim, trying to reconcile herself to Edward. As her advances are rejected and her sexual power declines in the homoerotic atmosphere of Edward's court, she attires herself in increasingly more outrageous *designer* styles, heaping on costume jewellery, plastering on make-up and almost strangling herself with multiple strings of pearls. Wearing a different gown in each scene, she evolves from ice queens Grace Kelly and Joan Crawford to the more malevolent figures of Margaret Thatcher, Imelda Marcos, Ivana Trump and Lady Macbeth, eventually becoming the ultimate queen of the vampires.[14]

Rewriting the narrative as a flashback by Edward from his water-filled dungeon cell, Jarman shuffles chronology, excises superfluous incidents and plays with the text. Isabella's observation, 'Is it not strange that he [Edward] is thus bewitched?', becomes 'Is it not queer ... ?' The famous death-by-poker climax is staged as a lurid red-lit fantasy, with Edward being reprieved. The film is interspersed with scenes from the end of the play, where Edward and his murderer-to-be, Lightborn, converse in his prison.[15] Throughout the film, a murderous end is foreshadowed, as homophobia, amply demonstrated in the violent hatred of Gaveston and the transformation of the barons into the moral majority, comes to a climax, only to be thwarted by Jarman, who, as a result of his own fight against death, has contrived a happy ending. As Lightborn approaches the king for a second time with the poker in his hand (Lightborn representing the homophobic working class), he rejects his role as executioner and instead kisses Edward, thereby annulling a whole history of violence and homophobia. Ken Butler writes, 'This scene, the surprise, the "happy ending". Derek says Marlowe is lucky to have us: we have rescued the play!' (Jarman, 1991, p. 162).

Although such heterogeneous cutting-and-pasting of a 'classic' might appear cavalier, Jarman's *Edward II* is actually a close reading of the original text. However, where Marlow's play ends with a return to order, the young Edward III reasserting authority, Jarman's movie suggests something else. One of the final scenes has the seven-year-old king in lipstick, earrings and high heels conducting the 'Dance of the Sugar Plum Fairies', while dancing on top of the cage imprisoning his mother and her lover. By using Tchaikovsky for the sound track in this particular scene, Jarman reinforces the idea of Isabella and Mortimer as wind-up dolls, at the same time cross-referencing to Eisenstein's *Ivan The Terrible* (1958), where the child Ivan's feet dangle from the throne and fail to reach the ground (O'Pray, 1991, p. 11).

In his remarkable final tracking, Jarman, returning to the defeated army of gays and lesbians, resurrects them. At the same time Edward's voice is heard reciting Marlowe's most powerful lines,

> And what are Kings when a regiment is gone
> But perfect shadows on a sunshine day ...
> Come death and with thy fingers close my eyes
> Or if I live, let me forget myself.

Culturally, Marlowe's *Edward II* could be seen as a direct response to Shakespeare, whose trilogy on Henry VI had produced a version of English history which sought to find ethical and political meaning in the bloody shambles that had produced the Tudor dynasty. Jarman's *Edward II* has similar objectives, but is concerned with responding to the more contemporary foundations of power and sexual representation: for example, demanding the repeal of all anti-gay laws by referring in his work to the formation of these liminal 'objects of discourse'. Since Jarman was sick during most of the production and post-production, *Edward II* was an acknowledged collaboration between his lover, intimate friends and people who had worked on his previous films. The dispersal of meaning produced by this collaboration works equally importantly for the audience. Jarman is not an unknown figure but is encountered in a variety of genres and media. One of the most prominent examples of this media involvement is his published screenplay of the film, which contains not only very private marginal notes but also a string of Outrage slogans (the Outrage movement providing the main body of Edward's army).

It is due to the complexity of the film's address that it is impossible for the audience to feel separate; reaction is not only demanded but inescapable. Actions in the film are removed from purely aesthetic abstraction and made analogous to contemporary life experience. Furthermore, formal barriers are shattered by the disruption of cinematic space, in the articulation of shots and scenes and in terms of costume and sets. This, together with the fragmentation of the narrative, produces a lack of closure (Derrida, 1982a, pp. 130–1), and the inclusion of Jarman's subjective fears and desires calls for active identification and participation by the spectator.

However, in Jarman's ambiguous delineation of his characters, this identification is not intended to produce an empathy for the characters: for example, Gaveston is not unproblematically presented as a victim. In one scene, accompanied by a gang of thugs, he carries out a particularly violent revenge, with Edward's permission, on the bishop who had instigated his initial exile; this is out of proportion to the offence. This would be incongruous if Gaveston were to be presented as a victim. Edward is not without bloodied hands either, as he murderously disembowels Gaveston's assassin. Their violence is further complicated by its erotic overtones. Isabella's character is also ambivalent: until her central soliloquy she is the wronged, wounded wife, but once she rebels, she becomes a political monster. At the same time, Jarman's *Verfremdung* or 'defamiliarization' effects distance the spectator and prevent character identification in favour of awareness. For example, in an early scene in the film, Jarman has two sailors making love in the background, upstaging the florid language of Gaveston's soliloquies. Rather than empathy for the characters, which would be quite difficult under the circumstances, Jarman appears to aim for emotional involvement in the formation of the problem. This appears to be a feature of much liminal performance

Finally, it would seem that Jarman's cinema does share certain traits with the cinema of Greenaway, although being far less extravagant in its methods and more 'transparent in its creation' (Skwara, 1990, p. 30). Jarman, like Greenaway, has created works that are parodic, metacinematic and questioning, and that in many ways appear complicit with what they seek to deconstruct (Derrida, 1978c, p. 281); in fact, traits that embody a liminal aesthetic. His constantly contradictory discourse foregrounds the issues of the ideological construction of subjectivity and of the way that history can be known, at the same time challenging the spectator's expectations. His contradictions, like Greenaway's, though not really resolved, are stylized in the extreme.

Transgressing borders: *Der Himmel über Berlin/Wings of Desire*

The film *Der Himmel über Berlin/Wings of Desire* (1987) begins with a shot of a hand writing, while a disembodied voice recites 'als das Kind Kind war ...' ('when the child was a child ...'). As the speaker continues with the poem, narrated in the style of a child's nursery rhyme, the hand dissolves, initially into a panorama of a cloudy sky and then into a close-up of a human eye. Following this, the spectator is provided with a bird's eye view (or in this instance an angel's eye view) of the city of Berlin.

The cinematic production *Der Himmel über Berlin/Wings of Desire*, a collaboration between Austrian writer Peter Handke and German director Wim Wenders, was an international success. This lyrical, romantic and at times surreal film of the angel Damiel and his love for the French trapeze artist Marion won eight awards, including one for best director at the 1987 Cannes Film Festival.

Photographed mainly in black and white by Henri Alekan, who had been the cinematographer on Jean Cocteau's classic surrealistic film *Beauty and the Beast* (1946), it features the veteran German dramatic actors Bruno Ganz, who plays Damiel, the central character, and Otto Sanders, who plays Cassiel, his angelic companion. Also featured is the well known American actor Peter Falk, famous for his characterization of the detective Colombo in the seventies television series of the same name, who portrays himself (at least an interpretation of himself). The central female character, Marion, is a French trapeze artist played by Solveig Dommartin.

The film essentially concerns the two angels Damiel and Cassiel, who are unseen by mortals but are able to hear their innermost thoughts. Damiel falls in love with Marion and decides to leave his heavenly abode for her. To the sound of Nick Cave's 'From Her to Eternity', he moves from 'eternity' to 'her'.

Primarily, the angels' abilities to read minds and to pass through physical barriers provides an opportunity for Wenders to portray Berlin as a spectacular panorama of images, sounds and associations.[16] The film explores the significance of Berlin as a symbol of the post-Second World War international order of borders (or transgressing those borders), no-man's land, desire and, most of all, German history and Nazism. The angel Cassiel listens to an old writer, Homer, whose memory is enmeshed with Nazi Germany.[17] Homer ponders the connections between the storyteller and his listeners (Homer represents 'the immortal singer abandoned by his mortal listeners'), and worries about humankind losing its memories. This is, perhaps, a reference to the collective German amnesia regarding Nazism, leading to the rise of nationalism taking place in Germany today. As part of Homer's and Cassiel's memories, old newsreel footage of wartorn Berlin is included in the film.

Another strand of Wenders's film is a film-within-a-film, with Peter Falk as himself in Berlin to make a detective movie set in Nazi Germany. By 'playing' with Falk's character, the film destabilizes identity, at the same time questioning 'origins' of that 'identity' formation (Derrida, 1982a, pp. 130–1). For Falk, the significance of the German past is forgotten, vague or reduced to trivialities. His muddled thoughts on arriving in Berlin include 'Emil Jannings', 'Kennedy' and 'von Stauffenberg', whom he refers to as a 'Helluva guy. . . . What difference does it make it happened?' Damiel follows him to the set, where extras wear yellow stars and SS uniforms and stand side by side, chatting nonchalantly (Falk is apparently not alone in his ignorance of history). Falk muses on the question of 'extra human beings' and why the Nazis chose the colour yellow, 'a sunflower'. Falk, it eventuates, is a fallen angel who enjoys his human state to such an extent that he tries to recruit other angels to join him.

The angels are not merely the disembodied spirits of individuals, they carry traces of knowledge and memory. Their favourite haunts include the towering 1871 Siegessäule (the Victory Monument in the Tiergarten), the ruins of the Kaiser Wilhelm Gedächtniskirche (Kaiser Wilhelm Memorial Church) and the

Staatsbibliothek (the public library), where the camera pans the orb-like lights to suggest the celestial connection.

For an English title to the film, Wenders decided not to use a literal translation of *Himmel über Berlin*, which is 'Heavens over Berlin', because he felt it did not quite work in either English or French, unlike 'in German [where] the word *Himmel* means both sky and heavens so it is almost like a little poem, a little haiku'. According to Wenders, in English

> 'The Sky Over Berlin' sounded like a war movie and 'Heavens Over Berlin' was too romantic. I tried to look for a title that was also a little poetic in French and English. ... *Wings of Desire* or *Les Ailes du Desir* seemed to work. ... I tried to retranslate this into German because I would have liked to have just one title, but there is no word in German for desire. (Paneth, 1988, p. 4)

It is a pity that Berlin was left out of the English and French titles, since the film is a beautiful and sensitive evocation of that city, although it soon becomes apparent that Berlin, however special, is one city among many in a global interactive space. We see Peter Falk, instantly identifiable as an American media person whose television persona of Colombo is directly referenced several times throughout the film, coming in to land at Berlin airport. His thoughts – 'Tokyo, Kyoto, Paris, London, Trieste ... Berlin!' – as he locates the place for which he is bound are read by Damiel. People in the film think their thoughts in German, French and English, with other languages occasionally used. References to the international space of 'seductive' media are everywhere (Baudrillard, 1979, pp. 221–2).

The film initially examines Berlin through the monochromatic eyes of the angels. Outside human time, they exist in the realm of pure spirit. They can move freely in space, frequently appearing and disappearing at the sites of accidents, in trains, in buses, in cars, in apartments, and effortlessly materializing in the Wall's no-man's land, where they like to walk 'because it is so peaceful'. Their presence is each time heralded by the black and white of the film. Time and space for them are conflated into a monochromatic world. The angels cannot voice the 'here' and 'now' precisely because they live in a world of 'always' and 'forever'. As Damiel laments, 'I wish I could say at each step, at each gust of wind "now". Say "now" and "now" and no longer "forever" and "for eternity".'

From the angels' perspective, Berlin emerges as an 'extraordinary landscape of fragmented spaces and ephemeral incidents' (Harvey, 1989, p. 315). The opening shots pan from the heavens down to the housing blocks of postwar Berlin. From there the labyrinthic apartments are entered. The film's spectator is led to isolated spaces and alienated individuals. One youth contemplates suicide because of a broken love affair; his parents, also isolated from one another, wonder what will happen to him. Children are seen watching television in the afternoon in the cramped apartments. Out on the streets a motor bike rider is dying following a street accident. A teenage girl is working as a prostitute following the death of her boyfriend. A pregnant woman is rushed to hospital in labour. Throughout all these incidents the angels are there bearing testimony, trying to sooth the shattered feelings of the individuals. Sometimes they succeed but just as often they do not: the unhappy youth, for example, does eventually commit suicide.

This wonderful evocation of an urban landscape of alienated individuals in divided spaces caught in transitory, diverse incidents is aesthetically powerful. The images are 'stark, cold but bestowed with all of the beauty of old-style still photographs, though set in motion through the camera lens' (Harvey, 1989, p. 316). The identity of Berlin is constituted through this disparate but quite marvellous imagery. The images of fragmented spaces are especially effective, and they are stylistically juxtaposed against each other in the manner of montage and collage. The Berlin Wall is one such spatial divide, and it is evoked again and again as a symbol of this fragmentation. Marion claims that 'it is impossible to get lost in Berlin because you can always find the wall'. However, it would seem that all divisions in this film are there to be in some ways transgressed, as the angels demonstrate by freely passing through the wall and, of course, as life reflects art in this instance, there is now no longer a wall to transgress, at least not physically.[18]

Fred Pfeil has argued that in ' "high" postmoderist' art

> One is confronted ... by a discontinuous terrain of heterogeneous discourses uttered by anonymous, unplaceable tongues, a chaos different from that of the classic texts of high modernism precisely insofar as it is not recontained or recuperated within an overarching mythic framework. (Pfeil, 1988, p. 384)

According to Pfeil, the 'quality of utterance and performance' is 'deadpan, indifferent, depersonalized, effaced', leading to the obliteration of 'the possibility of audience participation' (Pfeil, 1988, p. 384). It could be argued that certain of these points are relevant to the film *Der Himmel über Berlin/ Wings of Desire*. However, other features need to be considered. For instance, there is a strong need to transcend perceived divisions and boundaries; there is also a need to transcend the burden of the past by creating a new present, as Damiel demonstrates by leaving his spiritual limbo for a very real earthly existence. This theme is also expressed by Homer, whom we first meet in the library looking at photographs of damage done to the city during the war. With Cassiel, he sets off in search of Potsdamer Platz, which no longer exists except in name, the area flattened and overgrown with weeds. His search for an 'origin' leads only to 'différance' (Derrida, 1982a, pp. 130–1). He recalls when history turned ugly, 'und dann hingen plotzlich fahnen, dort ... und die Leute waren gar nicht mehr freundlich und die Polizei auch nicht' ('and then all of a sudden the flags appeared and the people were unfriendly and so were the police'). But this recollection is not enough, Homer requires more. He desires to taste and experience again the coffee and tobacco once sold in what is now wasteland in the middle of Berlin. It is significant that Homer's otherwise good memory should fail between the years of 1933 and 1945. Like Damiel, Homer would like greater vision or foresight (*Ahnung*); he needs to understand why no one has written the great 'epic of peace'. While Damiel descends to earth to live a sensual life, we see Homer puffing his way up the library steps, aspiring to angelic knowledge. In the upper reaches of the library his bald head seems to fit well among the planetary globes, which have the appearance of celestial orbs. It would seem that he and Damiel are reciprocals, eclipsing traditional boundaries, blurring the division between humans and angels.[19]

Peter Falk demonstrates an ignorance about the past, but this ignorance implies a freedom to define himself in the present. This becomes apparent in a somewhat humorous scene, when he tries on numerous hats before finding the right one for the role he is going to act in the detective film. Each search is a change of identity, one a 'Jewish Rabbi', another 'Humphrey Bogart'. However, this freedom is short-lived, as Berliners seeing him in the street refer to him as 'Colombo'. It would appear that *Der Himmel über Berlin/Wings of Desire* both meditates on the past and affirms the present.

Rather than 'obliterating audience participation', as Pfeil suggests, it would seem that this particular film does the opposite, and encourages the audience's participation.[20] The cold, starkly beautiful monochromatic imagery of Berlin actually forces the audience to participate by seeing the space and time of the city in ways that would otherwise have been ignored. The aesthetics of Wenders, in this instance, provide a Brechtian *Verfremdungseffekt*, in the way that certain 'natural' features, such as the depiction of urban spaces and institutions, the use of media, even the identities of the main protagonists, are highlighted and subverted. For instance, it seems ironic that the Victory Monument in the Tiergarten and the Memorial Church of Kaiser Wilhelm should be the abode of the gentle and sensitive angels. Similarly, Peter Falk, an American media person, is parodied and parodies himself as his identity becomes increasingly destabilized. Since he appears as 'himself' in this film, his fictional detective role of 'Colombo' is proved to be 'unreal' and is supplanted by his 'real' identity. However, this 'real' identity is dubious if it is to be believed that Peter Falk is indeed a fallen angel. Which particular media construction is true, if any? In this way the film points self-consciously to its own artifice. In the library, as Homer looks at the photographs from the war, we are provided with actual film footage from that period, we see the bodies of dead children in the ruins of their bombed home. A function of this paratextual insertion of actual historical documents into historiographic metafictions can also be related to Brecht's defamiliarization effect. As Linda Hutcheon writes, 'Like the songs in his plays, the historical documents dropped into the fictions have the potential effect of interrupting any illusion, of making the reader into an aware collaborator, not a passive consumer' (Hutcheon, 1989, p. 88).

David Harvey argues that 'death, birth, anxiety, pleasure, loneliness are all aestheticized on the same plane, empty of any sense of class struggle or of ethical or moral commentary' (Harvey, 1989, p. 316). I would strongly disagree with this statement. Wenders's film is obviously not suggesting a revolution, but it is quite innovative in its techniques of illustrating the alienation within urban spaces and individual lives in our cities. Furthermore, I would argue that there is a strong ethical commentary, though probably a redefinition of Harvey's notion of ethics, if only in the way that the film ultimately points to a celebration and affirmation of life.

Der Himmel über Berlin/Wings of Desire is an allegory of the artist as angel Damiel, who relinquishes immortality for the sensual pleasures of loving, living and dying in the here and now. He gives up his narcissistic, internal, knowing art for an art that captures only the surface of the world, but at the same time suggests its depths, its interiorities and its secrets, without actually revealing them. Cassiel, the other angel, remains angelic, immortal and self-enclosed, his role in the film being mainly one of contrast to Damiel. Cassiel goes nearly everywhere that Damiel goes — to the film set, the rock club, the coffee stand — but he always remains an interested observer and never has the impassioned urge to 'enter history', as Damiel does. He is the artist as self-pronounced seer and spends most of his time accompanying Homer in his search for people to listen to his tales.

Damiel and Cassiel appear as pleasant middle-aged men wearing dark overcoats. The only concession to their angelic state is that they both wear their hair long and tied back. There is one shot of Damiel with wings as he stands on top of the Kaiser Wilhelm Memorial Church. Other than that, only a quiver of a disembodied wing is seen, followed by a rapid panning of the camera, suggesting that the angels are in flight. They are seen only by children, but their presence is sensed by adults who have remained childlike, and of course by fallen angels such as Peter Falk. Other angels, in similar attire to Damiel and Cassiel, appear in the film, both males and females. They are seen mainly in the public library, though the film does not focus on them for too long. Since the angels already know everything, they are often content to watch mortals read and look at pictures. Yet Damiel is frustrated: he wants to know less and experience more; he wants to leave the realm of spirituality and eternity to enter the one of materiality and temporality; he wants to become mortal. He tells Cassiel, 'I want to enter history, if only to hold an apple in my hand.' He wants a more complete existence. Making this change will enable him not only to know things but also to guess, suspect and foresee.

While visiting the Alekan Circus (named after the film's photographer), Damiel meets Marion. Marion provides a certain blurring of the boundaries between humans and angels, being elfin and ethereal. Her initial appearance in the film is in flight wearing wings, as she rehearses on her trapeze. During the rehearsal she is told that the circus is out of money and has to close, providing another transitory image to the film. Yet while Marion is clearly distressed at the news, she still insists she 'has a story', she is going to continue 'creating', though not in the circus. She imagines going into a photo-automat and emerging with a new identity. Since her present history is composed of family photographs pinned to the wall, why not create a new identity with new photographs? However, these images are suffused with the desire to become a whole rather than a fragmented person. She longs to be 'complete' but believes this is only possible through a relation with another. However, any notion of a pure identity, even through a relation with another, can only be a myth, since identity, as Derrida has shown, is formed through 'différance', 'iterability' and 'trace' (Derrida, 1981a, p. 25). After the circus has left and the site is deserted, Marion sits alone and ruminates on her situation of being without roots, without history and without a country. Yet this emptiness for her holds out strong possibilities of transformation and affirmation: 'I can become the world,' she says.[21]

Damiel is attracted to Marion's energy and beauty. He becomes caught up in her inner imaginary, sharing her thoughts and her feelings. For the first time he gets a glimpse of what the world would be like in colour, and is increasingly drawn into the idea of entering human 'history'. Marion dreams of him as a resplendent 'other', and he sees himself reflected in her dream. Later, he follows her to a night club, where he touches her thoughts, providing her with a sense of blissful well-being. Her voice-over echoes her feelings: 'a hand is softly tightening within my body'.

Damiel's final catalytic moment comes when Falk senses his presence at a coffee stand: 'I can't see you but I know you're there.' Falk offers him his hand, which Damiel accepts. Damiel's decision to enter humanity is taken ironically, in the Wall's no-man's land, a place betwixt and between, a liminal state. Luckily for him, Cassiel has the presence of mind to carry him to the Western side of the Wall. There, Damiel wakes up with a jolt after being hit by angelic armour, which every fallen angel is provided with so that it can be sold, thereby propelling the angels fully into the material world. He awakens to a world rich in vibrant colours, happy to see and taste the blood from his cut head. He approaches the set where Falk is filming. Falk, seeing him and guessing who he is, asks, 'How long?' Damiel replies, 'Minutes, hours, days, … time.'

The physical coming together of Damiel and Marion takes place in The Esplanade, a nightclub where previously Marion had been followed by the invisible Damiel. To the strains of Nick Cave's 'From Her to Eternity', the two search for each other. After a slow sequence depicting the stark alienation among the nightclub's audience, they finally come together in the bar. They begin in an almost ritualistic way. Marion speaks a fairly lengthy monologue before surrendering to Damiel's embrace. In her monologue she insists on the seriousness of their situation even though 'the times may not be serious'. She wants to get rid of chance and coincidence: 'now is the time for decision … temporary contracts are over'. Finally, their coming together has a 'universal meaning' beyond this particular 'time and place'. She claims that although there is no longer destiny, there is decision, a decision to say 'my man' in such a way as to open up a whole world to fresh insight and interpretation. It seems that she is seeking to answer the questions that were asked at the beginning of the film, 'questions that children ask'. 'Why am I me and not you?' 'Why am I here and not there?' 'Where did time begin and where does space end?' In the final scene of the film, Damiel affirms that what is born of their coming together 'is not a child but an immortal image that all can live by'.

In the film, the collaboration between Peter Handke and Wim Wenders has produced noticeable tensions between word and image. At the beginning of the film a polarity is established between optical images, handwriting and voice-over narration. From the outset an interplay is established between the spoken and written language and between words and images. The angels write down their observations in their journals. They appear to love words but long to see, putting aside their journals to observe the people of Berlin. Falk can always find an audience when he speaks, but struggles to express himself visually through drawing: 'this picture stinks', he remarks of one of his drawings. Likewise, Homer, the writer and storyteller, turns to examining photographs in Berlin's Staatsbibliothek. Angels and humans alike feel the limits of both word and image and seek fuller means of perception. As Homer searches vainly for Berlin's Potsdamer Platz in what is now an empty space, he knows and recalls the former Platz though it can no longer be seen. It is this knowledge that evokes the need for foresight or intuition. In fact, not only fore-sight, but also fore-having and fore-conception are required, all 'presuppositions' of the hermeneutic situation, where each turn of the interpretive spiral produces fresh insights (Heidegger, 1978, p. 195).

Handke and Wenders not only emphasize visual and verbal signification in their film, drawing attention to the need for an aesthetic judgement that is not primarily restricted to the linguistic, as is Lyotard's theorization on the *differend* (1988, p. xiv), they also make reference to divergent cultural sources. This intertexuality is a central feature of liminal performance. Allusions are made to Rilke's *Duino Elegies*.[22] For Rilke, the angel represents not a Christian entity but the essence of pure being, at home in a vast open world that knows neither past, present or future. It represents the messenger and gatekeeper of the invisible, and perhaps most importantly it represents the terrifying demon of artistic creation; in Nietzschean terms, 'the will to art' (Nietzsche, 1924b, p. 289).

Allusions to Rilke and the German literary canon occur in a film that features a contemporary American character actor best known for his work in a popular television detective series. By focusing on angels, the film inevitably conjures up links with that genre of films which concentrates upon celestial visitors interacting with mortals, such films as *Here Comes Mr Jordan* (1941), *It's a Wonderful Life* (1946) and *Heaven Can Wait* (1979). Again, a liminal sensibility is apparent in the film's utilization of a broad and divergent range of cultural references. In fact, so diverse and wide is the scope that no distinct centre can be located. Its traces, which inscribe differences between its terms and entities, 'cannot be pinned down' by the concept of a single 'signified' (Derrida, 1981a, p. 25).

The question of how to acquire knowledge forms what could be seen as the theoretical focus of the film. As with Derrida's deconstruction of the 'myth of presence',[23] Handke and Wenders seem to realize that oral transmission has fallen into decline. They are faced with the problem of deciding whether to emphasize the written word, despite lingering questions about the ability of language to convey ideas, or to emphasize the primacy of visual evidence: 'seeing is believing' (Caldwell and Rea, 1991, p. 50). They ascribe ascendancy to neither, balancing both the written and the visual. The characters in their film demonstrate that an overreliance on merely one form of comprehension of reality distorts an understanding of past and present. Homer's name suggests he is a blind poet, a man of words. The amount of time in which the film dwells on Homer's quest for stories from the past might indicate that language is the only way to gain meaning. However, Marion balances this by creating her present life history, and invents a new visual life history with a collection of photographs. The film's scepticism about the reliability of all means of discourse is reminiscent of Linda Hutcheon's postmodern view that all forms of discourse are marginal or ex-centric. As she writes, 'Difference and ex-centricity replace homogeneity and centrality as the foci of postmodern social analysis' (Hutcheon, 1990, p. 5).

If there is emphasis placed anywhere, it is on intuition and *Ahnung*, especially in the second half of the film. A form of 'romanticism' is functioning, brought about by the deconstruction of oppositions, not between man and woman or angel and mortal, but between old and new relationships (Caldwell and Rea, 1991, p. 52). Marion's and Damiel's search leads to a relationship with future implications not just for them but for the 'whole world'. *Der Himmel über Berlin/Wings of Desire*, then, celebrates growth and implies a positive future. It could be argued that Nietzsche paved the way for such liminal performances with his writings on creative 'destruction', by which new hybridized styles can be created out of the remnants of the old ones (Nietzsche, 1956, p. 26). By transcending and deconstructing oppositions in a divided city, Handke and Wenders have heralded an era of reconciliations, celebrating life and affirming a future. In keeping with its liminality, the film ends with an anti-conclusion, thereby denying closure and at the same time creating a space for future possibilities.[24] The film ends with the words 'To be continued'. As Wenders remarked, 'I felt the film ended with its beginning' (Fusco, 1988, p. 17).

Limits of fragmentation: *Europa/Zentropa*

Danish director Lars von Trier's film *Europa/Zentropa* (1991) is about the present thinly disguised as the past. The European, post-Second World War setting presents a decaying continent in chaos searching for unity, just like present-day Europe. In fact, the film's European title is *Europa*, but it was changed by American and later Australian distributors to avoid confusion with Agnieszka Holland's *Europa Europa* (1991), which was released at the same time. Zentropa is the name of a fictional German railroad corporation headed by Max Hartmann, a German industrialist who used Zentropa trains to transport Jews to death camps, then collaborated with the American military to rebuild the new Germany.

Europa/Zentropa might be seen as a portrait of a fragmented world approaching a new millennium. This gloomy yet humorous thriller is set in Germany in 1945, shortly after the catastrophic conclusion of the war. It is a Danish/Swedish/German co-production. It is also a bilingual film, in English and German, that satirizes the national characteristics of Germans and Americans by a director from Denmark, the small Scandinavian country known for its protection of its Jewish population under Nazi occupation. Von Trier, when asked why *Europa/Zentropa* takes place in Germany during 1945 to 1946, replied,

I am obsessed by Germany. For Denmark it is a very big neighbour. Germany is a symbol. It is Europe. German Society has always demonstrated the most extreme passions: in the character and relationships of individuals and with other countries. ... My films show my obsessions with the universe of war. The ultimate setting for films and dreams. (Interview with Lars von Trier, 1992, p. 5)

It was shot with a multinational cast, using contemporary Poland to depict devastated Germany.[25] The main male lead is Canadian, another male lead is Franco-American, the main female lead is German and the hypnotic voice-over, interspersed throughout the film, belongs to the Swedish actor Max von Sydow.

The film, 'a deliciously mischievous primer of twilight-imperial Teutonic tones from Wagner to Wedekind to Kafka ... [which] stylistically pays homage to *film noir*' (Kennedy, 1991, p. 68), is a mixture of heterogeneous disparate influences and 'traces' (Derrida, 1976, p. 62). Intimations of Fassbinder's political cynicism and casting; allusions to Fritz Lang's *Metropolis* (1927) in the crowd scenes and the tangled railroad technology; to Alfred Hitchcock's *Vertigo* (1958) – 'I love Hitchcock. *Vertigo* is one of my favourite films' (Interview with Lars von Trier, 1992, p. 6) – with Joakim Holbek's emotionally tortured score practically quoting from Bernard Herrman, who provided the music for that film; all are blended with the visual styles (colour and monochrome mixes to suggest different moods) of Wim Wender's *Der Himmel über Berlin/Wings of Desire*. *Europa/Zentropa* is a film so excessively playful that it seems like a concoction of liminal tropes. Interspersed with 'narrative non sequiturs and casual apocalypses', it presents marks of 'dissemination' that cannot be contained by any single 'signified' (Derrida, 1981a, p. 25).

Europa/Zentropa borrows techniques from both Hollywood and MTV. These stylistic embellishments include the juxtaposition and layering of colour on black and white images (accomplished with rear screen projection and the use of multiple lenses), cameras mounted and tilted at surprising angles and skilfully layered montages, suggestive of German expressionist and surrealist paintings. This emphasis on style and technique is a principal feature of liminal performance. One scene, almost verging on the sublime, takes place in the shell of a bombed out cathedral where a candlelit midnight mass is taking place in the falling snow. The atmosphere is strongly evocative of some unearthly Wagnerian ritual. Another scene, perhaps the most striking in the whole film, is set around the suicide of Max Hartmann. The sequence starts and ends with two single stunning shots. In the first, the camera descends from the model railway room, where the male and female leads are about to make love, through the floor into the bathroom below, where the monochrome image (now revealed as a back projection) is broken up by a hand holding a razor in the foreground. As the razor slashes into the body, the wounds become bright red, while the background remains black and white. In the scene's final shot, colour seeps into a black and white shot of the other characters rushing to the locked bathroom door, while the camera simultaneously rises to a point above the wall to watch a sea of scarlet blood flood under the door. When the door is opened the whole bathroom floor is submerged in an ocean of redness.

Von Trier's use of techniques such as colour and black and white film, superimposition and back projection is not new. Eisenstein, several years earlier, used colour to emphasize the ideological foundations of the narrative and to concentrate on psychological states in *Ivan The Terrible* (1958); and Wim Wenders, in *Der Himmel über Berlin/Wings of Desire*, also employs colour to emphasize, distinguish and heighten various levels of meaning, articulation and modes of being. However, in *Europa/Zentropa* von Trier has gone even further: the film is simultaneously monochrome and colour. At times, the image consists of three or four (or more) planes and colour is used not just to highlight but also to suggest states of arousal, contrasts, time shifts and so on, and to act as a kind of structural scheme of presaging. For instance, bullets belonging to a child assassin are dropped on the floor. As they fall, a change of focus shows them magnified and coloured in the foreground, while a monochrome projection depicts the startled passengers in the background. The succeeding shots show the visual effect in a whirling montage, adding surreal distortions of perspective as the boy, who is filmed in colour in the foreground, fires at gigantic military personnel filmed in black and white and back projected.

The camera passes through walls, descends through floors or moves from a house into a train with no visible 'seams'. During one astonishing moment in the film, the camera pulls back from a close shot of an elaborate model train set, through a gaping hole in the roof of the house and back through the window of a passing train as a character originally in the house carries on a conversation with another character on the train.

Multiple back projections create a three-dimensional-like layering of scenes, and are used in the creation of the magnificent narrative ellipses which abound in the film. For example, as the two lead actors, standing on a bridge above a stream late at night, decide to marry, they turn to the sky and water behind them, which 'dissolves' into the magnified face of the priest officiating at their marriage. The scene once again is set in the shell of the cathedral, but now butterflies are fluttering in the background, greenery abounds and there is a sense of spring and new beginnings.

Von Trier uses back and front projection and superimposition to vary the visual dynamics of conversation scenes. In one scene, as the two leads are talking to each other in a train compartment, they take turns in being filmed on a rear screen. 'What you say seems to come from a place far away', says the female, filmed in colour, to the forlorn looking male, rear projected in black and white. Such strategies and techniques establish a fundamental system of differences within an image, a system of tensions, for instance, reflecting disparities and irreconcilabilities between the film's characters.[26] Von Trier, commenting on his film, explains:

> Each of my films contains a technical innovation. In *Zentropa* ... We are working on image superimposition (front—back projections and super-imposition). Sometimes, we have up to seven layers of image in black and white and colour. We can thus combine two or more images filmed with different lenses. ... We can create an unsettling effect that isn't immediately noticeable but which marks the audience. The same thing goes for the camera movements. We are making images that seem perfectly realistic but which turn out to have that element which leads the film off in the planned direction. (Interview with Lars von Trier, 1992, p. 56)

At the Cannes Film Festival in 1991, von Trier won a Prix de Supérieur Technique and Prix du Jury. This utilization of and emphasis on new technology is again typical of much liminal performance.

As could be expected, commodification, in its creation of desire and satisfaction of that desire, finds support in the syntax of the liminal and the latest types of computerized technology alike. However, although international hi-tech companies provide the means necessary for this and therefore provide the link between technology and commodification, the real challenge of technology concerns its aesthetic possibilities, as demonstrated in such liminal works as *Europa/Zentropa*: that is, in the production of an infinity of new aesthetic meanings.

If *Europa/Zentropa* is fertile on metacinema, it is also rich on metaphysics. Its young American hero is coming to play his part in rebuilding Europe, but he is also coming, though unconsciously, to help to infuse the West into a crumbling culture of doom and romanticism enhanced by a postwar *Götterdämmerung* that has become excessive, dissipated and putrefied. The film opens with a shot of railway tracks, as a deep voice-over draws the audience into a hypnotic trance: 'you will listen to my voice. I shall count from one to ten ... on the count of ten you will be in Europa'. The film thereby introduces its two main motifs, hypnosis and trains.

The use of an omniscient, third person narrator/hypnotist is a striking strategy; it is like the film itself, at one and the same time both serious and also completely nonsensical. It undermines the authority of the author, while challenging the 'speaking' subject's position (Foucault, 1972, p. 50). This concern with *énonciation* is a central feature of liminal performance, with its self-conscious awareness of the production of art. The theme of mass hypnosis suggests that a whole nation under Nazism came under the charismatic spell of Hitler. The hero is eventually drowned following a train explosion. Surprisingly, the hypnotic voice-over continues addressing the hero, as the body is swept along by the river current, eventually finding its freedom in the ocean and at the same time refuting any narrative closure (Derrida, 1978, p. 301). This narrator, who addresses not only the hero but also the audience, is never seen, only heard, and seems to have a foreknowledge of events. This raises an interesting point: if the hero is apparently faced with several choices, yet at the same time his choices are apparently made, is von Trier trying to suggest that, like the hero in his film, Europe has no choice but to be swept into a collective sea of unconsciousness? In other words, is he metaphorically arguing for a pessimistic, human determinism, or is he going beyond a rationalist view and arguing for an escape into the emotions or the instincts?[27]

The second cardinal motif, trains, literally propels the story along and exemplifies the stereotypical German regard for mechanical order, postwar economic recovery and Nazi atrocities to Jews. In an arresting scene, workers use ropes to pull a refurbished Zentropa carriage out of storage, a carriage once used to carry Jews to concentration camps. The scene is highly suggestive of forced labour camps, especially evoking recorded scenes of Jews forced to haul heavy containers along rail tracks.

The story unfolds from the perspective of a new Zentropa employee, Leopold Kessler, a naive and idealistic American of German descent, who avoided military service during the war but has gone to Europe to make a contribution as a civilian or, as he claims, 'to show a little kindness towards Germany'. Kessler's uncle, who works for Zentropa and helps him secure a position as a sleeping car attendant, is an alcoholic, perhaps signifying some Europeans' inclination to insulate themselves from unpleasant realities. He continuously instructs Kessler not to look out of the train's window, this introverted admonition summing up the general ambience of postwar Europe.

The passive Kessler is captivated by the decadent Hartmann family, who represent the deterioration of Germany. Katharina, a cool Marlene Dietrich lookalike, seduces (in a scene where the train is shot from a front angle as it travels through a narrow dark tunnel, providing a strong, almost parodic, allusion to the act of sexual intercourse) and subsequently marries Kessler. Katharina is eventually unmasked as a member of the neo-Nazi partisans known as 'werewolves'; her brother Laurence, portrayed as an ineffectual homosexual who refused to fight during the war, is consequently murdered by the 'werewolves', and her father Max Hartmann, an industrialist who owns the Zentropa railroad, is eventually consumed by guilt because of his Nazi past

(Katharina has also been blackmailing her father, unbeknown to him, because of his collaboration with the Americans, indirectly causing him to commit suicide).

Colonel Alex Harris, a pre-war friend of Max Hartmann, representing American collusion with dubious German interests, blackmails a starving Jew, whose only crime has been to steal food, to exonerate Hartmann of war crimes. Harris believes Hartmann is the key to protecting American transport interests in Germany. The Jew, played by von Trier himself, expresses his gratitude to Hartmann in front of witnesses for supposedly sheltering him from Nazis during the war. However, this only compounds Hartmann's sense of guilt, which culminates in his suicide. When Katharina's true identity as 'werewolf' is finally revealed, she cloaks herself in the concept of German collective guilt. She believes there is no such thing as an innocent German, since during the war everyone saw or committed atrocities; why now should it be criminal to kill when her organization is only fighting for its country? For Katharina, there is no contradiction in committing atrocities against other human beings while at the same time remaining a devoted and caring wife.

In the film, there are ambiguous references to links between the Church and the Nazis. In one scene, Kessler is asked by a priest to remove Max Hartmann's coffin from a secret compartment on the train which is filled with refugees and concentration camp survivors. Kessler maintains that he was unaware of this part of the train, an allusion to standard claims of ignorance concerning the Holocaust. This denial of responsibility is followed by a funeral procession, which resembles a celebration of some pagan Teutonic myth more than a Christian funeral.[28]

The film eventually evolves into a parody of American incompetence and gullibility and German bureaucratic pettiness, culminating in Kessler's farcical attempt to bomb a Zentropa train. After planting the bomb, believing he is protecting Katharina, Kessler changes his mind and dismantles it. However, there is still a bomb explosion leading to his death, a death pointing not to an end, but almost to a new beginning.

Von Trier's dreamscape conveys a sense of stylistic freedom. One technique follows another, yet the film never degenerates into pure fantasy. This is probably because of his skill in the utilization of those techniques and also his subject matter, being a representation of present-day Europe, a Europe thinly disguised as the past and to do with chaos and fantasy. The broken boundaries and human flux in contemporary Europe are much the same as those in 1945; only the historical crisis is changed.

The film demonstrates an essential liminal aesthetic in its employment of such traits as intertexuality, 'defamiliarization' techniques, parody, pastiche, fragmentation, lack of closure, self-reflexivity and a pursuit of chthonic. *Europa/Zentropa*'s self-consciousness foregrounds the fact that cinema is a signifying system within an economic and social context. As a self-conscious signifying system it is open to double encoding and double decoding, as the audience is forced to accept responsibility for the fact that it must make meaning and is, therefore, the only possible site of social change through art (Gasché, 1979, pp. 192–3). Like much poststructuralist theoretical discourse today, films like *Europa/Zentropa* point to the relation of power to knowledge and discourse. The difference between the purely nostalgic and the liminal becomes evident in the role of double-voiced, ironic parody. What liminal/postmodern parody does is to evoke what Hans Robert Jauss calls the 'horizon of expectation' of the audience, a horizon formed by recognizable conventions of genre style or form, which is then destabilized and dismantled (Bahti, 1982, p. 24). Multiple and overt parody can paradoxically foreground social issues by its very baring and challenging of conventions (Hutcheon, 1990, p. 131). The blending of the fictive and historically real in the film signals the spectator to beware of institutionalized genre boundaries, to refuse to let art and life be separated. Genre boundaries are structurally analogous to social borderlines, and both are called into question (Hutcheon, 1990, p. 131). Derrida's critical tools, the 'undecidables', are important, since they help to explain how genres are formed and how unstable these formations are (Derrida, 1980, p. 211). However, as Derrida inquires, can we 'identify a work of art ... if it does not bear the mark of a genre?' Therefore, it would seem that there can be 'no genreless text ... yet, such participation never amounts to belonging' (Derrida, 1980, pp. 211–12).

Finally, von Trier, discussing his work and its audience, writes:

> The fact of writing a film with a realistic background enables me to hypnotise the audience much more easily. ... The cinematographic language is based on a series of cliches that must be totally respected until you wish to make a change, a shift. ... I believe very powerful feelings are hidden in the subconscious. ... And I'd like to communicate these feelings to the cinema. ... I invite them [the audience] on a little train ride. The station is the movie theatre but I'd like to take them to many different places. (Interview with Lars von Trier, 1992, p. 5)

Notes

1. In conventional film to tape editing, the tape version is too low fidelity to be transferred back to film.
2. According to Greenaway, 'Obviously what clinched it was the opportunity we were offered to have the last grand classic English

Shakespearian actor, Sir John Gielgud, to play what presumably is the last performance of his life – he's 86. So we can have an identity cross-referencing Shakespeare, Prospero and Gielgud ... as the film progresses, we actually see Gielgud/Prospero as Shakespeare writing *The Tempest*' (Rodman, 1991, p. 38).

3. Greenaway's Ariel is portrayed as a small child, an adolescent and an adult; all bear a striking cherubic resemblance to each other.

4. Hi-Vision is NHK's propriety name for high definition television, and offers a film-style aspect ratio and several times the resolution of standard television.

5. Chris Wyatt (1992) recalls 'the irony behind *Prospero's Books.* with its high definition publicity is that 90% of the film's opticals were done in a conventional film optical house and only the last 14 minutes of the film is pure 100% high definition post-production.'

6. Wyatt (1992) explained: 'I am used to approaching a problem in a physical sense ... it's wrong ... try again etc. In Japan if the first attempt wasn't perfect, we would stop, machines ground to a halt and we would discuss it for an hour.'

7. The concept of 'interpellation' originates from Louis Althusser (1971, pp. 170–7), where he theorizes about the process by which the subject is 'interpellated' or hailed by ideology, so that it recognizes and implicates itself in that ideology.

8. Isabella's role is played by Tilda Swinton, who also helped to rewrite the play's script.

9. Jarman did die from AIDS in 1993.

10. Jarman writes, 'I was ill today with temp of 102° so Ken stepped in. ... My chemical life splutters on. Each morning I swallow with increasing difficulty: a cordial of Ritafer, Fansidar, AZT, Pirodoxin, one Calcium Folinate (to counteract the Ritafer) and two Carbamazapine to stop any fits my damaged brain might bring' (1991a, p. 28).

11. Jarman remarks, 'the actors insisted on Marks and Spencer's pyjamas. There was a sense of humour in the whole thing. The film needed a lightness of touch in places and this has been misinterpreted as my quirky campness. But I don't think it's true' (O'Pray, 1991, p. 8).

12. Jarman writes: 'Gaveston is working class and not French as he is in Marlowe ... what you have is a situation where two people have obviously fallen in love and one can't understand just what the attraction is. Gaveston is sexuality and class merged. I wanted to have the North/South divide – so Edward has a northern accent too' (O'Pray, 1991, p. 9).

13. The song sung by Lancaster in Marlowe's original text is turned into a football chant by Jarman (Marlowe, 1959, p. 314).

14. Tilda Swinton speaks about her role: 'I set myself a-pondering as to *why* is it that Imelda Marcos had a thousand pairs of shoes, why we want anyone to furnish us with details about Ivana Trump and the Princess of Wales' (Feay, 1991, p. 16).
15. The role of Lightborn is played by Kevin Collins, Jarman's companion.
16. Wenders believes that the movie 'could take place nowhere else. It is only in Berlin that I could recognize what it means to be German ... for history is both physically and emotionally present. ... No other city is to such an extent a symbol, a place of survival. It is a site more than a city' (Paneth, 1988, p. 2).
17. Homer is performed by Curt Bois, an actor who worked with Max Reinhardt and Bertolt Brecht and fled from Germany in 1933.
18. See Derrida on 'dissemination' (1981a, p. 25) and see Nietzsche on 'transvaluation'. Nietzsche writes,' the fate of nations ... [is] susceptible of the most varied interpretation and turns *for different purposes*' (1924b, p. 103).
19. See Caldwell and Rea for a more detailed discussion of the deconstruction of binary oppositions within this film (1991, pp. 46–54).
20. Lyotard writes: 'The destination of the subject ... is to supply a presentation for the unpresentable ... in regard to Ideas, to exceed everything that can be presented' (1988, p. 166).
21. See Nietzsche on Dionysian 'affirmation' (1979, p. 79).
22. See Rilke (1966). In 1912, at Castle Duino on the Adriatic coast, Rilke had a vision of the world as seen by an angel, and conceived the cycle of ten elegies, which he completed in 1922.
23. Derrida writes: 'Presence, in order to be presence and self-presence, has always already begun to represent itself, has always already been penetrated' (1978b, p. 249).
24. See Derrida's theorization of 'supplementarity' (1981a, p. 235).
25. The credits even contain an appeal to help rebuild a church where one key scene was shot.
26. See Derrida for a discussion of the instability of pure identity (1977, p. 175).
27. An emphasis on the 'instinctive' would mirror Nietzsche's theorization on 'artists': 'their work is an instinctive imposing of forms. They are the most spontaneous, most unconscious artists that exist' (1956, pp. 219–20).
28. These Teutonic rites offer an analogy to the 'rites of universal redemption, of glorious transfiguration' belonging to the 'Dionysian revelry' presented by Nietzsche (1956, p. 26).

6

Liminal music

Liminal music, like other liminal performance, accentuates heterogeneity, the experimental and the marginalized. Digital sampling creates exciting new hybrid styles of music which previous technologies have been unable to do. Although this is not without problems, it would appear that it is only in its infancy concerning its technological potential, and it can be described as being at the creative edge of contemporary music. Another quasi-genre of liminal music that can be said to be at the edge of innovation, although taking a much more theatrical form, is the neo-gothic. This hybridized genre concentrates on attempting to present the sublime through disruptive sounds, combined with tropical lyrics that produce wide metaphorical effects, blended with primordial visual imagery. Liminal music can therefore be seen as a marginalized, localized scene of experimentation that challenges traditional ideas of aesthetic judgement.

Digital sampling: the techno music scene

In an era of new technology and open plagiarism, old categories have virtually collapsed. There is more talk of rock or soul, the best songs are 'stolen moments and the best groups are a bunch of thieves' (Cosgrove, 1987a, p. 24). Digital sampling creates new heterogeneous aesthetic styles, at the same time questioning the legitimation of the old ones. Therefore, it foregrounds the notion of origin. 'Iterability' is of value, since it demonstrates how relations between repetition and alteration are marked, thus refuting any belief in pure identity (Derrida, 1977, p. 190).

Digital sampling likewise problematizes notions of authority, calling to account accepted socio-cultural and political belief systems. According to Nietzsche, 'something that thinks when we think, is merely a formulation of a grammatical custom which sets an agent to every action' (1924b, p. 14). This for Nietzsche ultimately leads to a 'plurality of perspectives' and a creative way of thinking, which is reflected in such liminal practices as digital sampling (1924a, p. 16).

'Hip-hop' is the cutting edge of pop theft, emerging in the seventies as a rap excursion played out against a series of stolen 'breaks' from old funk records. DJs noticed that crowds, especially the dancers, responded best to the drum breaks in some funk and Latin records. For the dancers, the percussion breaks appeared to be the high point of these records, yet some were only four bars long. These breaks, it was realized, could be extended by mixing two copies of the same record on twin turntables. By this method, DJs could elongate a ten-second drum break to two minutes and take the dancers, who developed wilder and more energetic routines, to higher levels of excitement. DJs became known and admired for their use of breaks and their skill in cutting two turntables. Eventually not only funk and soul were used; anything with a good drum beat could be plundered. Sometimes the DJs would play only the break and ignore the rest of the record (Cook, 1987, p. 25). It was not only what was played that was important, it was also how it was played. However, due to infringement of copyright laws, very few break beat records were ever released. Many of the rarer beats became so sought after that people began to bootleg them. Many artists have beaten copyright laws by using only snatches of beats over the top of drum machines.[1] While the limited appeal of 'drum breaks' as a pop form will ultimately restrict these recordings to a cult status, mixing, due to advances in music technology, has developed over the past few years into a heterogeneous, chaotic assembly of imagination and wholesale robbery. Metal guitars, disco machinery, synthetic sounds and disco breaks have clashed together in a new disruptive hybridized order that has finally displaced the shattered faith of punk: No more 'new wave'; only 'reused waves'.

As musical technology becomes increasingly more sophisticated and mixing becomes the normal process of making pop, theft is compulsory. In the sixties, although it was tolerated, stealing the riffs off 'rhythm and blues' was an amoral act. Black American music was systematically pillaged by white performers. However, in contemporary times, theft is more democratic, a two-way process in a desegregated dance hall; 'hip-hop' steals from heavy metal; 'house' music steals from Europop; and British indie (independent) bands steal from their own latterday heroes. Unlike punk, which reacted against the icons of decadent rock, hip-hop, house and sonic theft have waged war on the laws of property. Central to this is the art of digital sampling, which has only been possible since the advent of a more sophisticated music technology.

A sampler is a specialized digital recorder that converts sounds into a series of digits and stores them in memory chips. Editing and reversing or transposing sounds can be done at the touch of a button. Contemporary samplers are designed as musical instruments. They have a limited memory, typically holding under one minute of sound. Because musicians are concerned with changing the pitch of sounds, samplers normally have their own piano-type keyboards or can be connected to one. Unlike synthesizers, which generate their own sounds, the sampler can only store and then manipulate those sounds that are put into it. Whereas a synthesiser uses sounds that are located within its circuits and an electric guitar makes noise via vibration, a sampler simply 'takes'. The raw material is limited only by imagination, and any sound can be reproduced by a sampler.

In practice, samplers have been used in two ways. First, to emulate conventional instruments more effectively than synthesizers, most sampler buyers so far have simply used factory disks to give them new keyboard sounds. Drum sounds can be taken from sampler libraries or copied from favourite records. Most chart records are now made largely or completely from samples organized by a computer sequencer. The second obvious use of a sampler shows its creative possibilities. If, for example, drum sounds can be straightforwardly copied, then bigger chunks of these sounds can also be copied: a few bars, or even a whole verse, something that no ordinary keyboard can do. These sections of music can be cut up, looped and montaged into something completely new. This is an area that is only just beginning to be explored.

In the past musicians have pushed existing technologies to the limit in their quest for new music. John Cage wrote music that involved manipulation of the turntable in the thirties and forties (Gould, 1987, p. 14). Pierre Schaeffer, a sound engineer working for French radio, founded the *musique concrete* movement in 1948, with music collected from the recorded sound of steam trains, aeroplanes and other 'non-musical' sources (Gould, 1987, p. 14). Schaeffer started with turntables but as tape recorders became widely available his compositions were made entirely on tape. Producing such tapes often meant long periods of laborious copying and splicing; today they could be made with ease on a sampler.

All these devices not only provide a huge range of sounds, but also encourage an approach to making music that is based on consciously taking pieces or 'traces' (Derrida, 1976, p. 62) of pre-existing musical works and rearranging them into new ones. Another precursor was the development of collage and cut-up techniques by Andre Breton and William Burroughs, where pre-existing texts or artwork are cut, reordered and juxtaposed to create new works with new meanings. Current buzzwords like 'cultural theft' make this process seem the latest sensation, but music has always progressed by recycling and cross-fertilization. Western classical music has its pastiches, its themes and variations, its wholesale plundering of folk songs and hymn tunes. The creative skill is in the selection and arrangement of the source material. The difference today is of course the increased sophistication in technology which make this process a lot easier and quicker. And, of course, now musicians, quite happily, own up to the fact that much of 'their work' is purloined from other sources, realizing that the notion of an original piece of work is itself problematic. As Barbara Kirshenblatt-Gimblett points out, there can be no fixed originary meaning, only 'forces and relations' that help to form identity (1991, p. 433). Instead of an origin, there are only edges, such as 'supplement', 'margin' and 'mark' (Derrida, 1981a, p. 25). The only problem the musicians now have is avoiding the courts because of infringement of copyright.

Pop music is extremely adaptable because it draws on music from outside the mainstream, usually by simply taking superficial aspects of it. Genuine experimentation has been unfashionable since attempts at fusing rock and avant-garde in the sixties dwindled into self-indulgence. Most live circuits have been very reluctant to play any music other than guitar-based rock. It is only certain radio stations that have played sampled dance music. In Australia, for instance, only Triple-J has played 'more and more dance music as part of its regular programming since 1988' (Murphie and Scheer, 1992, p. 177). In contrast, a programme director for 2MMM-FM claims that 'triple-M has been, and always will be a rock 'n' roll station and, I mean, why should we change it? We don't bow to trends. The whole acid-house thing is fading now, and the dance music that we play seems to be less and less well-received' (Danielsen and Casimir, 1990, p. 2). As Murphie and Scheer write, 'in the light of the US sales of rap product, this seems a deliberate effort to close the door on dance music in favour of guitar rock' (Murphie and Scheer, 1992, p. 177). And 'most independent labels, instead of grasping new opportunities are falling over each other to assert traditional values and to wallow in nostalgia for the 1960s' (Gould, 1987, p. 14). In so doing, they are seeking to maintain the legitimation of these traditional 'discursive objects' (Foucault, 1972, p. 47) against the threat of innovation and experimentation.

As samplers and home computers became cheaper, they became the principal tools for many people already attuned to organizing sound, thus challenging existing 'institutional sites' (Foucault, 1972, p. 51) of music production. The end product is unique, harsh, aggressive, urban and minimal. The frantic search for new sounds and rhythms at the cutting edge of contemporary music is leading musicians to investigate and borrow from every type of music imaginable, creating an eclectic and explosive mix.

Samplers were an inevitable by-product of microcomputer technology, particularly with the fall in the price of memory chips.[2] A new technology has entered pop as previous technologies have not. Ten years ago, no ordinarily incomed band could afford a synthesizer, and using one was sufficiently complicated to ensure that the end product was either mundane or minimalist. It was only bands with technological backgrounds that seemed truly at ease with their machines. Microchips have democratized that access to technology and also to music itself, opening the road previously blocked by income or education. Digital sampling has brought technology from the studio to the street, seducing individuals not into 'inertia' and apathy but into creating new aesthetic possibilities.[3]

However, the very people who welcomed punk's gatecrashing of the music industry now fear the demise of pop. If there is such a thing as a conventional pop format, it is one based on the use of conventional musical instruments. It is not even necessary to play them. For example, Pete Townshend (The Who) got sounds out of his guitar when he smashed it and Little Richard got tones from his piano when he walked on it. In the theatre of pop, the instruments were there to be *seen*; the means of sound production had to be *visible*, thereby clearly demonstrating 'authorship' of the music. 'Whether or not sampling deskills the musician is not the issue; it allows non-musicians the possibility of performance by making *all* sounds musical' (Gray, 1987, p. 29). For instance, 'sampled' glass, motorbikes, traffic and the sounds of the inner city are contained in the 'Urban Hell' collage of London-based rappers The Three Wise Men (Gray, 1987, p. 29). No longer do artists need to secrete themselves in a 'garret scenario' to produce their sounds, or closet themselves with 'do-it-yourself' guides to learning the guitar; instead, the rebellion of the new generation is in sampling. Taking the ease of digital sampling to its logical conclusion, the sampling revolution is set to take on the quantifiable profits of studios. Contained in the accessibility of a sampler is the creation of new talents free of the notions of accepted musical techniques. As the demarcation between producer and musician disappears, no longer will 'musicianship' be defined by instrumental ability; instead, imagination will be the only limiting force.[4] House music is the ultimate producer dance language. The musicians who made the original snatches of sound are faceless and uncredited; the producer cum DJ is the vital element in the mix. The authorship of the record lies not in its origins but in its sonic splicing, foregrounding the issue of 'identity formation' (see Derrida, 1977, p. 175).

Media approaches to sampling have been consistently framed in the predictable language of 'irreverence' and 'subversion'. Sampling is invariably treated as an issue in terms of the politics of the music industry, a challenge to specific property rights, but also a shift in the struggle over who 'owns' the music culture. Thus, its 'surfaces of emergence' are mapped and its 'grids of specification' are demarcated, as it challenges these 'authorities of delimitation' (see Foucault, 1972, pp. 31–9, 40–9).

What are not usually considered are the formal possibilities and aesthetic implications of sampling, the way it makes difficult, time-consuming techniques – until now the preserve of the conscientious, 'engaged' avant-garde musician – attainable to ordinary individuals and not necessarily musicians; in short, it replaces the 'listening' subject with the 'performing' subject.[5] Sampling has been seized by a hungry rock culture/music press in its quest for a new opposition movement to provide some credence to the notion of the seriousness of pop music. Since the demise of punk, attempts have been made, with only limited success, to enlist other music movements, such as funk and then rap (seen as a proto-socialist street movement), for this purpose. The threat is directed outwards, seen in terms of damage to the record industry, 'the establishment', not as a disruption to personal value systems. Digital sampling allows an equivalence to be read between the 'violence' of a jarring edit and the outrage of a flagrant musical theft.

Sampling has been espoused as a new punk, both a repossession of control from the industry and a liberation from the inhibiting effect of expertise. There is even less need to gain musical expertise than in the days of punk's one-chord wonders. Instead of not sounding as good as James Brown, with a sampler one can simply appropriate his expertise. Commentors often link sampling with groups like Culturcide, Pussy Galore and Ciccone Youth (all have recorded catastrophic versions of classic songs), regarding both piracy and parody as acts of détournement, gestures against global pop hegemony. However, there are some problems with the idea of sampling as the consummation of punk's do-it-yourself ethic. Sampling may produce a largish number of bands making and producing their own music, but those individuals will still be buying music-making technology from companies that are linked to the major record companies. And although digital sampling makes certain effects more attainable, it cannot democratize the unequal distribution of talent, though not necessarily musical talent.

Contemporary use of computer technology in the popular music industry has generated an interesting discursive dilemma regarding technology as it pertains to performance, law and aesthetic judgement. What the law needs to decide is when collage/cut-up/scratch becomes outright theft: whether a two-second snatch of an old James Brown record is tantamount to ripping off the original artist; whether hip-hop collage is a valid form of music in its own right and, if so, what sort of copyright laws will protect against wholesale theft.

The issues that have arisen in the context of popular music echo other issues in the arts in recent years, especially the battles in the law courts on who owns what, fought out by playwrights and theatres over the use of texts, together with the appropriation of image in the visual arts. All are questions of textual ownership that engage with artistic practices, ethical questions and legal concepts such as that of intellectual property, at the same time problematizing the legitimation and authority of the author.[6]

The issues raised by digital sampling present new challenges to old debates. Through digital sampling, musicians can either incorporate parts of another's recorded music into their own or build a completely new performance from information sampled from another musician. In other words, by 'playing with the pieces' they create new hybrid aesthetic forms (Baudrillard, 1984b, p. 24). For example, the drumming in the 1984 recording of 'Relax' by Frankie Goes to Hollywood was sampled from the Led Zeppelin's drummer, John Bonham, who was deceased at the time. Therefore, the drumming on that recording is and is not Bonham's. Although he did not play on that particular performance, the 'drumming' was his, in that a new performance was electronically 'cloned' from a sample of his drumming. As Philip Auslander writes, digital sampling raises an issue that is unprecedented: that is, the commodification of 'performance itself' (1992, p. 31).

The term 'performance' here is not referring to a simple recording but to something much less tangible; in fact, to a new heterogeneous formation of aesthetic objects. In the case of 'Relax', it refers to John Bonham's performance 'performing itself', or genetic samples that encode his performance style, rather than any specific textual content, and in Nietzschean terms is therefore 'self (re-)generating' (1924b, p. 239). Digital sampling clearly challenges most of the traditional concepts of authorship and textual ownership. Who is the author? Who has the right to 'speak'? (Foucault, 1972, p. 50). Should a musician or his or her estate be entitled to compensation when someone else creates a completely different performance from a minute piece of electrical information extracted from a recorded performance? For that matter, is the author of the software used in cloning the author of the performance? Or is the author actually the machine that did the mixing? Simon Frith argues that sampling 'calls into question the principles that underpin copyright laws. ... Anglo-American copyright law is not a statement of ethical principle but a device to sustain a *market* in ideas', as the expression 'intellectual property' implies (1988b, pp. 123–4). Through textual appropriation samplers challenge the concepts of authorship and ownership that make such a market possible, and continue in the utopian belief that all are free to use the cultural environment as they wish. The 'authorities of delimitation' (Foucault, 1972, p. 41) – that is, the market and the legal establishment – have been slow to respond to this subversive challenge. Most lawsuits resulting from sampling have been settled in favour of the copyright holder, because most have been settled out of court, thereby establishing no legal method to regulate these practices. Therefore, the arguably outmoded copyright model is being imposed upon the products of the new technological environment, threatening freedom of expression. As

Auslander argues, 'a new aesthetic is in danger of being outlawed just as its expressive possibilities are beginning to be explored' (1992, p. 33).

A performance practice that takes on particular significance, even though it is not a product of technology, is the use of appropriated texts by some performance artists, challenging the 'rules of formation' (Foucault, 1972, p. 38) of the dominant performative discourses. One such example is The Wooster Group's appropriation of Arthur Miller's play *The Crucible* in their piece *L.S.D. (Just the High Points)* (1985), which resulted in a court battle between the group and Miller. The Wooster Group's use of Miller's text implies the same postmodernist attitude towards a literary text as digital sampling has towards recordings as musical texts: 'reproduction, pastiche and quotation, instead of being forms of textual parasitism, become constitutive of textuality' (Wollen, 1986, p. 169). The Wooster Group's use of Miller's text was not a simple matter of interpretation, as it incorporated parts of his text into another text. Neither was *The Crucible* appropriated for its narrative use, but for its style and cultural aura – its status 'as an icon that gathers together a network of associations and experiences' (Savran, 1985, p. 105). As Auslander notes, 'it is not clear that such a use of a play text constitutes a *performance* of the play, even legally' (1992, p. 34). As is apparent, The Wooster Group's appropriation of the Miller text is not easily incorporated into traditional understandings of the text–production relationship of the theatre, or into the legal institutions provided to protect the author's rights of ownership. Instead, it brings these issues into question in a similar way to the uses of digital technology. Samplers, too, choose their material for its stylistic and cultural aura. Furthermore, their work is regularly judged in terms of its cultural references and resonances.

It would seem, therefore, that it is more appropriate to envisage such performances as *L.S.D.* as performances *sampled* from a text, rather than to think of them as interpretations of that text. Although this does not clear up legal problems of authorship and ownership, it does provide a more contemporary description of the relationship between text and performance than traditional terminology such as 'performance of' and 'interpretation of'.

As well as questioning accepted conventions of authorship, ownership and intertexuality, digital sampling brings traditional assumptions of reproduction and representation into question. A recording is thought of as a representation of that performance; in other words, a recording transcribes an original but is not that original. All origin is a myth in any rigorous analysis, since instead of an origin, there is only a further chain of signification. In cases where a performance has been stored on a computer disc, the 'recording' can be made either before or after the 'original' performance using *MIDI* (musical instrument digital interface) technology. What is actually recorded through the MIDI cable is a set of instructions for recreating the original performance, rather than a transcription of that performance. A programmable keyboard produces an actual performance rather than a representation (recording) of a performance. Digital information need not be translated to be stored, and the computer and the synthesizer speak the same binary language. The recording is therefore an original performance: the same binary information that the keyboard produces in performance is entered on to the recording. When the stored information is subsequently decoded to produce sound, it is literally 'reproduced again', not 'represented'. This aspect of digital sound unquestionably shatters the valued distinction between 'live' and 'recorded' performance, as well as that between 'original' and 'reproduction'. In cases where the computer does not transcribe information generated by a manual performance, but is programmed to 'play' the instrument directly, the 'recording' actually precedes the event recorded, and the 'hyperreal' (Baudrillard, 1983a, p. 147) automated performance is the 'live' performance, deconstructing concepts of both 'live' and 'recorded' performance. As Nietzsche points out, without the 'real' there can be no 'apparent' (1990, p. 51).

In this way, digital technology challenges fundamental dualisms in its relation to performance, including those of original and reproduction, live and recorded, author and interpreter, and owner and user. The cultural tendency so far has been to reinscribe and redefine these dualisms. Critics condemn the use of programmed performance in 'live' settings (due to their problematization of these 'institutional sites'); traditional distinctions have been extended from the realm of specifiable texts to that of rudimentary style, in an attempt to bring new technological developments within the sphere of existing legal structures.

Not surprisingly, the cultural commodity market depends precisely on such distinctions, together with the concurrent maintenance of these dualisms, for its existence. These responses appear to be conditioned by the unspoken assumption that the authentic, originary and therefore privileged version of any performance is the 'live' version, and that recorded forms of performance are secondary, commodified versions of that 'authentic', 'originary' moment; pleasurable, but inauthentic. This privileging, which entails an idealization of the performer as the author of an authentic work, the source of the original style, and a reification of the performer's presence, is challenged and subverted by the practice of digital sampling technology and its attendant discourses.

The heterogeneous aesthetic practices facilitated by digital technology have created new perspectives and presented new challenges to the traditional critical and legal concepts of authorship, textual ownership and representation generally. These challenges constitute part of a larger cultural environment that contextualizes cultural practices which are not dependent on technology, but raise questions concerning the use and ownership of cultural texts. At present, these challenges are being negotiated and it remains to be seen whether the potential aesthetic creativity and freedom of expression offered by digital sampling and related practices, such as the ever increasing use of the Internet (bringing a different creative potential and opening a whole new can of worms, its 'superhighways' currently relish their freedom from any restrictions, including those of copyright laws), will become actualities.

However, it seems that the initial impulse has been an attempt to bring new technologies and their related possibilities under the authority of restrictive, outdated, legal definitions. Fortunately this, as yet, has been unenforceable on a large scale. Digital sampling, which has been seen as a threat to the music industry, will either be crushed in a series of test cases (which has not happened as yet), or lose its force by being allowed. When everyone can do something, the threat of opposition obviously disappears, which is the most likely scenario.

The only way to recharge sampling as an issue is by perpetual aesthetic innovation. The real 'politics' lie in the effects on a consciousness of formal futurism. Digital sampling facilitates the techniques of cut-up, collage and bricolage. In hip-hop, discontinuity and juxtaposition can induce a sense of play or a sense of impending doom. It can create a kind of dance psychedelia, disrupting consciousness by rupturing stylistic integrity. As Simon Reynolds notes, 'what a record documents is not an event but a phantasm constructed out of different takes. It never happened' (1990, p. 166). Digital sampling takes this fictitious nature of recording even further, creating heterogeneous, 'hyperreal' events that never could have happened.

Digital sampling can be regarded as a tribute to the old soul masters, which it is probably meant to be, or it can, which is often the case, be seen as creating irreverent and irrelevant music or 'taking the soul out of soul'. More than one media offering has concentrated on this supposed lack of content owing to the original work being divorced from its context. However, David Toop argues that the living spirit of communal improvisation is thriving. He writes: 'Diverse voices have contributed to this Greek chorus, all sharing a common project of technophobic humanism. Machines are killing music, they say' (1992, p. 34). Toop continues with the belief that rap is often the prime target of 'technophobes'. He argues that if recording technology's emphasis on isolationism, precision and technocratic, hierarchical control has squeezed the life out of much soul and jazz, the same qualities have been subverted by rap producers to reinvest African-American music with defiance and life. He writes:

In the hands of the Bomb Squad or Ice Cube's 'Lench Mob' mechanical precision becomes intensity and drive; fragmentation creates a theatre of interleaved signals; high audio fidelity allows deeper bass, sizzling highs, as well as a clear soundstage on which to place all the elements of a mix; hierarchical control enables the modelling of complex sound sculptures. ... At its best, *rap production plays with our grasp of authorship, our sense of time. Who is speaking?* Are all these contradictory messages intended to convey a unity of content or do they defy and question each other? Is this a fiction, a film, a private diary? (Toop, 1992, p. 36, emphasis added)

The future possibilities of sampling do not lie in it being proffered as a successor to the punk movement, a new opposition movement giving some credibility to the seriousness of pop. Instead, the real crisis or challenge to rock and pop posed by sampling concerns its aesthetic possibilities and the heterogeneous infinity of sounds only imagined by precursors such as Schaeffer. For the possibility of sampling is the removal of 'all historical reference points, together with an infinity of new musical meanings' (Gray, 1987, p. 29). Therefore, digital sampling, in creating such new exciting styles, indicates the need for an aesthetic analysis that can deal with its diverse significatory practices.

Digitized performance: the 'acid' rave

'Acid house' music is digitally sampled music, assembled not created, an extraction of the most heterogeneous dance-effective elements from English synthipop and early eighties' electrofunk. The gimmicks, special effects and extended breaks once added to spice up disco have become the whole body of 'house', forming exciting 'spectacles' and 'events' (Baudrillard, 1988, p. 192). Contemporary black music has abandoned narrative: both hip-hop and house exist in some kind of eternal present. They are the latest phases in an unwritten history of black music, a history conditioned by sophisticated changes in music technology. Instead of the song there is a kind of territory, a shifting ('shift-shape') dance environment without borders or destination. There is no charismatic centre to this music, just the relentless beat. There is a democracy of sounds and, rather than soul narrative, with its dynamic progression, resolution and catharsis, house offers an unrelenting 'seduction' (Baudrillard, 1979, p. 32). Instead of communication there is a plethora of catchphrases and buzzwords, and the sound of machines talking to one another. The listener is engaged through a fascination with an array of surfaces, there is a certain depthlessness, with no apparent social content to be divined, just an illegible, arbitrary alteration of twists and vectors whose obscurity is endlessly resistant to the attempts of white rock critics to interpret it in any way, thus creating its own form of local resistance.

Attempts have been made to salvage meaning out of 'acid' music by nationalizing it. For instance, in the UK there is Brit-funk, British jazz and so on. As Reynolds asks, why is there this strand of patriotism in an age when 'pop networks of distribution and reciprocal influence have made national boundaries irrelevant?' (Reynolds, 1990, p. 174). A band in Manchester can have more in common with a peer group in Chicago than a band living a few blocks away. The fact that 'acid house' is so widespread proves how irrelevant questions of nationality and location are in pop. These nationalistic responses derive partly from punk, which inspired an emotional commitment to the idea of creating oppositions in its attempt to produce a 'relevant' music movement.

However, listening to acid music indicates how unsuited it is to carry the mantle of the punk 'counter-culture' movement. It is difficult to imagine a genre more inappropriate as an indoctrination of nationality. Although it comes from Chicago, it does not draw anything from its origins, thereby pointing to the instability of pure 'identity'.[7] Nor can its producers be seen as authors. Producers like Curtis Mantronik are not authors but engineers or 'sound architects'. The music is a product of their expertise. Therefore, a Mantronik track, for instance, is not a song but a heterogeneous process, a space capable of endless extension and adaptation, a collection of resources to be reassembled and restructured and then 'dispersed' and 'disseminated' (Derrida, 1981a, p. 25).

The connotations of hallucinogenics that accompany the name 'acid' are denied by members of the Chicago scene as having anything to do with the sound of the music. The name, at least according to one version, comes from the slang term 'acid burn', which means to rip someone off, steal ideas or, in this case, sample sounds. However, many 'rave-goers' do take ecstasy or methylenedioxymetheamphetamine, as it is known by its generic name, a drug related to LSD which provides a euphoric sense of communion, together with strong aphrodisiac effects, without causing hallucinations.[8]

Unlike previous disco and club scenes, the bars in 'house' clubs are deserted and the dance floors are packed. Ecstasy is not a drug to mix with alcohol. One of the main features of the rave party, apart from the music, has been the techno-light shows. Each rave is proclaimed as the 'ultimate techno production' to end all techno productions. The metronomic beat of this Dionysian-like *Gesamtkunstwerk* continues well into the next day, with dancers still dancing, the 'ravers' still 'raving'. A smoke machine billows (or dry ice creates the same effect), producing a mise-en-scène reminiscent of the primeval swamp, where everyone is isolated but not alone in the ecstasy. A flickering strobe light matches the sustained beat of the music and everywhere arms are raised, pointing to some pagan deity.

Lyotard, in arguing that the sublime 'cannot demand even subjectively to be communicated to all thought', restricts his argument to merely the linguistic (1991, p. 239). Such performances as the rave abandon the purely linguist in favour of an intersemiotic signification. With the insertion of the body, together with the inclusion of certain Dionysian-like rituals that produce 'an outrage on the imagination' (Kant, 1978a, pp. 90–1), the 'unpresentable' can be presented in such performances, through the immediacy and ecstasy of the *gestus*.[9]

The excitement of the rave partly revolves around its underground connotations, revealed in its alternative performance sites, which challenge the dominant 'institutional sites' (Foucault, 1972, p. 51) of performance. Originally, the parties were held in obscure out-of-the-way places and the gatherings were relatively small. However, established entertainment entrepreneurs have begun to cash in on the trend in a big way and venues now tend to be in established clubs. Even though more and more raves are being held at city venues rather than in disused suburban warehouses and such like, there is still a feeling of mystery and intrigue surrounding the events, if it is only that the information regarding venues and locations remains veiled in secrecy until the prerequisite pre-rave party is attended and maps are provided. This gives the rave an unsettling sensation of a somewhat clandestine, marginalized social gathering.

Many of the original ravers have stopped going to the more commercial venues because they claim the age group is getting younger and they prefer 'mature' ravers. Since alcohol is not served at rave venues, no age limit is stipulated. Under the circumstances this, if the alcohol prohibition law for under eighteens is to protect juveniles, is fairly ironic, since raves usually last all night, frequently followed by a coming-down party the next day, and drugs like ecstasy or speed are the rule rather than the exception. Police raids are rare at the actual venues and when they do occur very few drugs are found. Drugs are taken before arrival at the rave venue (the likeliest reason for police intervention tends to be complaints from nearby residents regarding noise levels). Instead, dealers tend to hang around pre-rave venues or they are contacted by word of mouth.

Still, despite the obvious drawbacks of drug involvement, raves do tend to be fairly positive affairs. In contrast to the usual club and pub scene, everyone is very friendly and relaxed. It is not mandatory to take ecstasy to get the general effect of house experience, but as I realized when I attended a rave in Perth, Australia, it does help to understand fully what the movement is about. Ecstasy, at the time of writing, was selling for A$50–60 a tablet. That, together with a door price of approximately A$40, means that this entertainment is not cheap. At raves people are generally relaxed and happy, and this is not always owing to their chemical intake. Feelings of caring and sharing abound, in as much as each raver experiences his or her own individual sensations. Even the rave fashion scene is relaxed: anything goes as long as it is comfortable and allows plenty of dance movement. The point is not to be noticed but to be part of the collective scene. No designer labels are required and they would probably look out of place, which makes for a less status-conscious gathering. In fact, the rave fashion scene can be seen as a reaction against the 'cool' designer eighties.

The rave scene is more egalitarian than previous dance scenes. According to computerized lists of members attending raves in England, there is a surprising cross-section of individuals at these events (Garratt and Baker, 1989, p. 63). Professionals, teachers, bank workers, hairdressers, shop assistants, labourers, students and the unemployed; all frequent raves. Everyone is admitted, and for the same price.

Raves, although originating on the British scene, now tend to be a fairly international phenomenon (admittedly Western), especially in Australia and also in the United States. There has even been a five-day rave held in Amsterdam (apparently sponsored by that city's council). How long the rave scene will ultimately last is debatable but its evolution should be interesting. Raves could either return to being smaller intimate gatherings once again or become even bigger 'happenings' (Heidegger, 1971b, p. 57). However, whatever their transmutation may be, it is hoped that their egalitarianism and collectivism will be here to stay.

Destructive aesthetics: neo-gothic sound

'Neo-gothic' is a term I have coined for a sub-genre of liminal music that exhibits predominantly destructive aesthetics. The main features of this genre are disruptive sounds combined with lyrics which invoke images of passion, death, decay and a certain pursuit of the chthonic. These traits are best exemplified in the performances of Nick Cave and The Bad Seeds and Einstürzende Neubauten. With their dark, vampirish attire and overtly theatrical gestures, they accentuate a certain sardonic humour that parodies rather than merely (re)presents.

Nick Cave and The Bad Seeds

At the Metropolis night club in Perth, Australia, the house was focused and intense with expectation when Nick Cave walked on stage, black suited, grease-lined hair flicked back and cigarette in hand. Like a person demented with rage and intent on revenge, Cave performed with relentless energy while the rest of the band remained comparatively sedate, allowing him to be the focal point. He moves like the Bad Seeds' music, rising and falling, affronting the audience with his fallen preacher theatrics.

Nick Cave and The Bad Seeds are probably one of the most fashionable acts in the world today. However, while they have become the never-ending flavour of the month in the more sophisticated and decayed fashion centres of America, they have found it extremely hard to break into the wider American market. The American media have tended to write Cave off as a manic depressive. In a much discussed interview, Cave hung up after ten seconds on air when a radio DJ announced, 'Let's take a journey into doom and gloom, here's Nick Cave' (Collins, 1992, p. 4). Fellow Birthday Party (Cave's previous band) member and Bad Seed Mick Harvey remembers the excesses of both the Birthday Party (named after the Pinter play) and the Bad Seeds, the drug-taking that helped to form the twisted visions of horror, confession and medieval redemption that so often appear through Cave's analytical imagery, exposing his intoxicated 'reality' (Collins, 1992, p. 4).

As an article in *Rolling Stone* magazine mentions, few artists have inspired 'the reams of psychobabble from sycophantic adulation to hysterical sub-Jungian analysis nearly all of it on a personal level, that Cave has' (Walker, 1992, p. 64). He has never been too discreet, so no one has to look too far for family skeletons:

> I just did this phone interview with Czechoslovakia. The first question which was 'How ... does it feel now with your victory over drugs?' It's using this aspect of my life they know fuck-all-about, as if it's some public domain that everyone can stomp over. ... That side has become an increasing drag to me, to have to talk about. (Walker, 1992, p. 64)

As Walker writes in the *Rolling Stone* interview from which the above quote was taken, 'it's only natural he tries to downplay his "whole drug situation". Funny he should bring it up then.' However, as Walker points out, danger and glamour were crucial to Cave's image at that time. It was quite apparent to every one that going to see the 'Birthday Party in their heyday' was 'like sitting in a bad corner waiting for an accident to happen' (Walker, 1992, p. 64).

Cave's album *Henry's Dream* (1992), although abounding with iconic biblical imagery (even the name of his band, The Bad Seeds, provides biblical reference), is also stylistically evocative of the South American 'magical realist' text (e.g. Allende, Marquez, Borges), as demonstrated in the lyrics of 'John Finns' Wife':

> Well midnight came and a clock did strike
> And in she came, did John Finns' wife

With legs like scissors and butcher's knives
A tattooed breast and flaming eyes
and a crimson carnation in her teeth ...
I had brass knuckles and a bolo knife
Over near the bandstand with John Finns' wife
She got perfumed breasts and raven hair
Sprinkled with wedding confettis
And a gang of garrotters were all giving me stares
Armed as they were with machetes
And the night through the window was full of lights
Winking and awatching at John Finns' wife ...

The colourful and figurative use of language and the juxtaposition of
metaphors such as 'legs like scissors' with 'a tattooed breast and flaming eyes
and a crimson carnation in her teeth' evoke surreal images of passion, violence,
decay and death; an almost *Dionysian* intoxication with tragedy. This mixture
of wide metaphor, as in much of the liminal, produces a synaesthetic effect
caused by the interplay of various mental sense-impressions. These images
appear throughout Cave's lyrics, juxtaposed with equally strong mystical
'traces' (Derrida, 1976, p. 62) from the New Testament. For example, in
'Christina the Astonishing':

Christina the Astonishing
Lived a long long time ago
She was stricken with a seizure
At the age of twenty-two
They took her body in a coffin
To a tiny church in Liege
Where she sprang up from the coffin
Just after the Agnus Dei
She soared up to the rafters
Perched on a beam up there
Cried 'The stink of human sin is more than I can bear' ...

Images from the Old Testament are also presented as the lyrics of the song
'Straight to You', which carries traces of the *Songs of Solomon*, demonstrates:

All the towers of ivory are crumbling
and the swallows have sharpened their beaks
This is the time of our great undoing
This is the time that I'll come running

Straight to you
For I am captured ...

In an interview with Annette Shun Wah (*The Noise*), Cave was asked what
the source of his style of imagery was. Cave claims his imagery comes mostly
from his childhood growing up as a country boy in Australia. However,
judging by his colourful and strong imagery, it would seem that other places
where he has lived have strongly influenced his music, especially his two and
half years living in São Paulo in Brazil. While in São Paulo, Cave caught up on
crime fiction, especially James Ellroy's novels, which he admits have certainly
had some impact on *Henry's Dream* (Coupe, 1992, p. 42). This influence is
certainly manifest in the lyrics of 'Papa Won't Leave You Henry':

Well, I thought about my friend Michel
How they rolled him in linoleum
And shot him in the neck
A bloody halo like a think-bubble
Circling his head ...
Lynch mobs, death squads, babies being born without brains
The mad heat and the relentless rains
And if you stick your arm into that hole
It comes out sheared off to the bone ...

Cave, in his early work, used his voice to enhance the violence and revenge
inherent in his lyrics, lowering his pitch an octave, suggesting a raging and
tormented soul. When told his music appeared to be much softer and more
melodic now, Cave admitted that this was owing to his having developed his
voice while gaining new skills and improving his technical ability (Interview
with Nick Cave, 1992). Still, the theatrics, raging lyrics and the tortured
performer remain, producing a liminal aestheticizing of Brechtian techniques.
As Josette Féral writes,

The processes of alienation at work in the theatre of Brecht ... have been:
fragmentation of the narrative; rupture in the order of representation;
displacement of the subject of enunciation; decentering of the spectator's
point of view with respect to the event; passage from reality to fiction
and from fiction to reality; placement of the part within the context of
the whole. ... Contemporary theatre, and to a greater extent the multimedia arts, have transformed the bulk of these procedures into an
aesthetic form which today signals the contemporaneity of the
performance. (Féral, 1987, p. 469)

Cave prefers to have his performances recorded on video in a way that construes them as being 'natural', rather than allowing video directors to edit them and put in their own ideas of what the song is about. He has mentioned that he 'loathes MTV' and dislikes the idea that 'the life of a musician is put into the hands of a video director ... with a pressure to make a certain type of video. ... I will continue to make performance style video where we get up, play the song, and that's it' (Interview with Nick Cave, 1992).

Of course, any recorded performance is created using certain conventions, even if the desired effect is to produce a 'natural' performance, so it can never be quite as simple as Cave would appear to wish, and he draws attention to this fact in his video *At the Paradiso* (1992). The performance here is constructed as a staged concert, although there are some tracks which are obviously not recorded at this particular time and venue. This becomes apparent when Cave's clothes magically change during a song. It would seem that several performances have been recorded and the better ones selected to appear on the video. Each track is heralded with the appearance of a disembodied hand, which writes the name of the subsequent track with a texta pen, together with an ashtray overflowing and sometimes upturned (the cigarette butt is the obvious 'hallmark' of Cave, since during a performance he is rarely without one). When one of the tracks is seen to go quite wrong, the title of the track is again self-consciously written by the same disembodied hand, but this time it is scribbled out, drawing attention to the simulation of the performance. Almost a doubling effect takes place, with a performance ostensibly made to appear 'natural' but at the same time prepared to point out self-consciously that it is, after all, only a 'simulation' (Baudrillard, 1983a, p. 11).

Another strong component of Cave's performance is his use of parody, demonstrated by his lyrics, delivered with wild gesticulations and 'fallen preacher theatrics'. It could be argued that Cave's work takes the form of a self-conscious, self-contradictory, self-undermining statement, almost giving the effect of saying something while at the same time putting inverted commas around what is being said. The effect is to 'highlight' or 'subvert' and the mode is therefore a 'knowing' or even 'ironic' one (Hutcheon, 1989, p. 1).

One of the main features of liminal performance is this kind of partial commitment to duplicity. In this way the liminal ultimately installs and reinforces as much as it undermines and subverts the conventions it sets out to overturn. However, since the initial concern is to denaturalize some of the dominant features of our way of life — for example, those entities which we assume to be 'natural' (capitalism, liberal humanism and so on) — it can be said to have some resistant aspects. As David Wellbery mentions, 'postmodern aesthetic experimentation should be viewed as having an irreducible political dimension. It is inextricably bound up with a critique of domination' (Wellbery,

1985, p. 235). Yet this critique is bound up with a *complicity* with power and domination, one that acknowledges that it cannot escape implication in that which it nevertheless still wants to analyse and undermine. As Derrida writes, 'we cannot give up this metaphysical complicity without also giving up the critique we are directing against this complicity' (1978c, p. 281). The ambiguities of this position are translated into the 'shift-shape' style of liminal art, which therefore, self-consciously, at one and the same time provides and challenges ideology.

Nick Cave appeared in a film called *The Ghosts of the Civil Dead* (1988). He was also involved in the script writing. Asked about his involvement with the film, which offered acknowledgement to Michel Foucault's *Discipline and Punish*, Cave says, 'the penal system as it is, and the apparatus of judgement . . . does irritate, and upset me a lot. . . . I did a lot of homework when I started working on the script . . . what emerged was a particular vision of the whole penal system as almost a plot by the higher powers to perpetuate the whole system of crime' (Reynolds, 1990, pp. 68–9).

Foucault, in his research on the penal system, discovered that 'disciplines' such as criminology and psychiatry were not to do with revealing any 'truth'. Rather, the knowledge they generated was inseparable from and instrumental in techniques of 'power' (Foucault, 1986, pp. 300–3). As well as focusing on social control: (surveillance and segregation), Foucault concentrated on mental control: that is, the ways in which individuals become responsible for their own self-policing (1986, pp. 202–3). Most of Cave's characters are in some sense prisoners of obsessions or a claustrophobic environment. In describing his novel *And the Ass Saw the Angel* (1990), he claims,

> It's set in a small valley in a remote region somewhere in the world. . . .
> The fascination of these closed communities and hemmed-in lives, that recur in my work, is that they breed a certain ignorance, can be the breeding ground for very extreme, absurd emotional releases. (Reynolds, 1990, p. 70)

In his song 'The Mercy Seat' (1988) a condemned man is waiting to:

> Go shuffling out of life
> Just to hide in death awhile . . .

One of the accusations levelled at Cave is that of misogynism. During the interview with *Face the Press*, he was asked why so many of his songs evoked imageries of violence to women. By way of explanation, he says that he tended to write when he felt extremely emotional and when he was upset and jealous.

So, 'women have not fared well. ... I write some very violent things against them. ... I'm not violent to women as a person and I don't advocate that at all.'

Cave is estranged from the confining notion of 'humanity', stating again and again that 'the world is a disgusting place to live'. Morbidly inward, Cave refuses to be integrated: 'lyrically, thematically, my work is still charged to the same bowl of vomit' (Reynolds, 1990, p. 71). Cave appeared on the music scene towards the end of the punk era. Punk was seen as the demystification that would lead to enlightenment, together with a belief that it was possible through deconditioning by shock tactics to achieve some free flowing exchange. Against the predominant view of love as an idealistic state of being, Cave was almost alone in expressing love as a wretched dependence whose ultimate expression could only be violence.

Cave was the first writer in a post-punk climate of positivism to use biblical imagery (sin, retribution, curses, revenge, bad seed), claiming that 'things like revenge which you talk about as almost an Old Testament feeling, I see as completely now'. Asked if he therefore believed that certain kinds of violence, the crime of passion, for instance, had a kind of aesthetic integrity, he replied: 'There's something more noble in revenge than in ... sadism or violence through greed. Maybe, there's something more aesthetically pleasing about it ... the rewards of happiness and contentment and security ... have no aesthetic interest' (Reynolds, 1990, p. 76).

Cave goes on to say, 'then again my favourite song in the world is "Wonderful World" by Louis Armstrong ... but I would not attempt that because I wouldn't know how to begin'. In fact, Cave did 'attempt' this song which he sang with Shane McGowan of The Pogues (1992). However, the song appears to have sunk without a trace, probably because Cave's fans don't really expect or want to hear Cave singing about happiness and contentment. His audience, seemingly, would much rather hear him sing of revenge and violence leading to tragedy and affirmation. These emotions are far more identifiable with the present fragmentation and instability within their own lives.

Einstürzende Neubauten

Einstürzende Neubauten, since their inception as an 'industrial band' in the early eighties, have attempted to stretch the boundaries of their hybrid music.[10] Though now preferring the description of 'crossover', 'contemporary German folk music', or 'hardcore new age' (Laddish and Dippé, 1993, p. 92), they have long since dissolved the boundaries between art and everyday life, problematizing the notion of aesthetic purity, since even granting autonomy to the aesthetic is a way of limiting or 'framing' it (Derrida, 1987a). In Neubauten's early work the hum of machines and the dissonance of construction crews at work were harnessed by the group's destructive character to forge sounds that were exciting and overwhelming, demonstrating their Dionysian-like traits of intoxication, disruption, excess and the 'will to art' (Nietzsche, 1924b, p. 289). In their later work this has been succeeded by more conventional ways of creating music, though still performed at fairly unconventional sites, thus challenging the dominant 'institutional sites' (Foucault, 1972, p. 51) of performance; it remains equally disconcerting and thought provoking. Appropriating Walter Benjamin's belief that the destructive character is essentially cheerful (Ridgers, 1993, p. 221), Einstürzende Neubauten have obscured the division between music, performance and everyday life, thus bringing into question the accepted boundaries of those spheres. Their performances over the years have become more refined. The sheer noise and destructiveness with which they flattened their audiences have in recent years been replaced by an almost 'seductive' (Baudrillard, 1979) use of sound, creating tragic yet beautiful multilingual lyrics and sounds which dissolve into an almost breathtaking pastiche of aural and visual effects. According to Bargeld,

> What we are doing is already far enough away from music that nobody can tell you any more what the rules are for what we are doing. I could say tomorrow that we are no more a band, but a theatre group and still doing the same stuff. *Nobody can draw lines where the music ends or when the art ends or the performance or the art work or the installation ends, or where the next stage begins.* (Bohn, 1989, p. 51, emphasis added)

In *Halber Mensch* (*Half Man*) (1985), a performance directed by Sogo Ishii and filmed in Tokyo, long panning shots show scrap metal, junkyard remnants, seeping water oozing into slimy pools of filth, a revolting pile of worms that crawl over someone's foot and a dead cat on a stick. Interspersed is film footage of a foetus developing *in utero*. The effect is both threatening and sinister. Juxtaposed with this are the deafening sounds of machinery, road drills, concrete mixers, boiling furnaces, the hammering of walls which collapse and the sound and visual effects of something suspiciously like a Molotov cocktail: in fact, a cacophony of the sounds of chaos and destruction. Over the top of this are heard the unearthly screeches of Blixa Bargeld, who appears like some romantic vampirish character from a Teutonic post-holocaust fairy tale, screaming such lyrics as:

Halber Mensch
Halber Mensch
Geh weiter, in jede Rictung
Wir haben Wahrheiten für Dich
Aufgestellt
Halber Mensch
In ihren Rissen leuchten unsre
Sender
Zu jeder vollen Stunde senden wir
Deine Werte
Geh weiter, halber Mensch

Half man
Half man
Keep going in my direction
We've placed truths for you
Half man
Only your transmitters shine in their cracks
On the hour we broadcast your values
Keep going
We care for you
We sense for you
Half man

The culmination of the performance is the appearance of the dance troupe Byakko Sha, looking like some terrifying, grotesque, demonic caricatures that belong on the set of a Noh drama. In keeping with Einstürzende Neubauten's theme of destruction, these grim dancers of death hurl themselves against walls or brutally bash their heads together, long samurai knives held menacingly. To conclude this hybrid performance, Neubauten are filmed in the open amidst the sounds of what appears to be Tokyo's traffic. A competition appears to take place between the sound of the band and the sounds of trucks and buses, and other city noises. In fact, it is impossible to discern which is which. None the less, *Halber Mensch* presents a *Gesamtkunstwerk* of visual and aural wonder that emphasizes Neubauten's twin themes of destruction and chaos. Sensations of awe and disquiet are invoked by this performance, and these are closer to a 'negative pleasure' associated with the sublime experience (Kant, 1978a, p. 91) than to the sensation of 'disinterested delight' experienced with the 'beautiful' (Kant, 1978a, p. 50).

The themes of destruction and chaos are seen to permeate much of Neubauten's work, some of it impromptu, as when during a performance in Los

Angeles an onstage fire destroyed all the props for the second act (Maeck, 1989, p. 68). Some of it is not so impromptu, as during the *Concert for Machinery and Voice* at the London Institute of Contemporary Arts (1984), which was a one-off affair with concrete mixers, chain saws, cement breakers, jack hammers and pneumatic drills. It climaxed in a noisy crescendo which saw the band attempting to drill or break their way through the stage, the crowd throwing part of the sound system into the path of destruction and the ICA staff trying to maintain order. When the concert was brought to a premature close, a hardcore group of about thirty spectators refused to leave the hall and attempted to break up the stage. According to Neubauten, things started going wrong when a pounding machine malfunctioned and 'rationale went out of the window'. They attempted to get below to the tunnels running under the stage, which lead to Whitehall and Buckingham Palace: 'we decided to stop when it looked like someone might get hurt' (Maeck, 1989, p. 49). However, unfortunately the audience did not. Stevo (of the record label Some Bizarre), their producer at that time, remembers that they were sent a bill for three thousand pounds, which he refused to pay, since the ICA 'had booked a creative ... conceptual performance of destruction' (Maeck and Schenkel, 1993).

Bargeld has said, 'the reason I want to play live is because I want to lose control to experience something outside my normal consciousness. When I walk off I want to feel different than I did before. That's ritual I would say' (Dery, 1990, p. 10). Certainly a ritualistic performance can be seen in Neubauten's recording of *Dürstiges Tier* (*Thirsty Animal*) (1982), which consisted of Bargeld's body being miked, while his chest was pummelled by another band member. The blows were necessarily heavy to be picked up in the recording. To this was added the sound of meat being sliced: 'I tried to smash a bone with a sledge hammer but it didn't work, then I dabbled in the innards but you hardly hear it on the record' (N. U. Unruh, quoted by Maeck, 1989, p. 59). On this track it is not obvious what is being listened to – as Bargeld mentions, 'How do you mike up dead meat?' – but the experiment does have an effect on the record and the resultant sound 'leaves you with an undeniably weird, queasy feeling' (Maeck, 1989, p. 87).

According to Foucault, 'it would not appear to be possible ... to define a statement by the grammatical characteristics of the sentence' (1972, p. 82). As the above performance suggests, the emphasis in much liminal performance is on the intersemiotic: that is, narratives inscribed by the body which present a free association of themes. How does a primarily linguistic analysis account for sound created by punching an amplified chest, or the sounds produced by such percussion instruments as animal bones, hearts and meat? This is where Lyotard's theorization of the differend proves somewhat deficient. For how can a sublime based primarily on the incommensurability of phrase regimes[11] judge such non-linguistic significatory practices as those presented in the performances of Einstürzende Neubauten?

Another Neubauten performance, documented by Don Watson for *New Musical Express*, took place in a 'barn-like building on the outskirts of Vienna'. He writes:

> Neubauten ... Alternately mocking and arousing the audience ... cut through to the most basic instincts; fear, panic and excitement ... a 20 foot high petrol flame erupts, licking up the side of the speaker stack. ... Had it been a planned theatrical trick, it might have been a cheap shot. With Neubauten there's always the tantalising suggestion of real danger involved. (Watson, 1985, p. 34)

In *Liebeslieder* (1993), a video documenting Neubauten's performance history, Bargeld as a Faustian character recites a *'Prolog'* ('Prologue'). Originally from Neubauten's album *Haus der Lüge* (House of Lies, 1989), the *'Prolog'* is an internal dialogue between the two sides of the brain. The first tantalizingly advocates a poetry of impossible demands and desires to which the second, the voice of reason, counters with, 'we could, but ...'

> Meint ihr nicht:
> wir könnten unsere Züge
> zigtausendfach, in falschen Farben
> weltbewegend scheinen lassen ...
>
> Wir könnten, aber –
>
> Don't you think:
> that we could make our images appear
> – a thousand-fold, in false colours –
> earth-shattering ...
>
> We could, but –

'Die Interimsliebenden' ('The Interimlovers'), the opening song of *Tabula Rasa* (1992) and a videoed performance on *Liebeslieder*, is a whirlwind tour through Einstürzende Neubauten's thirteen-year history in the shape of compressed and compacted digital samples taken from their various releases. These traces can be seen to 'inscribe' difference and problematize identity and origin (see Derrida, 1992a, p. 32). Moreover, the lyrics are riddled with puns that play on the band's ambiguous alliance with chaos.[12] The band members are filmed in a studio playing with various forms of unconventional musical instruments, such as road drills and heavy chains, together with more conventional musical instruments, such as guitars. Interspersed with the studio scenes are filmed footage of disparate imagery. 'Die Interimsliebenden' is far more refined than the earlier performances; instead of loud noise and dangerous stunts, more conventional theatrical devices are utilized. For example, Bargeld intones the lyrics of the song with overly large gestures and mannerisms, almost reminiscent of Japanese Kabuki or Noh actors.

> in ihren gemeinsamen Mund
> lebt ein Kolibri
> mit jedem seiner Flügeischläge
> dafur das Auge viel zu träge
> Kulturen erbluhen und vergehen
> ganze kontinente untergehen
> hier gibt es keine harmiosen Worte
> alle viel zu gross
> Und das einfachste Beispiel explodiert
> in 10^{14} für
> die Interimsliebenden

> In their communal mouth
> lives a colibri
> with each humming beat of its wings
> too swift for the eye to see
> cultures flourish and perish
> whole continents vanish
> here are no harmless words
> all by far too large
> an example most simple explodes
> in 10^{14} for
> the interimlovers

Bargeld claims that he writes with 'the strange systematics of form'. The creation of this form takes up most of the time. He continues, 'I make up lists of words ... metaphors or structures. ... I put all this stuff together and get a complete form. .... For me it is just a provocation against the individualism and the romantic notion of writing. As a person, I always wanted to vanish behind the words, to disintegrate' (Maeck and Schenkel, 1992). This could almost be a parody of the Kantian concept of the 'purposiveness without purpose' of art (Kant, 1978a, p. 69), together with a problematization of the authority and activity of the author (Foucault, 1972, p. 50). It also questions the origin of the 'work of art', since, as is apparent from the above quote, this particular work is merely another signifier in an endless game of signification and 'dissemination' (Derrida, 1981a, p. 25), being 'unconcealed', in the Heideggerian sense, by its 'happening' (Heidegger, 1972b, pp. 72–3). Moreover, this focus on a certain 'shift-shape' form, pointing only indirectly to content, is a central feature of liminal performance.

'Wüste' ('Desert') is also a track from *Tabula Rasa*. It was originally recorded at the time of the Gulf War for the Canadian dance company La La Human Steps. For *Liebeslieder* it was performed in a television studio. To the rhythm of a special machine which slowly pumps out sand, flames leap out from what appears to be a hand-held welding tool. The whole *mise-en-scène* is bathed in a blue light, providing very formal imagery. Bargeld, dressed in his usual black, and appearing quite reserved in comparison to previous performances, but still evoking the image of a vampire-poet, provides the lyrics

> mir war
> als hieltest du
> in den Armen mich
> und·tausend Distein
> sag mir was das war
>
> mene, mene tekel, upharsin
>
> it was
> as if you held
> me in your arms
> and a thousand thistles
> tell me what that was
>
> mene, mene tekel, upharsin

The last line of the song is recited in a high-pitched Gregorian chant.[13] Another performance on *Liebeslieder* that presents multilingual lyrics is 'Salamandrina':

> Salamandrina Salamandrina Salamandrina
> not muses, fairies, elves, sylphs, nymphs or mermaids
> for you the moths I wish to understand
> you they just cannot withstand
> for you I am a mere phoenix, my history well-known
> only once again, never, never nothing new learnt . . .

IN GIRUM IMUS NOCTE ET CONSUMIMUR IGNI
at night we wander around in circles
and are consumed by fire

This provides the same formal imagery as 'Wüste', the scene being again bathed in a blue light. Interspersed between a strong vocal tenor are the unearthly screams of some small tortured animal, which creates an interesting juxtaposition, since Bargeld is by no means a small person.

Bargeld claims that Neubauten 'play to the edge of what is possible' (Watson, 1985, p. 34) and 'work with song structures in order to dissolve them' (Owen, 1985, p. 37). Their heterogeneous performances, in keeping with much of the liminal, often appear complicit with what they seek to dismantle.[14] Neubauten's multilingual lyrics can be seen as an attempt to decentre the language chauvinism that has developed in Germany since reunification. According to Bargeld, 'The point I am trying to make is that German culture is gone. We hate our culture and our language. All our philosophy and music was appropriated by the Nazis. ... We cannot redeem that tradition. We can only re-invent' (Laddish and Dippé, 1993, p. 95). However, Neubauten ultimately take no responsibility for the 'words, phrases and bits of sentences' that form their lyrics, since 'they just came out and because they sprang from an unknown source they had to be ok'. Since, according to Bargeld, there is no German tradition that 'one could refer to without feeling guilty', 'I have no song tradition as such. That is not a shortcoming but a strength ... not having this tradition gives me a kind of creativity. Like a Demiurg (creator of worlds) I can create the love song afresh according to my ideas' (Maeck and Schenkel, 1993).

The neo-gothic liminal epitomized in the above works appears to be centred on a Nietzschean 'will to power' developed by 'dissimulation' and the 'art of experiment' (Nietzsche, 1973, p. 54). The performance demonstrates the Dionysian features of disruption, immediacy and excess, all quintessential aesthetic features of liminal performance, and provides a scene of aesthetic intervention producing an immediate effect, though perhaps *indirectly*, on the social and political, in as much as it questions the cultural beliefs that sustain those systems.

Given the flexible grid of theoretical tools and details of liminal practice that has been discussed in the above performances (theatre, film and music), I am now in a position to provide a summary description of liminal performance as an emerging 'genre'. Chapter 7 offers such a description.

Notes

1. According to Norman Cook, 'Sweet Tee's "Its my Beat" features James Brown's "Funky Drummer", while Run DMC have cut Bob James' "Mardi Gras" and had their huge hit with a version of Aerosmith's "Walk This Way"' (1987, p. 25).

2. Gould explains that two Australians initally built the first commercial sampler in 1979, the 'Fairlight CMI'. The Fairlight was extremely expensive when it was first exhibited, and no one could quite work out what to do with it. Eventually it began selling to electronic music studios and rich liberal musicians like Peter Gabriel and Laurie Anderson, who gave mainstream pop consumers their first encounter with sampled sound. Other instruments followed, such as the Synclavier and Emulator, and prices soon began to fall, with most Japanese companies soon adding mid-price samplers to their range. Musicians such as Frank Zappa were the first to make albums entirely constructed from samples (Gould, 1987, p. 14).

3. Baudrillard claims that the society of 'simulation' exerts a 'cool' seduction which can lead only to apathy (1979, p. 221). However, the creative potential of digital sampling would seem to contradict this assertion.

4. According to Curtis Mantronik, creator of the first completely sampled album: 'It's real easy to do a sample, real easy to put something in a machine and sample it, but to make a good sample, make it work, it takes something else' (Gray, 1987, p. 29).

5. For a more detailed discussion of 'subject positions', see Foucault (1972, p. 52).

6. For Foucault, 'Commentary limited the hazards of discourse through the action of an identity taking the form of repetition and sameness. The author principle limits this same chance element through the action of an identity whose form is that of individuality and the I' (1972, p. 222).

7. In 'Limited Inc abc', Derrida discusses the formation of identity (1976, p. 190).

8. The drug was first used as a pharmaceutical sex aid to help couples who had problems with sexual intercourse. It appears to combine aspects of mescaline and amphetamine. The main problem is that no one knows what the effects of long-term usage of the drug are or whether there could be any delayed reactions. There have also been several reported deaths following its use. Other problems associated with it are morning-after sickness and recurring nightmares (O'Hagan, 1988, p. 47).

9. See Nietzsche (1956, p. 97): Dionysian art 'does not ... represent appearance, but the will directly'.

10. Bargeld claims in an interview with Laddish and Dippé (1993, p. 91) that the

term 'industrial' is no longer used except 'in America. The whole non-existent genre was conceived by your record industry as a marketing ploy.'

11. See Lyotard (1988, p. xii).

12. With the help of computerized technology, triple entendres and visual puns are inserted in the artwork of *Tabula Rasa*, which is from a Renaissance *stilleben* (still-life) by Ambrosius Bosschaert the younger (see Laddish and Dippé, 1993, p. 91).

13. Mene, mene, tekel, upharsin (Aramaic: numbered, numbered, weighed, divided).

14. See Owens (1980b, pp. 79–80) for a discussion of 'complicity' in contemporary art.

7

Conclusion: liminal performance

Liminal performance, a description of a range of experimental performative types which I have tentatively assembled under this heading, is an emerging genre that has surfaced only in the past few decades. Quintessentially, it combines recent digitized technology with a *corporeal* prominence, and, in many cases, the quest for the almost primordial. Paradigmatic liminal acts are: in theatre, the hybridized performances of Robert Wilson's operatic 'theatre of images', Pina Bausch's *Tanztheater*, the 'synthetic fragments' of Heiner Müller's *Hamletmachine* and the 'social sculptures' of the Viennese Actionists; in film, the 'painterly' aesthetics of Greenaway's *Prospero's Books*, transgressing borders with Wender's and Handke's *Der Himmel über Berlin/Wings of Desire*, the liminal politics of Jarman's *Edward II* and the limits of fragmentation in von Trier's *Europa/Zentropa*; and in music, the digitized performance of sampled music and the neo-gothic sound of Einstürzende Neubauten and Nick Cave and The Bad Seeds.

All liminal works confront, offend or unsettle. However, unlike traditional avant-garde performance, the liminal does not set itself up as an opposing structure to dominant ideologies. In fact, it appears at times to be complicit with mainstream trends. Nevertheless, it does display a parodic, questioning, deconstructive mode which presents a resistance, even when individual performances, such as Greenaway's *Prospero's Books*, because of their popularity, appear in danger of being appropriated by the mainstream. The liminal performs to the edge of the possible, a scene of immediate aesthetic intervention with an indirect effect on the political. As such, the liminal mirrors and is an experimental extension of our contemporary social and cultural ethos.

Liminal performances are hybridized and intertextual, and share common quasi-generic aesthetic features, such as heterogeneity, indeterminacy, self-reflexiveness, eclecticism, fragmentation, a certain 'shift-shape style' and a repetitiveness that produces not sameness but difference. Depending on the performance medium, varying emphasis is placed on different traits. As I have shown, liminal theatre displays distinctive aesthetic features, among them a blurring and collapsing of the barriers between traditional theatre, dance, music and art. Examples of this are the hybridized performances of Robert Wilson's operatic 'theatre of images' and Pina Bausch's *Tanztheater*. A distinctive aesthetic trait central to liminal film is the utilization of the latest media technology. Digitized high definition television is manipulated, for instance, by the 'painterly' aesthetics of Greenaway's *Prospero's Books*. Similarly, the introduction of new musical technology, which has taken the form of the digital sampler, must be regarded as a quasi-generic feature of liminal music. The neo-gothic exhibits an alternative form of this sub-genre. Characteristics of this music are the disruptive or tormented lyrics demonstrated in the overtly theatrical performance of Nick Cave and the utilization of diverse non-traditional or unconventional sound instruments in the *Gesamtkunstwerk* of Einstürzende Neubauten.

As I have argued, performative theory has proven deficient as a means of addressing the liminal. Aristotle's linear 'theatre of illusion', Brecht's political didactic theorization and Artaud's fixed essentialism are unable satisfactorily to address the aesthetics of this performance.[1] Similarly, current performative theories are equally ineffectual. In the absence of any effective critical tools with which to interpret such works, I have surveyed traditional aesthetics and current critical theory for an appropriate analysis. Kant is central to this theorization, since we cannot escape the structure of complex judgements. In reviewing aesthetic theorization, I have argued that the aesthetic is not a separate sphere but is a perspective that encompasses the whole of actuality. Kant tells us that the 'final analysis' of any concept, except formal ones, is always doubtful due to its inability to 'stand within safe limits' (1911, pp. 584–5). Therefore, it is impossible to argue, in any rigorous sense, that the aesthetic can ever be any kind of delimiting closure.

Aesthetic judgements for Kant are the result of 'reflective' and not of 'determinant' reason (1978a, p. 36), which means that when we make an aesthetic judgement, rules are created that can in no way be determined beforehand (1978a, p. 5). In other words, judgements have to be continually revised on each and every occasion, while no set judgement can be sustained (1978b, p. 35). This has exciting consequences for the liminal, since it is a scene of immediate and localized aesthetic intervention. By implication, it also has ramifications for any other judgement that must operate in the absence of closure.

Following Kant, Lyotard has emphasized the importance of the aesthetic as a prototype for all such judgements. Reflective reason is not invoked by Kant in the third *Critique* merely in its 'heuristic capacity'; instead, it invents its own principle. If the third *Critique* unifies the field of philosophy, it does so not by primarily presupposing an objective finality of nature but by revealing, by means of the aesthetic, the reflective method of 'thinking that is at work in the critical text as a whole' (Lyotard, 1991, pp. 2–8).

A retheorization of Kant's sublime is crucial to an analysis of liminal performance, since every performance strives for and some succeed in presenting the unpresentable. Lyotard has premised a revision of the Kantian sublime, primarily from a linguistic perspective (1988, 1991). For Lyotard, the silence that Auschwitz imposes is a sign for everyone. Signs are not, in their reference and signification, validatable by cognition; instead, they imply that something that should be put into phrases cannot be phrased (1993, p. 56). In his interpretation of the Kantian sublime, Lyotard has provided vital knowledge in this area. However, when tested against such phenomena as the liminal, Lyotard's linguistic bias lacks a satisfactory account of non-verbal signification. Given the importance of the *corporeal* in this kind of performance, Lyotard's 'linguistic turn' needs to be adjusted to allow for an intersemiotic analysis: that is, a significatory practice which includes but also goes *beyond* language. As I have argued from the perspective of liminal performance, it is only by such a broader analysis that a more appropriate interpretation of the liminal can be achieved which would allow for the prominence of the 'body'. And it is by such means that the sublime, which exceeds the linguistic and is 'an outrage to the imagination' (Kant, 1978a, pp. 90–1), can be presented in and through such performances as those of the liminal.

Hence, the 'direct art' of the Viennese Actionists requires the immediate spontaneity of the event itself, in which the naked body appears before the audience and, therefore, in a social context. Here an attempt is made to retrieve a chthonic identity by direct corporeal insertion into the creative act. In this sense, identity is supplemented by the body itself, thus compensating for a perceived lack. *Tanztheater*, too, derives everything from the *gestus*, itself strongly related to the actions of the body. The principle of presentation is the everyday process of understanding through 'body language', a process that is translated on stage by a distinctive corporeal semiotic. Bausch's performances become literally a 'writing of the body itself' (Derrida, 1978a, p. 191); and because the bodily gestures on stage originate directly in everyday life, art and everyday life become merged. This distinctive aspect of dance, the transmission of body signals, opens the way to defining a reality determined by corporeal conventions. *Einstein on the Beach*, with its eclecticism and mixing of codes, likewise produces signification mainly through the semiotics of gesture: kinetic, visual, aural, haptic, gravitational, proximic and tactile. Even the published 'text' for *Einstein on the Beach* is non-verbal; the pictographic text proceeds from and extends Wilson's ambition to offer a spectacle that cannot be contained in any verbal language alone.

Liminal performance demonstrates a need for a new form of aesthetic interpretation, given that beauty and harmony are not appropriate descriptions of liminal sensibilities. Rather, the exciting or unsettling are closer to the mark, nearer to sensations evoked by the sublime. The Kantian sublime produces feelings of 'negative pleasure', which prefigure the sensations of disquiet and discomfort produced by the liminal (Kant, 1978a, p. 91). Works such as Pina Bausch's performative dreamscape, which is filled with disparate images, movements and objects, and has been referred to as 'an image' that is 'a thorn in our eye', point to the fact that the liminal provokes and unsettles the audience (Müller, 1984, p. 30). Klaus Maeck, commenting on Einstürzende Neubauten's recording of *Dürstiges Tier* (*Thirsty Animal*), a performance that consists of the combinatory tones of the pummelling of a human body and the sound of meat being sliced, notes 'the disturbing quality of sound' that produces in us 'an undeniably weird, queasy feeling' (Maeck, 1989, p. 87).

Nietzsche's writings have been of considerable value in interpreting liminal performance. In order to enhance his species, the Nietzschean 'man' had to develop his unconditional 'will to power' by, among other things, 'his powers of invention and dissimulation' and 'the art of experiment' (Nietzsche, 1973, p. 54). This insistence on free creativity, invention and experimentation is central to liminal heterogeneity and indeterminacy. Such Dionysian features as immediacy, disruption and excess (Nietzsche, 1956) correspond to certain dominant traits in this kind of performance. The *Gesamtkunstwerke* of Einstürzende Neubauten have been described as 'conceptual' performances of 'destruction' (Maeck and Schenkel, 1993). *Halber Mensch* must be read as a cacophony of the sounds of chaos and destruction, climaxing in the appearance of the dance troupe Byakko Sha. These demonic dancers of death hurl themselves against walls or brutally bash their heads together, long samurai knives held menacingly. The digitized 'rave' performance likewise recreates a Dionysian ritual, with smoke machines billowing, providing a *mise-en-scène* reminiscent of the primeval swamp. The metronomic beat of sampled music and the flicker of the strobe light combine into one powerful audio-visual effect and everywhere arms are raised, pointing to some pagan deity.

Nietzsche's perspectival attitude, which led to a practice of *parole de fragment* (Hartman, 1970, pp. 97–103), is correspondingly mirrored in the fragmentation and hybridization of the liminal. Much hybrid theatre shatters traditional theatrical illusions. Bausch's work is separated from traditional dance by her particular type of realism, which avoids seamless impressions and standardized notions of beauty. No distinction is made between rehearsal and performance;

rather, the emphasis is on the process of adaptation and on exposing the dramatic process itself. Dance theatre destroys theatrical illusion *per se*. Heiner Müller's theatre, with its disseminated style of 'synthetic fragments', likewise destroys the illusion of theatre (Müller, 1984, p. 17). Seemingly disparate scenes are combined without a coherent plot to form an assemblage of intertextual fragments. The fragmentation of an event emphasizes its process-character, preventing the production's disappearance in the product, which is simply marketed, and turning the presentation of the event into an experimental experience in which the audience can participate in a productive way. As in Müller's *Hamletmachine*, liminal intertextuality continually disrupts the continuity of the text.

Liminal artists are 'ruthlessly, bare of pretext', their work 'is an instinctive imposing of forms' and they foreground the instinctual and emotive (Nietzsche, 1956, pp. 219–20). In *Tanztheater*, words are fragmentary and blurred, and only very seldom do they serve as communication or provide a basis for mutual understanding. Instead, dance theatre relies on the transmission of primarily emotive experiences. Likewise, Wilson in his 'theatre of images' points to an intuitive, non-verbal, non-rational mode of interpretation, and Müller, in comparable fashion, no longer tolerates 'a discursive dramaturgy'. Instead, the liminal can only work with 'inundation' (Müller, quoted by Fehervary, 1976, p. 96).

Liminal performance shares with Nietzsche the delegitimation of authority. Like Nietzsche, liminal performance undermines the notion of grammar in order to get rid of authority (Nietzsche, 1990, p. 48). In contrast to traditional performance, there is a loss of authority, together with a decline of the genius of the artistic producer, though not their disappearance. One consequence of this is a liberation of aesthetic response. The spectators' new freedom includes their emancipation from the specific textual interpretation of directors and actors, or what Wilson calls the 'fascist directing and acting' of Western theatre today (Dyer, 1985, p. A4). In *Hamletmachine*, Hamlet is beset by nausea at the privilege of the intellectual who ignores societal injustices under the auspices of 'reason'. In the context of Müller's liminal aesthetics, this problematizes the privileged author, his or her authorial activity and authority, and hence is a denial of Müller himself. Paradoxically, though, this symbolic rejection of privilege is a possibility that is itself open only to the privileged.

Liminal performance both illustrates and qualifies the hermeneutic perspective of Heidegger's aesthetic assumptions (1971b), which leads to the 'unconcealment' of 'truth' in the 'work of art' by way of a 'happening'. The recurrence of certain images in *Einstein on the Beach* implies a certain development, a 'happening' in process (Heidegger, 1971b, p. 57), its 'hermeneutic' situation revealing new insights at each stage of that development (Heidegger, 1978, pp. 192–3). This liminal aspect comes to the fore in the sequence of 'train' images, which are presented in a reductive order, each one becoming progressively less 'train-like'. Similarly, the Viennese Actionists, by their direct corporeal insertion in the creative act, strive to 'disclose' a chthonic identity by way of a 'happening' or 'event': with each turn of the interpretive spiral or 'hermeneutic helix' (Ruthrof, 1992, p. 141), new insights are revealed.

For a generic description of the liminal, Foucault's theorization of 'discursive formation' is equally useful, in that it explains how alternative discourses emerge, are delimited and specified.[2] Liminal film, for example, is usually screened in localized arthouses rather than in mainstream theatres, attracting a smaller audience and thereby producing alternative performative 'sites'. The excitement of the rave revolves around its underground connotations, revealed in its alternative performance locales, which challenge the dominant 'institutional sites' of performance (Foucault, 1972, p. 51).

Foucault's conjecture on *énonciation*, the positioning of the subject, is of similar significance (1972, pp. 51–5). In liminal performance, subjectivity is up for grabs. It is a *vacant* position filled by different individuals at different times. Thus, *Prospero's Books* places the audience in the same position as Prospero, as the conventions of movie-making are bared in a self-conscious way, thereby problematizing subject positions and challenging who is speaking and who is allowed to speak. Liminal film, while being stylized in the extreme, challenges spectators' expectations; no resolutions are offered and its contradictions are not really resolved. This lack of closure requires active identification and therefore a high degree of audience participation. Showing the formation process, not just of subjectivity but of narrativity and visual representation, is fundamental. This liminal self-reflexivity calls attention to the acts of production and reception of the film itself. In this sense, *Europa/Zentropa* is fertile on metacinema, its constantly contradictory discourse foregrounding the issues of the ideological construction of subjectivity and of the way that history can be known.

Liminal performance can also be seen as a critical practice of Derrida's deconstructive postulations. For Derrida, metaphysical complicity cannot be given up without also giving up the critique of the complicity that is being argued against (1978c, p. 281). The liminal parallels this, as many of the works appear complicit with what they seek to deconstruct (Owens, 1980b, pp. 79–80). In Derek Jarman's filmic works we are faced with performances that are parodic, metacinematic and questioning, and that in many ways appear to be in collusion with what they wish to dismantle. Similarly, the Actionists' apparent complicity with dominant means of media representation would seem to be at odds with their actions. Einstürzende Neubauten, in working 'with song structures in order to dissolve them', often appear complicit with what they seek to deconstruct (Owen, 1985, p. 37).

Derrida's notion of 'undecidables', such as the 'mark' (1978c, 1981a), has also proved productive in the analysis of the liminal, since it shows the formation and deformation processes of pure identity and origin. Digitized sampling is exemplary of this, for where a musical performance has been stored on a computer disc, the 'recording' can be made either before or after the 'original' performance. What is recorded is a set of instructions for recreating the original performance, rather than a transcription of that performance. Therefore, the 'recording' is an original performance, it is literally 'reproduced again' and not 'represented'. This shatters the distinction between 'live' and 'recorded' performance, as well as that between 'original' and 'reproduction'. In addition, since a new performance can be electronically 'cloned' from an existing one, digital sampling raises an issue that is unprecedented: that is, the commodification of 'performance itself' (Auslander, 1992, p. 31). In cases where the computer is programmed to 'play' an instrument directly, the 'recording' actually precedes the event recorded, and the automated performance is the 'live' performance, deconstructing concepts of both live and recorded performance and so bringing into question traditional notions of origin and identity. Each search for an origin leads only to edges, such as, 'différance', 'margin', 'supplement', 'mark' and 'trace' (Derrida, 1981a, p. 25).

The elucidation of the formative process of pure identity and origin has implications for generic construction of the liminal, where barriers and boundaries are continually being stretched and transgressed (Derrida, 1977, 1980). In *Der Himmel über Berlin/Wings of Desire*, allusions to Rilke and the German literary canon occur in a film that features a contemporary American character actor best know for his work in a popular television detective series. By focusing on angels, the film inevitably evokes links with the genre of films that focus on relationships between spiritual beings and mortals. Correspondingly, in *Europa/Zentropa*, the blending of the fictive and historically actual in the film signals the spectator to beware of institutionalized genre boundaries, which are structurally analogous to social borderlines, and so both are called to account (Hutcheon, 1990, p. 131).

Liminal music likewise demonstrates a new hybrid style. The boundaries of music, art, performance and installation are blurred. Music performance becomes dance theatre, which becomes performance and so on, undermining accepted boundaries and definitions. *Halber Mensch* is such a hybrid performance, demonstrating as it does a *Gesamtkunstwerk* of visual and aural stimuli, emphasizing Einstürzende Neubauten's twin themes of destruction and chaos. The 'rave' similarly produces highly stylized images of a *Gesamtkunst-*

werk of a new kind. Such blurring of the boundaries of performance points to a more general problematization of genres. New critical tools, such as the 'undecidables', help to explain how genres are formed and how unstable these formations are. At the same time, it is not possible to jettison the notion of genre altogether, since the stipulation of an 'open genre' makes demands which neither heterogeneity nor the emphasis on the local is able to meet. This is why I have argued that a work of art cannot be identified unless it carries the mark of some genre. There can be 'no genreless text ... yet, such participation never amounts to belonging' (Derrida, 1980, p. 112). This applies pre-eminently to liminal performance.

The employment of wide, jarring metaphors is a further central characteristic of the liminal (Derrida, 1982b, pp. 219–20). In Nick Cave's performance, the colourful and figurative use of language and the juxtaposition of metaphors evoke surreal images of sex, blood, violence and death. This mixture of wide metaphor produces a synaesthetic effect caused by the interplay of various mental sense-impressions. In Bausch's *Tanztheater*, similar tropical and figurative juxtapositions create inclusive, jarring metaphors. They unsettle the audience by frustrating their expectations of any simple interpretation, and in so doing they create a new kind of synaesthetic effect.

At the same time, liminal performance aims at the displacement of the borders between art and theory. The liminal suggests that the aesthetic resists theoretical closure from a space that is not entirely aesthetic, and even granting autonomy to the aesthetic is a way of limiting or 'framing' it.[3] This shows that there are important analogies between the liminal and recent theorizing, since much of this kind of performance seemingly opposes an autonomous aesthetic sphere. Thus Bausch's *Tanztheater* can be seen as a process rather than a product that provides a certain merging of the aesthetic with everyday life in resisting closure from within a place that is not entirely aesthetic. Einstürzende Neubauten, since their inception as an 'industrial band' in the early eighties, have likewise attempted to stretch the boundaries of their hybrid music. They have long since dissolved the boundaries between art and everyday life, and so problematized the notion of aesthetic purity. Their aim is to force 'people to keep redefining the boundaries' of music, art and performance (Bohn, 1989, p. 51).

By exploring the characteristic features of the liminal we also note the interesting phenomenon that its practice can function as a critique of theoretical positions. This applies particularly to Baudrillard, who argues for 'an aesthetic determinacy of things'. However, for Baudrillard, when everything is aesthetic, 'art itself disappears' (1992a, p. 10). He believes that new forms of technology and information have become central to a shift from a productive to a reproductive social order in which simulations and models increasingly constitute the world, so that distinctions between the real and appearance are being erased. According to Baudrillard, individuals are 'seduced' by the hyperreal, obscene 'spectacles' of 'cool' media objects, which produce an 'entropic inertia' (1979, p. 32). On this account, this must inevitably lead to the 'hyperreality' of art as it finds only its 'own empty essence' (1988, p. 187). By contrast, liminal performance suggests that this indicates an increased potentiality for new artistic creativity rather than an emptiness, and instead of a 'scene of nihilism' indicates a redefinition of 'meaning'.

This is supported by the observation that the latest multimedia technology is employed in much hybrid theatre. *Einstein on the Beach* was a huge musical undertaking, involving state of the art sound and lighting technology as well as sets to rival the biggest touring rock acts. Bausch, in her use of montage, appropriates various kinds of media technology, such as theatre, film and pantomime, in order to make her statements. Utilizing the latest media technology was equally important to the Viennese Actionists. Many of their actions were conceived only for film owing to their excessive radicality, which prevented them from being performed live for fear of arrest. The use of multimedia technology in liminal theatre causes a *Verfremdungseffekt*, which distances the spectator and prevents identification, in favour of awareness. Montage enhances this awareness with its concurrent formation of a (hyper)reality based on the juxtaposition of separate situations. However, unlike Brechtian defamilarization, which is founded upon the possibility of representing reality, multimedia liminal performance does not attempt to represent actuality, but rather, in presenting some kind of reality, questions its condition. And while not aiming for a transformation of society, it puts 'perceptive strategies into play' that allow for the decoding of that reality (Féral, 1987, p. 471). In this sense, liminal performance is also a political enterprise.

A distinctive aesthetic trait central to liminal film is the use of state of the art media technology. Digitized high definition television was successfully used by Peter Greenaway in his production of *Prospero's Books*. High definition television achieves better resolution, higher contrast and a wider range of colours than have been available to traditional genres. *Europa/Zentropa*, another liminal film utilizing new media technology, mixes techniques from both Hollywood and MTV. These stylistic embellishments include the juxtaposition and layering of colour on black and white images (accomplished with rear screen projection and use of multiple lenses) and skilfully layered montages.

The introduction of new technology, which has taken the form of the digital sampler, is also a distinctive aesthetic feature of liminal music. Through digital sampling, musicians can either incorporate parts of another's recorded music into their own or build a completely new performance from information sampled from another musician. By 'playing with the pieces' (Baudrillard, 1984b, p. 24), they create new hybrid aesthetic forms. Thus, deliberate plagiarism has become another major characteristic of new music production, which creates innovative heterogeneous styles and at the same time questions the legitimation of the old ones. Consequently, digital sampling clearly challenges most of the traditional concepts of authorship and textual ownership, shoring up the utopian belief that all are free to use the cultural environment as they wish.

The use of digital technology is foregrounded in much of the liminal (and in the postmodern), not only as an object of the technical but as a recognizable style. In fact, it can be argued to be the syntax of late 'secularization and an ironic fulfilment of Kant's project of determining the limits of concept formation' (Ruthrof, 1990, p. 185). The digital as a discourse cannot convert phenomena directly, but depends on a preceding production of meaning by non-digital technology. Thus, the digital sampler, which is dedicated to processing sound information, can either emulate conventional musical instruments or create new sounds by manipulating sections of music. Digitized high definition television likewise produces its meaning by transforming visual imagery. The digital, like all formal systems, has no semantics unless one is added, which means that its digitally processed contents require different habits of reading that can accommodate thinking in terms of indifferent differentiation. This, of course, clashes with the complex value hierarchization of traditional culture.

This is of fundamental significance for the role of the digital in liminal performance. Many traits of the digital, such as fragmentation, dehistoricization, 'dedifferentiation' and repetition, are mirrored in the liminal.[4] Not surprisingly, commodification finds support in the syntax of the liminal and digital alike: that is, in its creation of desire, satisfaction of that desire, mobility, its local and locatable surfaces and its dehistoricization of history. However, although, major record companies, for instance, still provide the music-making technology required for digital sampling and therefore provide the link between digital sampling and commodification, the real challenge of this liminal performance concerns its aesthetic possibilities and its heterogeneous infinity of sounds. For the potentiality of digital sampling lies in the production of an 'ahistorical amnesia', together with an 'infinity of new musical meanings' (Gray, 1987, p. 29). By the severing of some sound from its origins for individual sampling purposes, history not only is being created through collage, quotation and pastiche, but the hybridized fragments are, as a result, remotivated with new meanings. Therefore, I would argue that the emergence of new forms of technology, like those employed in such practices as the liminal, does not, as Baudrillard argues, necessarily lead to 'catastrophe' for the subject (1988, p. 192). Rather, it is part of an innovative project that creates new aesthetic styles, which demand active participation from their audience, thereby creating the potential for social performers to become non-'docile bodies' of non-performance (Foucault, 1986, pp. 135–69).

Clearly, such works as liminal performance demonstrate the need for a more sophisticated theorization than is available at present, a thinking that can address the liminal's new heterogeneous aesthetic criteria. As I have shown, the Viennese Actionists in their performances attacked the essence of representation itself. Their object was a form of catharsis by means of abreaction induced by the demonstrative, gestural act of overcoming illusion. However, unlike traditional notions of catharsis, it was not intended that this would ultimately provide some resolution; rather, the lack of closure of this performance, with its tension between representation of image and immanence of action, between distance and participation and between hierarchy and anarchy, prevented any such resolution from occurring and, as such, indicates a deconstructive process within the work as a whole.

Neo-gothic sound exhibits destructive aesthetics. The main features of this genre are disruptive sounds combined with lyrics which invoke images of passion, death, decay and a certain pursuit of the chthonic. Nick Cave and The Bad Seeds and Einstürzende Neubauten, with their dark, vampirish attire and overtly theatrical gestures, accentuate a certain sardonic humour that parodies rather than merely (re)presents. Unlike traditional aesthetic interpretations, their performances are neither 'beautiful' nor 'harmonious' (Kant, 1978a, p. 60); instead, they 'cut through to the most basic instincts; fear, panic and excitement' (Watson, 1985, p. 34).

Tanztheater, whose experimental mode of presentation is through 'body language', creates a scene of immediate localized aesthetic intervention and, in contrast to pleasing 'universally' (Kant, 1978a, p. 60), requires a new individual ruling for each and every performance.[5] And if Brecht's theatre brought about a 'proper consciousness' through intellectual insight, Bausch's theatre seeks to produce the same with emotive experience. Like Brecht's theatre, her performance derives everything from the *gestus*. However, in this instance, the *gestus* is strongly related to the actions of the body. It neither 'supports nor contrasts something spoken'; rather, it speaks itself (Servos, 1981, p. 440).

The notion of the sublime, even in its most recent redefinition by Lyotard, has proven inadequate as a means to interpret the liminal. Given the importance of corporeal *gesta* in liminal performance, the linguistic emphasis, prevalent in even the latest critical theory, needs to be adjusted. A new textual interpretive method is required, one that would allow for intersemiotic modes of signification and hence for an appropriate explication of such heterosemiotic practices as the liminal.[6]

Notes

1. See Aristotle (1947), Brecht (1964) and Artaud (1958).

2. See Foucault, in particular 'Discursive Formations' (1972, pp. 31–9) and 'The Formation of Objects' (1972, pp. 40–9).

3. Derrida, in 'Parergon', foregrounds the question of framing (1987a, pp. 15–147).

4. According to Scott Lash, 'If modernity and modernism result from a process of differentiation ... *Ausdifferenzierung*, then postmodernism results from a much more recent process of *de*-differentiation or *Entdifferenzierung*. There has been ... de-differentiation ... between literature and theory, between high and popular culture, between what is properly cultural and what is properly social' (1989, pp. 173–4).

5. Lyotard and Rogozinski assume a similar position when they write, 'precisely because it is immediate, because it operates ' "without the mediation of any concept", aesthetic judgement can only claim a subjective universality, the "indeterminate norm of common sense"' (1987, p. 26).

6. In contrast to formal semantics, which is homosemiotic, where meaning is determined by fixed stipulated rules, non-formal semantics is hetero-semiotic, its meaning being constituted from interpretive approximations where various kinds of non-linguistic readings are reconciled by the principle of linguistic expression (see Ruthrof, 1997, pp. 46–7).

References

Adorno, Theodor W. (1981) 'Schoenberg'. In *Prisms*, trans. Samuel Weber and Shierry Weber. Cambridge: MIT Press, pp. 141–72.

Adorno, Theodor W. (1983) *Negative Dialectics*, trans. E. B. Ashton. New York: Continuum.

Althusser, Louis (1971) 'Ideology and Ideological State Apparatuses'. In *Lenin and Philosophy and Other Essays*. New York: Monthly Review Press.

Arens, Katherine (1991) 'Robert Wilson: Is Postmodern Performance Possible?', *Theatre Journal*, **3**(1), 14–40.

Aristotle (1947) *Aristotle on the Art of Poetry*, trans. Lane Cooper. Ithaca: Cornell University Press.

Artaud, Antonin (1958) *The Theater and its Double*, trans. Mary Caroline Richards. New York: Grove Press.

Auslander, Philip (1986) 'Just Be Yourself: Logocentrism and Difference in Performance Theory', *Art and Cinema* (new series), **1**, 10–12.

Auslander, Philip (1992) 'Intellectual Property Meets the Cyborg', *Performing Arts Journal*, **14**(1), 30–42.

Bahti, Timothy (1982) *Toward an Aesthetic of Reception*. Minneapolis: University of Minnesota Press.

Barker, Adam (1991) 'A Tale of Two Magicians', *Sight and Sound*, **1**(2), 26–30.

Baudrillard, Jean (1979) *De la séduction*. Paris: Editions Denoel-Gonthier.

Baudrillard, Jean (1983a) *Simulations*, trans. by Paul Foss and Paul Patton. New York: Semiotext(e).

Baudrillard, Jean (1983b) *In the Shadow of the Silent Majorities*, trans. Paul Foss and Paul Patton. New York: Semiotext(e).

Baudrillard, Jean (1983c) 'The Ecstasy of Communication'. In Hal Foster (ed.), *The Anti-Aesthetic: Essays on Postmodern Culture*, trans. J. Johnston. Washington, DC: Bay Press, pp. 126–34.

Baudrillard, Jean (1984a) 'Clone Story of the Artificial Child', trans. Paul Foss. *Z/G*, **11**, 16–17.

Baudrillard, Jean (1984b) 'Games with Vestiges', trans. Ross Gibson and Paul Patton. *On the Beach,* **5** (Winter), 19–25.

Baudrillard, Jean (1984c) 'On Nihilism', trans. Paul Foss. *On The Beach,* **6** (Spring), 38–9.

Baudrillard, Jean (1985) 'The Masses: The Implosion of the Social in the Media', trans. M. Maclean. *New Literary History,* **16**(3), 577–89.

Baudrillard, Jean (1987) *Forget Foucault and Forget Baudrillard,* trans. Phil Beitchman, Lee Hildreth and Mark Polizzotti. New York: Semiotext(e).

Baudrillard, Jean (1988) 'Fatal Strategies'. In Mark Poster (ed.), *Jean Baudrillard: Selected Writings.* CA: Stanford University Press, pp. 185–206.

Baudrillard, Jean (1990) *Cool Memories,* trans. Chris Turner. London: Verso.

Baudrillard, Jean (1992a) 'Transpolitics, Transsexuality, Transaesthetics', trans. Michel Valentin. In William Stearns and William Chaloupka (eds), *Jean Baudrillard: The Disappearance of Art and Politics.* London: Macmillan, pp. 9–26.

Baudrillard, Jean (1992b) 'Revolution and the End of Utopia', trans. Michel Valentin. In William Stearns and William Chaloupka (eds), *Jean Baudrillard: The Disappearance of Art and Politics.* London: Macmillan, pp. 233–42.

Bausch Pina (chor.) (1978) *Café Müller* (video, 20 May). Wuppertal Dance Company: Suhrkamp Production.

Bazin, André (1967) 'The Myth of Total Cinema', trans. Hugh Gray. In *What is Cinema? Volume 1.* Berkeley: University of California Press, pp. 17–22.

Bell, Richard (producer) (1992) *Nick Cave and The Bad Seeds: Live at the Paradiso* (video). London: Mute Records.

Benjamin, Andrew (ed.) (1989) *The Lyotard Reader.* Oxford: Basil Blackwell.

Benjamin, Walter (1969a) 'The Work of Art in the Age of Mechanical Reproduction'. In Hannah Arendt (ed.), *Illuminations,* trans. Harry Zohn. New York: Schocken, pp. 217–51.

Benjamin, Walter (1969b) 'Theses on the Philosophy of History'. In Hannah Arendt (ed.), *Illuminations,* trans. Harry Zohn. New York: Schocken, pp. 253–265.

Birringer, Johannes (1991) *Theatre, Theory, Postmodernism.* Indianapolis: Indiana University Press.

Bohn, Chris (1989) 'Lets Hear It for the Untergang Show'. In Klaus Maeck (ed.), *Listen with Pain.* Hamburg: Freibank, pp. 50–5.

Brecht, Bertolt (1964) 'The Modern Theatre Is the Epic Theatre'. In J. Willett (ed.), *Brecht on Theatre.* New York: Hill and Wang, pp. 33–42.

Brecht, Bertolt (1966) *Mother Courage and Her Children: A Chronicle of the Thirty Years War.* New York: Grove Publications.

Brecht, Stefan (1978) *The Theatre of Visions: Robert Wilson.* Frankfurt: Suhrkamp.

Brenner, Eva (1991) 'Heiner Müller Directs Heiner Müller', *The Drama Review*, **36**(1), 160–8.

Bürger, Peter (1984) *Theory of the Avant-garde*. trans. Michael Shaw. Minneapolis: University of Minnesota Press.

Burroughs, William (1982) 'The Third Mind'. In *A William Burroughs Reader*. London: Picador.

Calandra, Denis (1983) *New German Dramatists*. New York: Grove Press.

Caldwell, David and Rea, Paul W. (1991) 'Handke's and Wender's Wings of Desire: Transcending Postmodernism', *The German Quarterly*, **64**(1), 46–54.

Carroll, David (1987) *Paraesthetics: Foucault, Lyotard, Derrida*. New York: Methuen.

Cave, Nick (1990) *And the Ass Saw the Angel*. London: Penguin.

Cave, Nick and The Bad Seeds (1988) 'The Mercy Seat', *Tender Prey*. London: Mute Records.

Cave, Nick and The Bad Seeds (1992) *Henry's Dream*. London: Mute Records, C30771.

Chambers, Iain (1987) *Urban Rhythms: Pop Music and Popular Culture*. London: Methuen.

Collins, P. (1992) 'Cult Status for Cave', *West Australian Revue*, 26 November, 4.

Cook, Norman (1987) 'Breaking and Entry', *New Musical Express*, 11 July, 25.

Corrigan, Robert W. (1984) 'The Search for New Endings: The Theatre in Search of A Fix, Part III', *Theatre Journal*, **36**(2), 153–63.

Cosgrove, Stuart (1987a) 'On The Wheels of Steal', *New Musical Express*, 11 July, 24.

Cosgrove, Stuart (1987b) 'House Breaking', *New Musical Express*. 11 July, 26.

Coupe, Stuart (1992) 'The Criminal inside Nick Cave', *X Press Magazine*, 26 November, 42.

Danielsen, S. and Casimir, J. (1990) 'Rap', *Sydney Morning Herald*, 10 August, 1–2.

Derrida, Jacques (1976) *Of Grammatology*, trans. Gayatri Spivak. Baltimore: Johns Hopkins University Press.

Derrida, Jacques (1977) 'Limited Inc abc', trans. Samuel Weber. *Glyph*, **2**, 162–254.

Derrida, Jacques (1978a) 'La parole soufflée'. In *Writing and Difference*, trans. Alan Bass. Chicago: University of Chicago Press, pp. 169–95.

Derrida, Jacques (1978b) 'The Theatre of Cruelty and the Closure of Representation'. In *Writing and Difference*, trans. Alan Bass. Chicago: University of Chicago Press, pp. 232–50.

Derrida, Jacques (1978c) 'Structure, Sign and Play in the Discourse of the Human Sciences'. In *Writing and Difference*, trans. Alan Bass. Chicago: University of Chicago Press, pp. 278–93.

Derrida, Jacques (1980) 'The Law of Genre', trans. Avital Ronell. *Glyph,* **7,** 202–32.

Derrida, Jacques (1981a) *Dissemination,* trans. Barbara Johnson. Chicago: University of Chicago Press.

Derrida, Jacques (1981b) *Positions,* trans. Alan Bass. Chicago: University of Chicago Press.

Derrida, Jacques (1982a) *Margins of Philosophy,* trans. Alan Bass. Chicago: University of Chicago Press.

Derrida, Jacques (1982b) 'White Mythology'. In *Margins of Philosophy,* trans. Alan Bass. Chicago: University of Chicago Press, pp. 209–71.

Derrida, Jacques (1987a) 'Parergon'. In *The Truth in Painting,* trans. Geoff Bennington and Ian McLeod. Chicago: University of Chicago Press, pp. 14–147.

Derrida, Jacques (1987b) 'Restitutions'. In *The Truth in Painting,* trans. Geoff Bennington and Ian McLeod. Chicago: University of Chicago Press, pp. 255–382.

Dery, Mark (1990) 'Meat Blixa Bargeld', *Guitar Play,* **24**(7), 10.

Dreyfus, Herbert L. and Rabinow, Paul (1982) *Michel Foucault: Beyond Structuralism and Hermeneutics.* Chicago: University of Chicago Press.

Dyer, Richard (1985) 'Wilson's LARGER-than-life-works', *The Boston Globe,* 24 February, A4.

Eidsvik, Charles (1988/9) 'Machines of the Invisible: Changes in Film Technology in the Age of Video', *Film Quarterly,* **42**(2), 18–24.

Einstürzende Neubauten (1982) *Dürstige's Tiet.* Berlin: Eigenprod.

Einstürzende Neubauten (1989) *Haus Der Lüge.* London: Some Bizarre.

Einstürzende Neubauten (1992) *Tabula Rasa.* London: Mute Records, 961458-4.

Esslin, Martin (1980) *Brecht: A Choice of Evils.* London: Eyre Methuen.

Feay, Suzi (1991) 'Edward II: Crimes of Fashion', *Time Out,* 16–23 October, 16.

Fehervary, Helen (1976) 'Enlightenment or Entanglement: History and Aesthetics in Bertolt Brecht and Heiner Müller', *New German Critique,* **8,** 80–109.

Féral, Josette (1987) 'Alienation Theory in Multi-media Performance', *Theatre Journal,* **39**(4), 461–72.

Foucault, Michel (1965) *Madness and Civilization: A History of Insanity in the Age of Reason,* trans. Richard Howard. New York: Pantheon.

Foucault, Michel (1972) *The Archaeology of Knowledge,* trans. Alan Sheridan. New York: Random House.

Foucault, Michel (1977) 'Nietzsche, Genealogy, History'. In Donald F. Bouchard (ed.), *Language, Counter-memory, Practice,* trans. Donald F. Bouchard and Sherry Simon. New York: Cornell University Press, pp. 139–64.

Foucault, Michel (1986) 'Docile bodies'. In *Discipline and Punish: The Birth of the Prison*, trans. Alan Sheridan. London: Penguin, pp. 135–69.

Foucault, Michel (1990) 'Contemporary Music and the Public', trans. John Rahn in L. D. Kritzman (ed.), *Politics, Philosophy, Culture: Interviews and Other Writings*. New York: Routledge, pp. 314–22.

Frith, Simon (1987) 'We Win Again', *The Voice*, 29 December.

Frith, Simon (1988a) *Music for Pleasure*. London: Polity Press.

Frith, Simon (1988b) 'Picking Up the Pieces'. In *Facing The Music*. New York: Pantheon.

Fusco, Coco (1988) 'Angels, History and Poetic Fantasy', *Cineaste* **16**(4), 14–17.

Garratt, Sheryl and Baker, Lindsay (1989) 'Clubland after Acid', *The Face*, **2**(15), 62–5.

Gasché, Rodolphe (1979) 'Deconstruction as Criticism', *Glyph* **6**, 177–215.

Gasché, Rodolphe (1986) *The Tain of the Mirror: Derrida and the Philosophy of Reflection*. Cambridge, MA: Harvard University Press.

Glass, Philip (1978) 'Notes on Einstein on the Beach', *Performing Arts Journal*, **3**(3), 63–70.

Glass, Philip (1988) *Opera on the Beach*. London: Faber and Faber.

Gould, Morris (1987) 'An Idiot's Guide to Sampling', *New Musical Express*, 14 November, 14.

Gray, Louise (1987) 'Fairlight Robbery', *New Musical Express*. 11 July, 28–9, 37.

Greenaway, Peter (director) (1991) *Prospero's Books*. London: Allarts.

Grundman, Roy (1991) 'History and the Gay Viewfinder: An interview with Derek Jarman', *Cineaste*, **18**(4), 24–7.

Hallett, Bryce (1992) 'Advances Make Einstein Smooth as Glass', *The Australian*, 17 September, 5.

Hartman, Geoffrey (1970) 'Maurice Blanchot: Philosopher Novelist'. In *Beyond Formalism: Literary Essays, 1958–1960*. New Haven, CT: Yale University Press, pp. 97–103.

Harvey, David (1989) *The Condition of Postmodernity*. Oxford: Basil Blackwell.

Hassan, Ihab (1978) 'Culture, Indeterminacy and Immanence', *Humanities in Society*, **1**(1), 51–85.

Heath, Stephen (1981) *Questions of Cinema*. London: Macmillan.

Heidegger, Martin (1967) 'Plato's Doctrine of Truth'. In William Barrett and Henry D. Aiken (eds), *Philosophy in the Twentieth Century: An Anthology*, trans. John Barlow, three volumes. New York: Random House.

Heidegger, Martin (1971a) 'Language'. In *Poetry, Language, Thought*, trans. Albert Hofstadter. New York: Harper and Row, pp. 187–210.

Heidegger, Martin (1971b) 'The Origin of the Work of Art'. In *Poetry, Language, Thought*, trans. Albert Hofstadter. New York: Harper and Row, pp. 17–87.

Heidegger, Martin (1978) *Being and Time*, trans. John Macquarrie and Edward Robinson. Oxford: Basil Blackwell.

Heisenberg, Werner (1971) *Physics and Philosophy: The Revolution in Modern Science*. London: George Allen and Unwin.

Hill, Leslie (1990) 'Julia Kristeva: Theorizing the Avant-garde?' In John Fletcher and Andrew Benjamin (eds), *Abjection, Melancholia and Love: The Work of Julia Kristeva*. London: Routledge, pp. 137–56.

Hoberman, J. (1992) 'Prisoners of Sex', *Voice*, 24 March, 57.

Hoghe, Raimund (1980) 'The Theatre of Pina Bausch', *The Drama Review*, **24**(1), 63–74.

Holden, Stephen (1985) 'When the Avant-garde Meets Mainstream', *New York Times*, 29 September, section 2.

Holmberg, Arthur (1988) 'A Conversation with Robert Wilson and Heiner Müller', *Modern Drama*, **31**(3), 454–8.

Hutcheon, Linda (1989) *The Politics of Postmodernism*. London: Routledge.

Hutcheon, Linda (1990) 'An Epilogue: Postmodern Parody: History, Subjectivity and Ideology', *Quarterly Review of Film and Video*, **12**, 125–33.

Interview with Nick Cave (1992) *Face The Press*. Australian SBS Television (9 December).

Interview with Lars Von Trier (1992) Dendy Press Release. Sydney: Dendy Films.

Ishii, Sogo (director) (1985) *Halber Mensch*. Tokyo: IDO Productions.

Jameson, Frederic (1984) 'Postmodernism, or The Cultural Logic of Late Capitalism', *New Left Review*, **146**, 53–92.

Jarman, Derek (1991a) *Queer Edward II*. London: British Film Institute.

Jarman, Derek (director) (1991b) *Edward II*. London: Working Title Productions.

Jaspers, Karl (1979) *Nietzsche: An Introduction to the Understanding of His Philosophical Activity*, trans. Charles F. Wallraff and Frederick J. Schmitz. South Bend, Indiana: Regnery/Gateway.

Jowitt, Deborah (1986) 'What the Critics Say about Tanztheater', *The Drama Review*, **30**(2), 80–81.

Kant, Immanuel (1911) *Critique of Pure Reason*, trans. Max Müller. London: MacMillan and Co. Ltd.

Kant, Immanuel (1978a) *The Critique of Judgement*, trans. James Creed Meredith. Oxford: Clarendon Press.

Kant, Immanuel (1978b) 'Part II: Critique of Teleological Judgement'. In *The Critique of Judgement*, trans. James Creed Meredith. Oxford: Clarendon Press, pp. 1–163.

Kaplan, Jay L. (1987) 'Pina Bausch: Dancing around the Issue', *Ballet Review*, **15**(1), 74–77.

Kennedy, Harlem (1991) 'Go Deeper', *Film Comment*, **27**(4), 68–71.

Kirshenblatt-Gimblett, Barbara (1991) 'Objects of Ethnography'. In Ivan Kamp and Steven D. Lavine (eds), *Exhibiting Cultures: The Poetics and Politics of Museum Display*. Washington, DC: Smithsonian Institution Press, pp. 386–443.

Kisselgoff, Anna (1986) 'What the Critics Say about Tanztheater', *The Drama Review*, **30**(2), 81–82.

Klocker, Hubert (1989a) 'The Dramaturgy of the Organic'. In Hubert Klocker (ed.), *Viennese Actionism 1960–1971, Volume 2*. Klagenfurt: Ritter Verlag, pp. 41–55.

Klocker, Hubert (1989b) 'The Shattered Mirror'. In Hubert Klocker (ed.), *Viennese Actionism 1960–1971, Volume 2*. Klagenfurt: Ritter Verlag, pp. 89–112.

Kripke, Saul (1980) *Naming and Necessity*. Cambridge, MA: Harvard University Press.

Kristeva, Julia (1974) *La Révolution du langage poétique. L'avant-garde à la fin du XIXe siècle: Lautréamont et Mallarmé*. Paris: Seuil.

Kristeva, Julia (1977) *Polylogue*. Paris: Seuil.

Kristeva, Julia (1984) *Revolution in Poetic Language*, trans. Margaret Waller. New York: Columbia University Press.

Kristeva, Julia (1985) 'The Speaking Subject'. In Marshall Blonsky (ed.), *On Signs*. Oxford: Basil Blackwell, pp. 210–20.

Kuhn, Annette (1985) *The Power of the Image: Essays on Representation and Sexuality*. London: Routledge and Kegan Paul.

Lacan, Jacques (1985) 'Sign, Symbol, Imaginary'. In Marshall Blonsky (ed.) *On Signs*. Oxford: Basil Blackwell, pp. 203–9.

Laddish, Kenneth and Dippé, Mark (1993) 'Blixa Einstürzende: Bargeld Harassed', *Mondo 2000*, **11**, 88–95.

Lash, Scott (1989) 'Discourse or Figure? Postmodernism as a "Regime of Signification"'. In *Sociology of Postmodernism*. London: Routledge, pp. 172–98.

Lyotard, Jean-François (1981) *Les fins de l'homme: à partir du travail de Jacques Derrida*. Paris: Galilée.

Lyotard, Jean-François (1984a) *The Postmodern Condition*, trans. Geoff Bennington and Brian Massumi. Manchester: Manchester University Press.

Lyotard, Jean-François (1984b) 'Answering the Question: What is Postmodernism?' In *The Postmodern Condition*, trans. Régis Durand. Manchester: Manchester University Press, pp. 71–82.

Lyotard, Jean-François (1984c) *Driftworks*. New York: Semiotext(e).

Lyotard, Jean-François (1986a) 'Defining the Postmodern', trans. Geoff Bennington. In Lisa Appignanesi (ed.), *Postmodernism: ICA Documents 4 and 5*. London: ICA, pp. 6–7.

Lyotard, Jean-François (1986b) 'A Response to Philippe Lacoue-Labarthe', trans. Geoff Bennington. In Lisa Appignanesi (ed.), *Postmodernism: ICA Documents 4 and 5.* London: ICA, p. 8.

Lyotard, Jean-François (1986c) 'Complexity and the Sublime', trans. Geoff Bennington. In Lisa Appignanesi (ed.), *Postmodernism: ICA Documents 4 and 5.* London: ICA, pp. 10–12.

Lyotard, Jean-François (1988) *The Differend*, trans. Georges Van Den Abbeele. Manchester: Manchester University Press.

Lyotard, Jean-François (1989) 'Anamnesis of the Visible, or Candour'. In Andrew Benjamin (ed.), *The Lyotard Reader*. Oxford: Basil Blackwell, pp. 220–39.

Lyotard, Jean-François (1991) *Lessons on the Analytic of the Sublime*, trans. Elizabeth Rottenberg. Stanford, CA: Stanford University Press.

Lyotard, Jean-François (1993) *The Postmodern Explained*, trans. Julian Pefanis and Morgan Thomas. Minneapolis: University of Minnesota Press.

Lyotard, Jean-François and Rogozinski, Jacob (1987) 'The Thought Police', trans. Julian Pefanis. *Art and Text*, **26**, 24–31.

MacCabe, Colin (1991) *Sight and Sound*, **1**(6), 12–14.

McClary, Susan (1989) 'Terminal Prestige: The Case of Avant-Garde Music Composition', *Cultural Critique*. **12** (Spring), 57–81.

Maeck, Klaus (ed.) (1989) *Listen With Pain.* Hamburg: Freibank.

Maeck, Klaus and Schenkel, Johanna (directors) (1993) *Liebeslieder* (video). Berlin: Studio 7.

Marlowe, Christopher (1959) *The Plays of Christopher Marlowe.* London: Oxford University Press.

Marranca, Bonnie (1985) 'Acts of Criticism', *Performing Arts Journal*, 10th Anniversary Issue, 36–9.

Megill, Allan (1985) *Prophets of Extremity: Nietzsche, Heidegger, Foucault, Derrida.* Berkeley: University of California Press.

Meisel, Perry (1984) 'Interview with Julia Kristeva', trans. Margaret Waller. *Partisan Review*, **51** (Winter), 131–2.

Mitry, Jean (1965) *Esthétique et psychologie du cinema, Volume 2.* Paris: Editions Universitaires.

Müller, Heiner (1979) 'Reflections on Post-Modernism', *New German Critique*, **6**, 55–7.

Müller, Heiner (1984) *Hamletmachine and Other Texts for the Stage*, trans. Carl Weber. New York: Performing Arts Journal Publications.

Murphie, Andrew and Scheer, Edward (1992) 'Dance Parties: Capital, Culture and Simulation'. In Philip Hayward (ed.), *From Pop to Punk to Postmodernism.* Sydney: Allen and Unwin, pp. 172–84.

Nietzsche, Friedrich (1924a) *The Will to Power, Volume 1, Books 1 and 2*, trans.

Anthony M. Ludovici. London: George Allen and Unwin.

Nietzsche, Friedrich (1924b) *The Will To Power, Volume 2*, trans. Anthony M. Ludovici. London: George Allen and Unwin.

Nietzsche, Friedrich (1956) *The Birth of Tragedy and the Genealogy of Morals*, trans. Francis Golfing. New York: Doubleday Anchor Books.

Nietzsche, Friedrich (1964) 'On Truth and Falsity in their Ultramoral Sense'. In Oscar Levy (ed.), *The Complete Works of Friedrich Nietzsche, Volume 2*, trans. M.A. Mügge. New York: Russell and Russell, pp. 171–92.

Nietzsche, Friedrich (1966) *The Birth of Tragedy and The Case of Wagner*, trans. Walter Kaufmann. New York: Vintage.

Nietzsche, Friedrich (1969) *Thus Spoke Zarathustra*, trans. R. J. Hollingdale. London: Penguin.

Nietzsche, Friedrich (1973) *Beyond Good and Evil*, trans. R. J. Hollingdale. Harmondsworth: Penguin.

Nietzsche, Friedrich (1974) *The Gay Science*, trans. Walter Kaufmann. New York: Vintage.

Nietzsche, Friedrich (1979) *Ecce Homo*, trans. R. J. Hollingdale. Harmondsworth: Penguin.

Nietzsche, Friedrich (1990) *Twilight of The Idols/The Anti-Christ*, trans. R. J. Hollingdale. Harmondsworth: Penguin.

Obenhaus, Mark (director) (1985) *Einstein on the Beach: The Changing Image of Opera* (film documentary). Brooklyn: The Brooklyn Academy of Music.

Oberhuber, Konrad (1989) 'Thoughts on Viennese Actionism'. In Hubert Klocker (ed.), *Viennese Actionism 1960–1971, Volume 2*. Klagenfurt: Ritter Verlag, pp. 17–23.

O'Hagan, Sean (1988) 'Turn on, Drop out', *New Musical Express*, 16 July, 47.

O'Pray, Mike (1991) 'Edward II: Damning Desire', *Sight and Sound*, **1**(6), 8–11.

Owen, Frank (1985) 'Guru Metal', *Melody Maker*, 14 September, 36–7.

Owens, Craig (1977) 'Einstein on the Beach: The Primacy of Metaphor', *October*, **4** (Fall), 21–31.

Owens, Craig (1980a) 'Robert Wilson: Tableaux', *Art in America*, **68** (November), 115–17.

Owens, Craig (1980b) 'The Allegorical Impulse: Towards a Theory of Postmodernism Part 2', *October*, **13**, 58–80.

Owens, Frank (1988) 'Bytes and Pieces', *The Voice*, 27 September, 82.

Paneth, Ira (1988) 'Wim and His Wings', *Film Quarterly*, **42**(1), 2–8.

Pfeil, Fred (1988) 'Postmodernism as a Structure of Feeling'. In Gary Nelson and Lawrence Grossberg (eds), *Marxism and the Interpretation of Culture*. London: Macmillan, pp. 381–403.

Price, David (1990) 'The Politics of the Body: Pina Bausch's Tanztheater', *Theatre Journal*, **42**(3), 322–31.

Reynolds, Simon (1990) *Blissed Out*. London: Serpent's Tail.

Ridgers, Derek (1993) 'Apocalypse', *New Musical Express*, 23 January, 20–1.

Rilke, Rainer Maria (1966) *Werke in drei Bänden*. Frankfurt am Main: Insel.

Rockwell, John (1980) 'Robert Wilson's Stage Works: Originality and Influence'. In Robert Stearns (ed.), *Robert Wilson from a Theatre of Images*. Cincinatti, Ohio: Contemporary Arts Centre.

Rodgers, Marlene (1991/92) 'Prospero's Books – Word and Spectacle', *Film Quarterly*, **45**(2), 11–19.

Rodman, Howard A. (1991) 'Anatomy of a Wizard', *American Film*, **15**(10), 35–9.

Ruthrof, Horst (1989) 'Narrative and the Digital: On the Syntax of the Postmodern', *Journal of the Australasian Universities Language and Literature Association*, Narrative Issues: Special issue of AUMLA, **74** (November), 185–200.

Ruthrof, Horst (1992) *Pandora and Occam: On the Limits of Language and Literature*. Bloomington: Indiana University Press.

Ruthrof, Horst (1995) 'Meaning: An Intersemiotic Perspective', *Semiotica*, **104**(1/2), 23–43.

Ruthrof, Horst (1997) *Semantics and the Body: Meaning from Frege to the Postmodern*. Toronto: University of Toronto Press.

Savran, David (1985) 'The Wooster Group, Arthur Miller and *The Crucible*', *The Drama Review*, **29**(2), 105.

Sayre, Henry M. (1989) *The Object of Performance*. Chicago: University of Chicago Press.

Schulte-Sasse, Jochen (1986/7) 'Modernity and Modernism, Postmodernity and Postmodernism: Framing the Issue', *Cultural Critique*, **5**, 5–22.

Schumann, Robert (1883) *Gesammelte Schriften über Musik und Musiker*, two volumes. Leipzig: Breikopf and Härtel.

Servos, Norbert (1981) 'The Emancipation of Dance: Pina Bausch and the Wuppertal Dance Theatre', trans. Peter Harris and Pia Kleber. *Modern Drama*, **23**(4), 435–47.

Servos, Norbert and Weigelt, Kurt (1984) *Pina Bausch: Wuppertal Dance Theater or the Art of Training a Goldfish, Excursions into Dance*, trans. Patricia Stadié. Cologne: Ballet-Buhnen Verlag.

Shun Wah, Annette (presenter) (1992) *The Noise*. Sydney: Australian SBS Television, 6 December.

Shyer, Laurence (1989) *Robert Wilson and His Collaborators*. New York: Theatre Communications Group.

Siegel, Marcia B. (1986) 'Carabosse in a Cocktail Dress', *Hudson Review*, **39**(1), 107–12.

Simmer, Bill (1976) 'Robert Wilson and Therapy', *The Drama Review*, **20**(1), 99–110.

Skwara, Anita (1990) '101 lat mieszczanskiej pewnosci siebie', *Kino*, **24** (July), 28–30.

Stauth, G. and Turner, B. S. (1988) *Nietzsche's Dance*. Oxford: Basil Blackwell.

Teraoka, Arlene Akiko (1985) *The Silence of Entropy or Universal Discourse: The Postmodernist Poetics of Heiner Müller*. New York: Peter Lang Publishing.

Toop, David (1992) 'High Tech Mindscapes. Is Technology Killing Music?', *The Wire*, 34–6.

Turner, Victor (1990) 'Are there Universals of Performance in Myth, Ritual, and Drama?'. In Richard Schechner and Willa Appel (eds), *By Means of Performance*. Cambridge: Cambridge University Press, pp. 1–18.

van Reijan, Willem (1992) 'Labyrinth and Ruin: The Return of the Baroque in Postmodernity', *Theory, Culture and Society*, **9**(4), 1–24.

van Reijen, Willem and Veerman, Dick (1988) 'An Interview with Jean-François Lyotard', *Theory, Culture and Society*, **5**(2/3), 277–309.

von Trier, Lars (director) (1991) *Europa/Zentropa*. Gunner Obel, Nordisk Film and TV A/S, Gérard Mital Productions–PCC, WMG, Swedish Film Institute.

Walker, Clinton (1992) 'Latter-day Alternative Renaissance Man', *Rolling Stone*, June, 62–5.

Watson, Don (1985) 'Trans-Europe Excess', *New Musical Express*, 6 April, 22–3, 34.

Watson, Lawrence (1987) 'Bytes and Pieces', *New Musical Express*, 14 November, 12–3.

Weber, Carl (1980) 'The Despair and the Hope', *Performing Arts Journal*, **4**(3), 135–46.

Wellbery, David E. (1985) 'Postmodernism in Europe: On Recent German Writing'. In Stanley Trachtenberg (ed.), *The Postmodern Moment. A Handbook of Contemporary Innovation in the Arts*. Westport, CT: Greenwood Press, pp. 229–49.

Wenders, Wim (director) (1987) *Der Himmel über Berlin/Wings of Desire*. West Berlin: Road Movies/Paris: Argos Film.

Wilke, Sabine (1991) 'The Role of Art in a Dialectic of Modernism and Postmodernism: The Theatre of Heiner Müller', *Paragraph*, **14**(3), 276–89.

Wittgenstein, Ludwig (1968) *Philosophical Investigations*, trans. G. E. M. Anscombe. Oxford: Basil Blackwell.

Wollen, Peter (1986) 'Ways of Thinking about Music Video (and Postmodernism)', *Critical Quarterly*, **22**(1/2), 169.

Wyatt, Chris (1992) 'Forum on *Prospero's Books*'. Melbourne Film Centre, Australia, 13 September.

Wyndham, Susan (1992) 'Opera's Nuclear Reaction', *The Australian* (Weekend Review), 29–30 August, 12.

Index

Adorno, Theodor W. 5, 61
  on Arnold Schoenberg 5
aesthetic intervention 2, 10, 69, 99, 165,
    168–9, 178
alternative institutional sites 142, 147, 151,
    159
Althusser, Louis 4, 137 n.7
Arens, Katherine 82, 89
Aristotle 2–3, 21, 169, 179 n.1
  drama of illusion 2
  praxis and *mythos* 2
Artaud, Antonin 3, 14, 23–4, 71, 80–1, 92,
    100, 103, 106 n.35, 107 n.43, 169, 179
    n.1
  essentialism 3, 169
  theatre of cruelty 3, 14, 71
  theatre of dreams 23
  theatre as 'writing of the body' 23
'aura' of work of art 1, 11 n.1, 13, 146
Auslander, Philip 3, 145–6, 174
  acting theories 3
  digital sampling and commodification of
    performance 145
  logocentrism in performance 3
  music 145

Bahti, Timothy 136
Barker, Adam 112
Baudrillard, Jean 8, 43, 55–9, 147, 156, 159,
    175–7
  aesthetic determinacy 10, 54, 58, 175
  catastrophe 57, 67 n.13, 177
  cloning 55, 57
  cool media 56, 113, 176
  cool seduction 56
  ecstasy 56, 58

entropic inertia 113
entropy 66 n.11
fatal strategy 57
fatal theory 57, 67 n.15
figures du transpolitique 57
hyperrealism 10, 54, 57–8, 67 n.14, 111,
    176
implosion of forms 56
language 54
media and masses 56
obscenity 58, 109
postmodernism 24, 57
resistance strategy 56
seduction 8, 10, 43, 55–6, 149, 159, 176
simulation 8, 43, 54–7, 175–6
spectacle 8, 56, 176
'textualist view' of world 54
theatre 58
'works of art' 58
Bausch, Pina 2, 13–14, 69–82, 168–72,
    175–6, 178
  Arien 74–7, 80
  Artaudian influence 14, 71, 80–1
  Brechtian influence 71, 77–9, 81
  Café Müller 14, 71–4, 79–81
  corporeal language 77–8, 170
  use of defamiliarization devices
    (*Verfremdungseffekt*) 14, 71, 73–4, 77–8
  dreamscape 80, 171
  epic theatre 14, 71, 77–8
  Expressionism (*Ausdruckstanz*) 70, 73, 79
  gestus 14, 73, 78–9, 178
  hybrid dance theatre 14, 71
  use of media technology 78,
  montage and collage 73, 77–8, 80, 176
  Palermo, Palermo 69–70

pantomime 77–8, 176
rejection of linear narrative 77, 80
Tanztheater 2, 13–14, 69–82, 104 n.3, 168–72, 175–6, 178
use of wide jarring metaphors 76, 175
writing of the body 80, 170
Wuppertal Dance Theatre 70–2
Bazin, André 4
Benjamin, Walter 11 n.1, 54, 66 n.8, 97, 159
Birringer, Johannes 3, 71, 76, 78
Blanchot, Maurice 35
Bohn, Chris 159, 175
Boulez, Pierre 5
Brecht, Bertolt 2–3, 11 n.5, 14, 20–4, 71, 77–9, 81, 91–3, 98–9, 118, 125–6, 155, 169, 176, 178, 179 n.1
'A–B–C dramaturgy' 91
defamiliarization (*Verfremdungseffekt*) 22, 71, 77–8, 118, 121, 176
double political strategy 2, 23
epic-dialectical structural principles 21
epic theatre 2, 14, 20, 23
Mother Courage and Her Children 22–3, 25 n.7
'not ... but rather' (*nicht-sondern*) 78
political theatre 2, 20, 23–24
Brecht, Stefan 105–6 n.22
Brenner, Eva 91
Bürger, Peter 25 n.2
Burroughs, William 6, 141

Calandra, Denis 91
Caldwell, David 129, 130, 138 n.19
Carroll, David 62
Cave, Nick 2, 5, 122, 128, 152–8, 168–9, 175, 178
And the Ass Saw the Angel 157
biblical imagery 153–4, 158
complicity 157
Dionysian 154
figurative use of language 175
Foucault, Michel 157
The Ghosts of the Civil Dead 157
Henry's Dream 153–5
At the Paradiso 156
parody 156
synaesthetic effect of 154
Tender Prey 157
violent imagery 155, 158
use of wide metaphors 154, 175
Chambers, Iain 6
chthonic 1, 12–13, 32, 99–100, 103, 135, 170, 173, 178

circulus vitiosus 48
cloning 55, 57, 145
collage 6, 13, 38, 89, 95, 102, 109, 124, 141, 143–4, 148, 177
complicity 2, 4, 9, 11 n.3, 16, 48, 58–9, 103, 108, 121, 157, 165, 167 n.14, 168, 173
Cook, Norman 140
corporeal *gestus* 14, 46, 64–5, 69, 73, 79, 102, 151, 170, 178
corporeal semiotic 1, 6, 9, 12, 45–6, 59, 69, 77–8, 102–3, 110, 168, 170, 173, 178
Corrigan, Robert W. 11 n.4
Cosgrove, Stuart 139

defamiliarization (*Verfremdungseffekt*), use of 14, 22, 71, 73–4, 77–8, 89, 121, 126, 135, 176
Derrida, Jacques 8–10, 23–4, 41, 43, 47–53, 78, 80, 86–7, 90, 92, 96–7, 102, 110, 112, 116–17, 120–2, 125, 127, 129, 131, 134, 136, 139, 141–3, 150, 154, 157, 159, 162, 164, 170, 173–5
aesthetic framing 52, 104 n.9
on art 52
circulus vitiosus 48
deconstruction 9, 44, 47–53, 173–4
de hors texte 47, 51
différance 10, 43, 49, 51, 104 n.2, 125, 127, 174
dissemination 48, 51
écriture 47
genre 51, 104 n.1, 136, 174–5
hymen 51
iterability 10, 43, 50, 117, 127
margin 50–1
mark and re-mark 48, 50
metaphor as extension of Heidegger's 'as-structure' 53
metaphor and metaphoricity 8, 52–3, 104 n.8
metaphysical complicity 2, 9, 11 n.3, 48, 103, 108 n.49, 157, 168, 173
parergon 52
supplementarity 49–51, 67, 105 n.18, 142, 174
trace 50, 174
trace as adaptation of Heidegger's '*die frühe Spur*' 50
syncategoremata 51
undecidables (infrastructures) 8–10, 44, 48–53, 174
digital sampling 6, 10, 139–49, 174, 176–7
aesthetic potential of 139, 148

authorities of delimitation 143, 145
Burroughs, William 141
Cage, John 141
concerns with authorial authority 6, 139,
    148
hip-hop 140, 144, 148–9
house music 143, 149
intellectual property 145
microcomputer technology 142
plagiarism 6, 139, 177
problematizing origin and identity
    formation 139, 142–3, 146–7, 150, 174
digitized technology 2, 4, 6, 10, 13–14, 46,
    56, 139–151, 162, 168–9, 171, 174, 176–7
Dionysian features 8–9, 13, 26, 31–32,
    99–100, 105 n.12, 138 n.21, 150–1, 159,
    165, 166 n.9, 171
dreamscapes 15, 23, 80, 99, 135
Dreyfus, Hubert L. 66
Dürer, Albrecht 15
Dyer, Richard 89, 106 n.28, 172

Eidsvik, Charles 4
Einstürzende Neubauten 2, 5, 15–16, 152,
    158–65, 168–9, 171, 174–5, 178
  Byakko Sha 160, 171
  complicity 16, 165
  corporeal *gestus* 160–1, 163, 174
  'cross-over' and 'hardcore new age'
    music 16, 158
  destructive character of 16, 159–60
  Dionysian traits 159, 165, 171
  dissolving boundaries 158, 174
  Durstiges Tier 15, 161
  Gesamtkunstwerk 160, 169, 171, 174
  Halber Mensch 159–60
  Haus Der Lüge 162
  heterogeneous performance 165
  'industrial' sound 16, 158, 167, 175
  on language 16,163, 165
  Liebeslieder 162–5
  'strange systematics of form' 163
  Tabula Rasa 16
  Viennese Actionism, influence of 15
Esslin, Martin 20, 25 n.7

Feay, Suzi 138 n.14
Fehervary, Helen 92, 107 n.40, 172
Féral, Josette
  alienation theory 155
  Brechtian alienation 155
  perceptive strategies 2, 176
Foucault, Michel 1–5, 8–9, 17, 24, 43–7, 69,
    71–2, 78, 84, 93, 95, 110, 115–18, 133,
    142–3, 145–6, 151, 157, 159, 161, 163,
    173, 178
  authorities of delimitation 45
  discourse as perspectival process 43–4
  discursive formations 8–9, 43–4, 118, 173
  docile bodies 2, 69, 178
  énonciation 8–9, 47, 93, 173
  grids of specification 45, 143
  institutional sites 46, 72, 109–10, 116, 173
  ordering of objects 46
  speaking subject 45, 47, 106 n.29
  subject position as vacant site 4, 9, 47, 84,
    93, 95, 173
  subject positioning 4, 8–9, 45–7, 78, 95,
    115, 133, 144, 173
  surfaces of emergence 44–5, 71, 117, 143
Frith, Simon
  postmodern music and the postmodern 5
  sampling 145
Fusco, Coco 130

Gasché, Rodolphe 48, 49, 51, 66, 136
  deconstruction as criticism 48, 66
  infrastructures or undecidables 49
genre destabilization 14, 20, 51, 59, 61–5,
    71, 73, 106 n.32, 129, 136, 139, 175
Glass, Philip 69, 82–90
  Einstein on the Beach 82–90
  repetitiveness 86
  rhythmic structure 85
  text as description of music 85
  see also Wilson, Robert
Gould, Morris 141–2, 166 n.2
Gray, L. 143, 149, 177
Greenaway, Peter 2, 14, 109–116, 121,
    168–9, 176
  énonciation 15, 115
  use of high definition television 13–14,
    109, 111, 113–14, 137 n.4–6, 169, 176–7
  metacinematic 115, 121
  and 'paint box' 13, 114
  painterly aesthetics 2, 14, 109–115, 168
  Prospero's Books 2, 14, 109–115, 168–9, 176
  adaptation of *The Tempest* 14, 109–12,
    116, 137 n.2
Grundman, Roy 115

Hallett, Bryce 105 n.16
Handke, Peter 2, 121–30, 168
  Der Himmel über Berlin/Wings of Desire 2,
    121–130, 168, 174
  see also Wenders, Wim

Hartman, Geoffrey   11, 35, 104 n.5, 106
    n.32, 171
Harvey, David   123–4, 126
Hassan, Ihab   13
Heath, Stephen   4
Heidegger, Martin   8–9, 17, 24, 26, 34–40,
    48, 50, 52–3, 84, 111, 128, 152, 172–3,
    Auslegung 37, 111
    becoming or happening of truth   8–9, 26,
        36, 42 n.15, 84, 103, 111, 164, 172–3
    Dasein   36–38
    hermeneutic circle   8–9, 26, 35, 37–8, 48,
        84, 103, 111, 128, 172–3 (*see also circulus
        vitiosus*)
    poetic language   38
    primordial way of knowing   36–7, 41, 107
        n.43
    truth value of art   38
    understanding as interpretation   37
    Unheimlich   36
    'work of art'   8–9, 16, 26, 35–6, 38, 172
Heisenberg, Werner   59
heterogeneity   1, 10, 12, 20, 29, 33, 45,
    61–3, 139, 168, 171, 175
heterosemiotic   178, 179 n.6
Hill, Leslie   11 n.11
Hoberman, J.   116
Hoghe Raimund   73–5, 82
Holden, Stephen   74
Holmberg, Arthur   90
homosemiotic   179 n.6
Hutcheon, Linda   15, 114, 126, 129, 136,
    156, 174
hybridized performance   10, 51, 69, 71, 99,
    139, 145, 158, 160, 174–7

identity formation   10, 15, 43, 50–1, 122,
    143, 166 n.7, 174
immanence   13, 103, 178
immediacy   2–3, 5, 9–10, 13, 23–4, 31, 59,
    69, 101–2, 165, 168–70, 178, 179 n.5
indeterminacy   1, 10, 13, 33, 168, 171
indirect political effect   2, 10, 24, 59, 69, 99,
    165, 168
interpretative spiral (hermeneutic helix)   38,
    103, 111, 173
intersemiotic   1, 6–10, 13, 25 n.1, 31, 43, 46,
    59, 65, 69, 81, 90, 94, 101, 151, 161, 170,
    178
Irigaray, Luce   81
Ishii, Sogo   159

Jameson, Frederick   13, 41 n.3

Jarman, Derek   2, 115–21, 168, 173
    AIDS   137 ns.9–10
    Bertolt Brecht   118
    Edward ll 2, 109, 115–21, 168
    Greenaway, Peter   116, 121
    Marlowe, Christopher   115, 119
    problematizing origin and identity
        formation   117
    Outrage   120
    queer politics   115–21
Jowitt, Deborah   104 n.3

Kant, Immanuel   7–9, 11, 16–20, 23–4,
    26–32, 40, 52, 59, 61–5, 117, 151, 160,
    169–70, 177–8
    aesthetic idea as representation of
        imagination   18
    centrality of aesthetic judgement (invents
        its own principle)   7, 17, 20, 24, 26–7,
        29, 32, 58, 129, 139, 144, 169
    determinate reason   20, 28, 63
    'disinterested' aesthetics   17, 28, 160
    finality without end (purposiveness without
        purpose)   17–18, 20, 27–9, 163
    moments in the judgement of beauty   27
    morally good   9, 18, 29
    negative pleasure   8, 30, 71, 106 n.31,
        117, 160, 171
    reflective reason   7, 19–20, 27, 29, 63, 169
    reflective teleology   20
    sensus communis   29
    the sublime   8, 26–7, 29–31, 71, 160, 170
    transcendental schemata   18, 28
    universal validity   9, 17–19, 27, 29, 40 n.2,
        178
Kaplan, Jay   81
Kennedy, Harlem   122, 131
Kirshenblatt-Gimblett, Barbara   142
Klocker, Hubert   100–3, 107 n.45,
Kripke, Saul: on naming and rigid
    designators   64
Kristeva, Julia   6–7, 11 n.10
Kuhn, Annette   4

Lacan, Jacques   6
Lash, Scott: de-differentiation
    (*Entdifferenzierung*) in
    postmodernism   179 n.4
Limen   12
liminal, features of   1–2, 8–9, 12–14, 18, 38,
    43, 59, 69, 74, 116, 131, 156, 165, 168–9
localized resistance   18, 23, 59, 109, 139,
    149, 169, 173, 175, 178

Lyotard, Jean-François 8–10, 17, 24, 30–31, 43, 59–65, 90, 94, 129, 150, 161, 169–70, 178
  aesthetic judgement 17, 61–3, 179 n.5
  agonistic environment 59
  anamnesis 60
  art 60
  regarding artist and philosopher 63
  corporeal semiotic 64
  determinate reason 63
  differend 8–9, 31, 60, 61–5, 94, 129, 161, 167 n.11
  ethical-political community 63
  extra-linguistic permanence 60, 67 n.17
  genre 59–65
  joyful sublime 60
  Immanuel Kant 8, 17, 59, 61, 63
  linguistic bias 9–10, 31, 170
  linguistic model 8, 43, 64–5, 90, 129, 161, 178
  motoricity 60
  naming and rigid designators 64
  nostalgic sublime 60
  ostension 64
  paralogisms 59
  philosophy of phrases 62
  phrase linkage 62
  political dimension 59–63
  postmodern condition 59–60
  postmodernity 65
  reflective reason 8, 63
  silence as sign 61, 170
  sublime 8, 30, 59–60, 63, 90, 94, 150, 161, 170, 178
  symbolization 8, 63
  taste 63

MacCabe, C. 117
McClary, Susan 11 n.7
Maeck, Klaus 16, 161, 163, 165, 171
Mantronik, Curtis 150, 166 n.4
Marlowe, Christopher 115–20, 137 n13
Marranca, Bonnie 3
Megill, Alan 17
metacinematic 4, 10, 109, 115, 121, 173
Miller, Arthur: *The Crucible* and author's right of ownership 146
Mitry, Jean 4
montage 13, 38, 54, 77–78, 109, 124, 132
Müller, Heiner 2, 69, 71, 73, 81, 90–9, 168, 171–2
  Artaudian influence 92, 106 n.35
  authorial authority 91, 98

Brechtian influence 91–3, 98–9
deconstruction of text 90–4
disruption of narrative 94
Foucauldian influence 148
fragmentation 90, 92, 94, 97
Grotowski, Jerzy 92
Hamlet 90, 93
Hamletmachine 2, 90–9, 168, 172
intertextuality 91, 94, 99
perceptive strategies 99
Wilson, Robert 92
synthetic fragments 2, 69, 71, 91, 168, 172
Murphie, Andrew 142

neo-gothic sound 152–65
neo-gothic traits 2, 5, 10, 15, 139, 152–4, 160, 164–5, 169, 175, 178
  chthonic 152
  destructive aesthetics 152–65, 178
  disruptive sounds 10, 139, 152, 155, 159, 161, 165, 178
  parody 156, 163, 178
Nietzsche, Friedrich 8–9, 16–17, 26, 31–6, 44, 99–100, 113, 113, 129–30, 139–40, 147, 159, 165, 171–2
  Apollonian 31
  art as experiment 33
  artist-philosopher 32
  artists as instinctive and emotive 41, 138, 172
  delegitimation of authority 33, 172
  Dionysian 8, 13, 26, 31–2, 171
  genealogy 33–34
  Kant, Immanuel 32
  language as work of art 35
  metacritique of truth 17, 26, 33
  nihilism 33–4
  perspectival attitude 8, 34–5, 171
  'transvaluation' 34–5, 138
  Übermensch (superman) 35
  will to art 8, 31, 100, 129, 159
  will to power 33, 41, 165, 171
  world as self-generating work of art 16, 32
non-'docile bodies' 2, 69, 178

Obenhaus, Mark 82, 86, 90
Oberhuber, Konrad 99–101
O'Hagan, Sean 166 n.8
O'Pray, Mike 117, 119, 137 ns.11–12
Owen, Frank 6, 16, 165, 174
Owens, Craig 16, 85, 173

allegory 16
deconstruction and postmodern art 11
n.3, 16, 108 n.49
'impossible complicity' 11 n.3, 16, 167

Paneth, Ira 123, 138 n.16
parody 1, 13–14, 25 n.2, 38, 71, 135–6, 144,
156, 163, 168
pastiche 1, 5, 13, 35, 38, 59, 109, 135, 146,
159, 177
perceptive strategies 2, 4, 69, 99, 176
Pfeil, Fred 124, 125
plagiarism 139–40, 144–6, 177
Price, David 23, 73, 80–1

Rabinow, Paul 66 n.1
rave 46, 149–52, 171, 173–4
'acid house' 5, 142, 149–52
alternative performance sites 142, 147,
151, 173
Dionysian aspects 150, 171
ecstasy 150–1, 166 n.8
egalitarianism 152
Gesamtkunstwerk 150, 174
hallucinogenics 150
happening 152
hip-hop 149
identity formation 150, 174
immediacy 151
seduction 149
shift-shape 149
use of technology 149
Rea, Paul W. 129–30, 138 n.19
Reynolds, Simon 148, 150, 157–8
Rilke, Rainer Maria 129, 138 n.22, 174
Rockwell, John 82
Rodgers, Marlene 112
Rodman, Howard A. 110–11, 114, 136–7
n.2
Rogozinski, Jacob 63, 179 n.5
Ruthrof, Horst
constraints of language 24–5 n.1
digital technology as syntax 177
extra-linguistic permanence 65, 67 n.18
homosemiotic and heterosemiotic 179 n.6
interpretive spiral (hermeneutic helix) 38,
103, 111, 173
intersemiotic semantics 24–5 n.1
non-verbal systems 24–5 n.1, 65
'textualist' positions 66 n.7

Savran, David 147
Sayre, Henry M. 87

Scheer, Edward 142
Schulte-Sasse, Jochen: on avant-garde and
parody 25 n.2
Schumann, Robert 5
self-reflexiveness 3, 5, 169
Servos, Norbert 70, 74, 77–9, 81, 104 n.4,
178
shift-shape 1, 11 n.2, 13, 32, 71, 101, 149,
157, 164, 169
Shyer, Lawrence 83, 85, 92–3, 106–7 n.36
Siegel, Marcia B. 105 n.13
Simmer, Bill 83
Skwara, Anita 121
Stauth, G. 34
subject formation 5, 11 n.10, 15, 47, 90,
114–15, 121, 173
subject positioning 4, 8–9, 45–7, 57–8, 78–9,
95, 98, 106 n.29, 115, 133, 144, 155, 173
sublime 8, 10, 26–7, 29–31, 40–1 n.5, 43,
59–60, 63, 65, 67 n.6, 71, 90, 94, 105
n.17, 131, 139, 150, 160, 161, 170–1,
178
surface depthlessness 13, 34, 41 n.3, 149
Swinton, Tilda 137 n.8, 138 n.14
synaesthetic 11 n.6, 76, 100, 102–3, 154,
175

Teraoka, Arlene Akiko 107 n.38
Toop, David 148
transcendental procedural 19, 28
Turner, Bryan 34
Turner, Victor 12–13
limen and liminality 12

van Gennep, Arnold 12
van Reijen, Wilhem 61, 67 n.16
Veerman, Dick 67 n.16
Viennese Actionism 2, 15, 69, 99–103, 168,
170, 173, 178
abreaction and catharsis 100, 107 n.44,
178
analytical shamanistic 100
Artaudian influence 100, 103
Brus, Günter 99–100, 102–3
chthonic 100, 103, 170, 173
complicity 103, 173
deconstruction 99, 103, 178
Dionysian rituals 100
direct art 102–3, 170, 173
documentary-voyeuristic 101
Gesamtkunstwerk 100, 103
happenings 100, 103, 173
Mühl, Otto 99–103

mysterium 100
Nitsch, Hermann 99–102
psycho-archaeological existentialism 100
Reich, Wilhelm 15
ritualistic dramaturgy 15, 99–100
Rudolf Schwarzkogler 99–102
social sculptures 2, 69, 99, 168
synaesthetic-alchemistical 100
von Triers, Lars 2, 130–6, 168, 174, 176
Europa/Zentropa 2, 109, 130–6, 168, 173–4
fragmentation 130, 135, 168
destabilization of genre 136, 174
metacinematic 109, 133, 173
parody 109, 135–6
pastiche 135
and style 131, 136
subject positioning 133
technical innovation 132–3, 176
use of technology 131–3, 135, 176

Walker, Clinton 153
Watson, Don 11 n.8, 16, 162, 165, 178
Weber, Carl 92–4, 106 n.5
Weigelt, Kurt 70, 74, 81, 104 n.4
Wellbery, David 156
Wenders, Wim 2, 109, 121–30, 132, 168, 174
Alekan, Henri 121, 127
Berlin 121–4
Bois, Curt 138 n.17
Cave, Nick 122, 128
use of defamiliarization techniques 125–6
destabilization of identity 122, 125, 127
Falk, Peter 122–3, 125–8
fragmentation 123–4, 127
Der Himmel über Berlin/Wings of Desire 2, 109, 121–32, 168, 174

Rilke, Rainer Maria 129, 138 n.22, 174
and style 121, 123, 125
transgressing borders 2, 121–2, 124, 168
see also Handke, Peter
Wilke, Sabine 107 n.42
Wilson, Robert 2, 13, 69, 71, 82–90, 92, 168–9, 171–2
acting technique as metronomic repetition 85–6, 90
auteur 82
dance 83, 87
use of defamiliarization techniques 89
corporeal *gestus* 85, 87–8, 90
disruption of narrative 89
dream play 82, 89
eclecticism 83, 89, 170
Einstein on the Beach 2, 13, 82–90, 170, 172, 176
Hamletmachine 92
'happening' 84
heterogeneous theatre 83, 89
hybridized performance 2, 82, 168
Müller, Heiner 92
non-verbal language 84–5, 89–90, 171–2, opera 82–3, 169
use of technology 83, 176
theatre of images 69, 71, 82, 169, 172
visual and oneiric images 84, 89
see also Glass, Philip
Wittgenstein, Ludwig 59, 62, 63–4
language games 59, 61
Wollen Peter 146
Wooster Group, The 146
and Arthur Miller 146
L.S.D. (Just the High Points) 146
Wyatt, Chris 114, 137 ns. 5–6
Wyndham, Susan 82

Printed in Great Britain
by Amazon.co.uk, Ltd.,
Marston Gate.